What readers are saying about
Programming Groovy 2

If you ever wondered why dynamic languages in general, and Groovy in particular, are so popular and how you can leverage them in your own work, this is the book for you.

➤ **Joe McTee**
Developer, JEKLsoft

Whether you're a Java developer starting to dabble with Groovy, an intermediate Groovy developer looking to improve your understanding of the language, or an experienced Groovy developer looking for an introduction to the latest features in Groovy 2, this book is the perfect way to take your skills to the next level.

➤ **Peter Bell**
hackNY

In this update for Groovy 2, Venkat has done a great job showing you both the theory and the practice of using Groovy. From basic, everyday tasks to advanced usage like compile-time metaprogramming and AST transforms, method interception and synthesis, and creating DSLs, you'll find a ton packed into this relatively thin book. Best, it won't become a desk anchor since you'll constantly refer to its many great examples!

➤ **Scott Leberknight**
Co-founder and senior software architect, Near Infinity Corp.

I'm delighted that Venkat has revised this essential Groovy tutorial to reflect the developments in the language and ecosystem since the first edition. Everyone learning Groovy should have this book in the library.

➤ **Tim Berglund**
  GitHub trainer and evangelist

Many other programming books assume too much. What makes Venkat's books unique is that they welcome various levels of readers without insulting their intelligence. *Programming Groovy 2* is no exception—it is crafted with small palatable examples that guide the reader in a natural and incremental learning experience from novice to expert.

➤ **Daniel Hinojosa**
  Consultant, programmer, speaker, author of *Testing in Scala*

Programming Groovy 2
Dynamic Productivity for the Java Developer

Venkat Subramaniam

The Pragmatic Bookshelf

Dallas, Texas • Raleigh, North Carolina

Many of the designations used by manufacturers and sellers to distinguish their products are claimed as trademarks. Where those designations appear in this book, and The Pragmatic Programmers, LLC was aware of a trademark claim, the designations have been printed in initial capital letters or in all capitals. The Pragmatic Starter Kit, The Pragmatic Programmer, Pragmatic Programming, Pragmatic Bookshelf, PragProg and the linking *g* device are trademarks of The Pragmatic Programmers, LLC.

Every precaution was taken in the preparation of this book. However, the publisher assumes no responsibility for errors or omissions, or for damages that may result from the use of information (including program listings) contained herein.

Our Pragmatic courses, workshops, and other products can help you and your team create better software and have more fun. For more information, as well as the latest Pragmatic titles, please visit us at *http://pragprog.com.*

The team that produced this book includes:

Brian P. Hogan (editor)
Potomac Indexing, LLC (indexer)
Candace Cunningham (copyeditor)
David J Kelly (typesetter)
Janet Furlow (producer)
Juliet Benda (rights)
Ellie Callahan (support)

Printed in the United States of America.
ISBN-13: 978-1-937785-30-7
Printed on acid-free paper.
Book version: P1.0—July 2013

To Mythili and Balu—for being much more than an aunt and an uncle—for being there when I needed them most.

Contents

Part II — Using Groovy

Part IV — Using Metaprogramming

Foreword to the Second Edition

As the saying goes, time flies. In the first edition of this book, Venkat guided you through all the nice features of Groovy 1.5 and turned you into a proficient "Groovy-ist," but it's now time to discover what Groovy 2 has in store. Of course, your favorite author has you covered!

The Groovy team worked on three major themes for the 2.0 version. First of all, we brought Groovy in line with JDK 7: we added the Java 7 "Project Coin" syntax enhancements, and we also powered Groovy's runtime with the "invoke dynamic" bytecode instruction and APIs under the hood. That way, you can use the latest syntax additions in Groovy even on older JDKs, but by running JDK 7 you'll benefit from performance improvements.

Secondly, we broke up Groovy into smaller modules, a core and several API-related ones, so you can pick the pieces you are interested in to compose your application. We also extended the Groovy Development Kit to allow you to create your own extension methods—just like Groovy does with its enriched JDK with the famous DefaultGroovyMethods class!

Last but not least, we introduced a "static" theme with two key novelties: static type-checking and static compilation. With the former, you can catch typos and other errors easily at compile time and even allow your domain-specific languages to be type-checked, while with the latter you can get the same performance as Java for critical parts of your application that request the highest level of speed.

With all those additions to the language and APIs, Groovy continues to mature like good wine, and just as a sommelier would share his expertise, Venkat dispenses his knowledge of all the power features of Groovy through the nice flavors of the chapters you are going to read, helping you get up to speed with the language and transport you to the next level.

Guillaume Laforge
Groovy project manager
June 2013

Introduction

The Java platform is arguably one of the most powerful and widely adopted ecosystems today. It has three significant pieces:

- The Java Virtual Machine (JVM), which has become increasingly powerful and more performant over the years

- The Java Development Kit (JDK), the rich set of third-party libraries and frameworks that help us effectively leverage the power of the platform

- The set of languages on the JVM—the Java language being the first—that help us program the platform

Languages are like vehicles that let us navigate the platform. They let us reach into various parts of this landscape with ease. The Java language has come a long way; its libraries have been refactored and expanded. It's gotten us this far, but we need to look beyond the Java language to languages that are lightweight and that can make us more productive. When used correctly, dynamic languages, the functional style of programming, and metaprogramming capabilities can help us navigate the landscape much faster. When viewed as vehicles, these newer languages aren't faster cars; they're flying machines, giving us the capability to be several orders of magnitude more productive.

The Java language has been flirting with metaprogramming and the functional style of programming for a while and will support some of these features to various degrees in future versions. We don't have to wait for that day, however. We can build performant JVM applications with all the dynamic capabilities today, right now, using Groovy.

What's Groovy?

Merriam-Webster defines *groovy* as "marvelous, wonderful, excellent, hip, trendy." The Groovy language is all of that—it's lightweight, low-ceremony, dynamic, object-oriented, and runs on the JVM. Groovy is open sourced under the Apache License, version 2.0. It derives strength from various languages, such as Smalltalk, Python, and Ruby, while retaining a syntax familiar to Java programmers. Groovy compiles into Java bytecode and extends the Java API and libraries. It runs on Java 1.5 and newer. For deployment, all we need is a Groovy Java archive (JAR) in addition to the regular Java stuff, and we're all set.

Groovy is a "language that has been reborn several times."[1] James Strachan and Bob McWhirter started it in 2003, and it was commissioned into Java Specification Request (JSR) 241 in March 2004. Soon afterward, it was almost abandoned because of difficulties and issues. Guillaume Laforge and Jeremy Rayner decided to rekindle the efforts and bring Groovy back to life. Their first effort was to fix bugs and stabilize the language features. The uncertainty lingered for a while. A number of people, including committers and users, simply gave up on the language. Finally, a group of smart and enthusiastic developers joined forces with Guillaume and Jeremy, and a vibrant developer community emerged.

The release of Groovy version 1.0 was announced on January 2, 2007. It was encouraging to see that, well before it reached 1.0, Groovy was put to use on commercial projects in a handful of organizations in the United States and Europe. Organizations and developers are beginning to use Groovy at various levels on their projects, and the time is ripe for major Groovy adoption in the industry. Groovy version 2.0 was released in mid 2012.

Groovy shines in tools and frameworks like Grails, CodeNarc, easyb, Gradle, and Spock. Grails, a dynamic web-development framework based on "coding by convention," exploits Groovy metaprogramming.[2] Using Grails, we can quickly build web applications on the JVM using Groovy, Spring, Hibernate, and other Java frameworks.

Why Dynamic Languages?

Dynamic languages have the ability to extend a program at runtime, including changing types, behaviors, and object structures. With these languages, we can do things at runtime that static languages do at compile time; we can even execute program statements that are created on the fly at runtime.

For example, if we want to compute a five percent raise on an $80,000 salary, we could simply write the following:

---

1. See "A bit of Groovy history," a blog post by Guillaume Laforge at http://glaforge.free.fr/weblog/index.php?itemid=99.
2. http://grails.org

```
5.percentRaise(80000)
```

Yes, that's the friendly java.lang.Integer responding to our own dynamic method, which we can add quite easily, like so:

```
Integer.metaClass.percentRaise = { amount -> amount * (1 + delegate / 100.0) }
```

As we see here, it's easy to add dynamic methods to classes in Groovy. The dynamic method we added to the Integer instance, referred using the delegate variable, returns the dollar amount increased by the appropriate percentage.

The flexibility of dynamic languages gives us the advantage of evolving programs as the applications execute. This goes far beyond code generation. We should consider code generation to be soooo twentieth century. In fact, generated code is like an incessant itch; if we keep scratching it, it turns into a sore. With dynamic languages, there are better ways. Dynamic languages make it easier to prefer *code synthesis*, which is in-memory code-creation at runtime. The code is synthesized based on the flow of logic through the application and becomes active *just in time*.

By carefully applying dynamic languages' capabilities, we can be more productive as application developers. This greater productivity means we can easily create higher levels of abstractions in shorter amounts of time. We can also use a smaller yet more capable set of developers to create applications. In addition, greater productivity means we can create parts of our application quickly and get feedback from our fellow developers, testers, domain experts, and customer representatives. And all this leads to greater agility. Tim O'Reilly observes the following about developing web applications: "Rather than being finished paintings, they are sketches, continually being redrawn in response to new data." He also makes the point that dynamic languages are better suited to web development in "Why Scripting Languages Matter" (see Appendix 1, *Web Resources*, on page 309).

Dynamic languages have been around for a long time, so why is now a great time to get excited about them? There are at least four reasons:

- Machine speed
- Availability
- Awareness of unit testing
- Killer applications

Let's start by talking about machine speed. Doing at runtime what other languages do at compile time raises a concern about dynamic languages' speed. Interpreting code at runtime rather than simply executing compiled code adds to that concern. Fortunately, machine speed has consistently increased over the years—handhelds have more computing power and memory today than large computers had decades ago. Tasks that were quite unimaginable using a 1980s processor are easy to achieve today. The performance concerns of dynamic languages are greatly eased because of processor speeds and other improvements in our field, including better just-in-time compilation techniques and JVM support for dynamic languages.

Now let's talk about availability. The Internet and active "public" community-based development have made recent dynamic languages easily accessible and available. Developers can now easily download languages and tools and play with them. They can even participate in community forums to influence the evolution of these languages. The Groovy users mailing list is very active, with constant discussions from passionate users expressing opinions of, ideas about, and criticisms of current and future features.[3] This is leading to greater experimentation, learning, and adaptation of languages than in the past.

Next let's look at awareness of unit testing. Most dynamic languages are dynamically typed. The types are often inferred based on the context. There are no compilers to flag type-casting violations at compile time. Since quite a bit of code may be synthesized and our program can be extended at runtime, we can't rely upon coding-time verification alone. From the testing point of view, writing code in dynamic languages requires greater discipline than writing in statically typed languages. Over the past few years, we've seen increased awareness among programmers (though not sufficiently greater adoption yet) in the area of testing in general and unit testing in particular. Most of the programmers who have taken advantage of these dynamic languages for commercial application development have also embraced testing and unit testing.

Finally, many developers have in fact been using dynamic languages for decades. However, for the majority of the industry to be excited about them, we had to have killer applications—compelling stories to share with our developers and managers. That tipping point, for Ruby in particular and for dynamic languages in general, came in the form of Rails.[4] It showed struggling web developers how they could quickly develop applications using Ruby's dynamic capabilities. In the same vein came Grails, a web framework written in Groovy and Java that offers the same productivity and ease.[5]

---

3. Visit http://groovy.codehaus.org/Mailing+Lists and http://groovy.markmail.org to see.
4. http://rubyonrails.org
5. http://grails.org

These frameworks have caused enough stir in the development community to make the industrywide adoption of dynamic languages highly probable.

Dynamic languages, along with metaprogramming capabilities, make simple things simpler and hard things manageable. We still have to deal with the inherent complexity of our application, but dynamic languages let us focus our effort where it's deserved. When I got into Java after years of C++, features such as reflection, a good set of libraries, and evolving framework support made me productive. The JVM, to a certain extent, provided me with the ability to take advantage of metaprogramming. However, I had to use something in addition to Java to tap into that potential—heavyweight tools such as AspectJ. Like several other productive programmers, I found myself left with two options: use the exceedingly complex and not-so-flexible Java along with heavyweight tools, or move on to using dynamic languages such as Ruby that are object-oriented and have metaprogramming capabilities built in. (For instance, it takes only a couple of lines of code to do aspect-oriented programming—AOP—in Ruby and Groovy.) A few years ago, taking advantage of dynamic capabilities and metaprogramming while being productive meant leaving behind the Java platform. (After all, we use these features to be productive and can't let them slow us down, right?) That is not the case anymore. Languages such as Groovy, JRuby, and Clojure are dynamic and run on the JVM. Using these languages, we can take full advantage of both the rich Java platform and dynamic-language capabilities.

Why Groovy?

As Java programmers, we don't have to switch completely to a different language. Groovy feels like the Java language we already know, with a few augmentations.

Dozens of scripting languages can run on the JVM—Groovy, JRuby, BeanShell, Scheme, Jaskell, Jython, JavaScript, and others. The list could go on and on. Our language choice should depend on a number of criteria: our needs, our preferences, our background, the projects we work with, our corporate technical environment, and so on. In this section, we discuss when Groovy is the *right* language to use.

Groovy is an attractive language for a number of reasons:

- It has a flat learning curve.
- It follows Java semantics.
- It bestows dynamic love.
- It extends the JDK.

Let's explore these in detail. First, we can run almost any Java code as Groovy (see Section 2.11, *Gotchas*, on page 46 for known problem areas), which means a flat learning curve. We can start writing code in Groovy and, if we're stuck, simply switch gears and write the Java code we're familiar with. We can later refactor that code and make it groovier.

For example, Groovy understands the traditional for loop. So, we can write this:

```
// Java Style
for(int i = 0; i < 10; i++) {
        //...
}
```

As we learn Groovy, we can change that to the following code or one of the other flavors for looping in Groovy (don't worry about the syntax right now; after all, we're just getting started, and very soon you'll be a pro at it):

```
10.times {
        //...
}
```

Second, when programming in Groovy we can expect almost everything we expect in Java. Groovy classes extend the same good old java.lang.Object—Groovy classes are Java classes. The object-oriented paradigm and Java semantics are preserved, so when we write expressions and statements in Groovy, we already know what those mean to us as Java programmers.

Here's a little example to show that Groovy classes *are* Java classes:

Introduction/UseGroovyClass.groovy
```
println XmlParser.class
println XmlParser.class.superclass
```

If we run groovy UseGroovyClass, we'll get the following output:

```
class groovy.util.XmlParser
class java.lang.Object
```

Now let's talk about the third reason to love Groovy. Groovy is dynamic, and it is optionally typed. If we've enjoyed the benefits of other dynamically typed languages, such as Smalltalk, Python, JavaScript, and Ruby, we can also enjoy those in Groovy. For instance, if we want to add the method isPalindrome() to String—a method that tells whether a word is spelled the same forward and backward—we can add that easily with only a couple of lines of code (again, don't try to figure out all the details of how this works right now; we have the rest of the book for that):

Introduction/Palindrome.groovy

```groovy
String.metaClass.isPalindrome = {->
  delegate == delegate.reverse()
}

word = 'tattarrattat'
println "$word is a palindrome? ${word.isPalindrome()}"
word = 'Groovy'
println "$word is a palindrome? ${word.isPalindrome()}"
```

Let's look at the output to see how the previous code works:

```
tattarrattat is a palindrome? true
Groovy is a palindrome? false
```

That's how easy it is to extend a class—even the sacred java.lang.String class—with convenient methods, without intruding into its source code.

Finally, as Java programmers, we rely heavily on the JDK and the API to get our work done. These are available in Groovy. In addition, Groovy extends the JDK with convenience methods and closure support through the Groovy JDK (GDK). Here's a quick example of a GDK extension to the java.util.ArrayList class:

```groovy
lst = ['Groovy', 'is', 'hip']
println lst.join(' ')
println lst.getClass()
```

From the output of the previous code, we can confirm that the JDK is being used, but in addition we're able to use the Groovy-added join() method to concatenate the elements in the ArrayList:

```
Groovy is hip
class java.util.ArrayList
```

Groovy augments the Java we know. If a project team is familiar with Java, is using it for most of the organization's projects, and has a lot of Java code to integrate and work with, then Groovy is a nice path toward productivity gains.

What's in This Book?

This book is about programming with Groovy; it is aimed at Java programmers who already know the JDK well but are interested in learning the Groovy language and its dynamic capabilities. Throughout this book we'll explore the Groovy language's features with many practical examples. The objective is to make programmers quickly productive with this interesting and powerful language.

The rest of this book is organized into four parts, as follows:

In the chapters in Part I, "Beginning Groovy," we focus on the whys and whats of Groovy—the fundamentals that'll help us get comfortable with general programming in Groovy. This book is for experienced Java programmers, so we won't spend any time with programming basics, like what an if statement is or how to write it. Instead, we directly dive into the similarities of Groovy and Java, and topics that are specific to Groovy.

In Part II, "Using Groovy," we'll see how to use Groovy for everyday coding—working with XML, accessing databases, and working with multiple Java/Groovy classes and scripts—so we can put Groovy to use right away for the day-to-day tasks. We'll also discuss the Groovy extensions and additions to the JDK so we can take advantage of both the power of Groovy and the JDK at the same time.

In Part III, "MOPping Groovy," we dive into Groovy's metaprogramming capabilities. We'll see Groovy really shine in these chapters and you'll learn how to take advantage of its dynamic nature. We'll start with the fundamentals of the metaobject protocol (MOP), cover how to do AOP-like operations in Groovy, and discuss dynamic method/property discovery and dispatching. We will also explore the compile-time metaprogramming capability and see how it can help extend and transform code during the compilation phase.

In the last part, "Using Metaprogramming," we'll apply Groovy metaprogramming right away to create and use builders and domain-specific languages (DSLs). Unit testing is not only necessary in Groovy because of its dynamic nature, but it's also easy to do—we can use Groovy to unit-test Java and Groovy code, as you'll see in this part of the book.

You're reading the introduction now, of course. Here's what's in the rest of the book:

In Chapter 1, *Getting Started*, on page 3, we'll download and install Groovy and take it for a test-drive using groovysh and groovyConsole. We'll also see how to run Groovy without these tools—from the command line and within an integrated development environment.

In Chapter 2, *Groovy for Java Eyes*, on page 11, we'll start with familiar Java code and refactor that to Groovy. After a quick tour of Groovy features that improve our everyday Java coding, we'll talk about Groovy's support for Java 5 features. Groovy follows Java semantics, except in places it does not—we'll also discuss gotchas that'll help avoid surprises.

In Chapter 3, *Dynamic Typing*, on page 53, we'll see how Groovy's typing is similar to and different from Java's typing, what Groovy really does with the type information we provide, and when to take advantage of dynamic typing versus optional typing. We'll also cover how to take advantage of Groovy's dynamic typing, design by capability, and multimethods. For tasks that need better performance than we can get from dynamic typing, we'll see how we can instruct Groovy to statically type parts of code.

In Chapter 4, *Using Closures*, on page 71, you'll learn all about the exciting Groovy feature called *closures*, including what they are, how they work, and when and how to use them. Groovy closures go beyond simple lambda expressions; they facilitate trampoline calls and memoization.

In Chapter 5, *Working with Strings*, on page 97, we'll talk about Groovy strings, working with multiline strings, and Groovy's support for regular expressions.

In Chapter 6, *Working with Collections*, on page 109, we'll explore Groovy's support for Java collections—lists and maps. We'll explore various convenience methods on collections, and we'll never again want to use collections the old way.

Groovy embraces and extends the JDK. We'll explore the GDK and see the extensions to Object and other Java classes in Chapter 7, *Exploring the GDK*, on page 127.

Groovy has pretty good support for working with XML, including parsing and creating XML documents, as we'll see in Chapter 8, *Working with XML*, on page 143.

Chapter 9, *Working with Databases*, on page 151, presents Groovy's SQL support, which will make our database-related programming easy and fun. In this chapter, we'll cover iterators, data sets, and how to perform regular database operations using simpler syntax and closures. We'll also see how to get data from Microsoft Excel documents.

One of Groovy's key strengths is its integration with Java. In Chapter 10, *Working with Scripts and Classes*, on page 159, we'll investigate ways to closely interact with multiple Groovy scripts, Groovy classes, and Java classes from within our Groovy and Java code.

Metaprogramming is one of the biggest benefits of dynamic languages in general, and Groovy in particular; with this feature we can inspect classes at runtime and dynamically dispatch method calls. We'll explore Groovy's support for metaprogramming in Chapter 11, *Exploring Metaobject Protocol (MOP)*, on page 175, beginning with the fundamentals of how Groovy handles method calls to Groovy objects and Java objects.

With Groovy we can perform AOP-like method interceptions using GroovyInterceptable and ExpandoMetaClass, as we'll see in Chapter 12, *Intercepting Methods Using MOP*, on page 185.

In Chapter 13, *MOP Method Injection*, on page 193, we'll dive into Groovy metaprogramming capabilities and learn how to inject methods at runtime.

In Chapter 14, *MOP Method Synthesis*, on page 215, we'll go through how to synthesize or generate dynamic methods at runtime.

Chapter 15, *MOPping Up*, on page 225, covers how to synthesize classes dynamically, how to use metaprogramming to delegate method calls, and how to choose between the metaprogramming techniques from the previous three chapters.

Groovy goodness does not end with runtime metaprogramming. Groovy now offers some of the same benefits at compile time, using abstract syntax tree (AST) transformation techniques, as we'll see in Chapter 16, *Applying Compile-Time Metaprogramming*, on page 235.

Groovy builders are specialized classes that help create fluent interfaces for a nested hierarchy. We discuss how to use them and how to create our own builders in Chapter 17, *Groovy Builders*, on page 253.

Unit testing is not a luxury or an "if we have time" practice in Groovy. Groovy's dynamic nature requires unit testing. Fortunately, Groovy facilitates writing tests and creating mock objects, as we'll cover in Chapter 18, *Unit Testing and Mocking*, on page 271. We will play with techniques that will help us use Groovy to unit-test our Java code and our Groovy code.

We can apply Groovy's metaprogramming capabilities to build internal DSLs using the techniques in Chapter 19, *Creating DSLs in Groovy*, on page 295. We'll start with the basics of DSLs, including their characteristics, and quickly jump into building them in Groovy.

Finally, in Appendix 1, *Web Resources*, on page 309, and Appendix 2, *Bibliography*, on page 315, you'll find all the references to web articles and books cited throughout this book.

Changes Since This Book's First Edition

This book's first edition covered Groovy version 1.5. Groovy has come a long way since then. This second edition is up to date with Groovy 2.1. Here's how the updates in this edition will help you:

- You'll learn Groovy 2.x features.

- You'll learn about Groovy code-generation transformations like @Delegate, @Immutable, and so on.

- You'll learn the benefits of the new Groovy 2.x static type-checking and static compilation facilities.

- You will pick up tips for creating your own extension methods with the new support for extension modules in Groovy 2.x.

- Closures in Groovy are quite exceptional, and you'll learn about their new support for tail-call optimization and memoization.

- You'll learn how to integrate Java and Groovy effectively, pass Groovy closures from Java, and even invoke dynamic Groovy methods from Java.

- You'll find new examples to learn about the enhancements to the metaprogramming API.

- You'll learn how to use Mixins and implement some elegant patterns with them.

- In addition to runtime metaprogramming, you can grasp compile-time metaprogramming and abstract syntax tree (AST) transformations.

- You'll see the details for building and reading JSON data.

- Additionally, you'll learn the Groovy syntax that facilitates fluent creation of DSLs.

Who Is This Book For?

This book is for developers working on the Java platform. It is best suited to programmers (and testers) who understand the Java language fairly well. Developers who understand programming in other languages can use this book as well, but they should supplement it with books that provide them with an in-depth understanding of Java and the JDK. For example, *Effective Java [Blo08]* and *Thinking in Java [Eck06]* are good resources for Java.

Programmers who are somewhat familiar with Groovy can use this book to learn some tips and tricks that they may not have the opportunity to discover otherwise. Finally, those already familiar with Groovy may find this book useful for training or coaching fellow developers in their organizations.

Online Resources

Web resources referenced throughout the book are collected in Appendix 1, *Web Resources*, on page 309. Here are two that will help you get started:

- The Groovy website for downloading the version of Groovy used in this book: http://groovy.codehaus.org.

- The official homepage for this book at the Pragmatic Bookshelf website: http://www.pragprog.com/titles/vslg2. From there you can download all the example source code for this book. You can also offer feedback by submitting errata entries or posting your comments and questions in the forum for the book.

If you're reading the book in ebook form, you can click on the link above a code listing to view or download the specific example.

Acknowledgments

It's been a real pleasure watching the Groovy ecosystem grow over the past four years. I thank the Groovy committers for creating a language and a set of tools that help programmers to be productive and have fun at the same time.

I'd like to thank everyone who read the first edition of this book. Special thanks to Norbert Beckers, Giacomo Cosenza, Jeremy Flowers, Ioan Le Gué, Fred Janon, Christopher M. Judd, Will Krespan, Jorge Lee, Rick Manocchi, Andy O'Brien, Tim Orr, Enio Pereira, David Potts, Srivaths Sankaran, Justin Spradlin, Fabian Topfstedt, Bryan Young, and Steve Zhang for taking the time to report errors on the book's errata page.

My sincere thanks and appreciation go to the technical reviewers of the second edition of this book. They were kind enough to give their time and attention to read through the concepts, try out the examples, and provide me valuable feedback, corrections, and encouragements along the way. Thank you, Tim Berglund, Mike Brady, Hamlet D'arcy, Scott Davis, Jeff Holland, Michael Kimsal, Scott Leberknight, Joe McTee, Al Scherer, and Eitan Suez.

A few more people deserve to be called out. I thank Guillaume Laforge for his encouragement and for taking the time to write the foreword. Cédric Champeau and Chris Reigrut were generous to quickly read through the beta of the second edition and provide valuable feedback. I am indebted to you; thank you. I also thank Thilo Maier for reporting errors on the errata page for the second edition.

Special thanks to Brian Hogan, editor for the second edition, for his reviews, comments, suggestions, and encouragement. He provided much-needed guidance throughout the creation of this edition.

Thanks to the entire Pragmatic Programmers team for taking up this edition and for their support throughout the production process.

Part I

Beginning Groovy

CHAPTER 1

Getting Started

Before we can crank out some Groovy code, we need to get Groovy installed. In this chapter you'll learn how to quickly install Groovy and make sure everything is working well. Taking care of these basics now will help us move quickly to the fun things ahead.

1.1 Installing Groovy

Getting a stable working copy of Groovy is really simple: just visit the Groovy home page at http://groovy.codehaus.org, and click the Download link. We can download either the binary release or the source release. Download the source release to build Groovy locally or to explore the source code. Otherwise, download the binary release. For Windows, we can also get the Windows Installer version. While we're there, let's also grab the documentation for Groovy.

For programmers on the Groovy users mailing list who're bleeding-edge types, the previously mentioned releases will not suffice. They'll want the latest prerelease version of the language implementation. We can get the snapshot release from http://groovy.codehaus.org/Git.

We also need the JDK 1.5 or newer, so we need to make sure Java is installed on the local system.[1]

Let's get Groovy installed.

Installing Groovy on Windows

We can use the one-click installer for Windows—simply run it and follow the instructions. Programmers who prefer more control over the installation can use the binary distribution package.

---

1.   http://java.sun.com/javase/downloads/index.jsp

Next we have to set the GROOVY_HOME environment variable and the path. Edit the system-environment variables (by going into Control Panel and opening the System application). Create an environment variable named GROOVY_HOME, and set it to the location of the Groovy directory (for example, I set it to C:\programs\groovy\groovy-2.1.0). Also, add %GROOVY_HOME%\bin to the Path environment variable to set the location of the Groovy bin directory in the path. Remember to separate directories in the path using a semicolon (;).

Next, confirm that the environment variable JAVA_HOME is pointing to the location of the Java Development Kit (JDK) directory (if it's not present, set it).

That's pretty much all we have to do. Remember to close any open command window, because the changes to environment variables don't take effect until we reopen command windows. In a new command window, type groovy -v, and make sure it reports the correct version.

Installing Groovy on Unix-like Systems

Unzip the downloaded binary distribution. Check http://groovy.codehaus.org/Download to see if there are special distributions and instructions for different flavors of Unix. Move the groovy-2.1.0 directory to a desired location. For instance, on my Mac system, I have it in the /opt/groovy directory.

Next, set the GROOVY_HOME environment variable and the path. Depending on the shell you use, you have to edit different profile files. You probably know where to go—refer to the appropriate documentation if you need help figuring out what to edit. I use bash on OS X, so I edited the ~/.bash_profile file. In that file, I added an entry export GROOVY_HOME="/opt/groovy/groovy-2.1.0" to set the environment variable GROOVY_HOME. Also add $GROOVY_HOME/bin to the path environment variable.

Next, confirm that the environment variable JAVA_HOME is pointing to the location of the JDK directory (if it's not present, set it). ls -l `which java` should help determine the location of the Java installation.

Installation of Groovy is complete and we're ready to use the language. Close any open terminal windows—changes to environment variables don't take effect until we reopen the windows. We may source the profile file instead, but it's simple and easy to open a new terminal. In a new terminal window, type the command groovy -v, and make sure it reports the correct version. That's all there is to it!

1.2   Installing and Managing Groovy Versions

We often have to work with multiple versions of the language for various projects. The task of managing the right version for a project can quickly turn into a time sink if we're not careful. GVM, the Groovy environment manager, can manage not only the versions of the Groovy language, but also versions of Groovy-related libraries and tools, like Grails, Griffon, Gradle, and so on.

The tool is a breeze to install and is supported on various flavors of xnix and on Windows through Cygwin.[2] Once you install GVM, you can see a list of available and installed versions of the language by simply running the command gvm list groovy. If you want to use a particular version of Groovy, say version 2.1.1, you can specify that. For instance, to run the examples in this book, we can type the command gvm install groovy 2.1.1. GVM will then download the version and install it for use. If we have installed multiple versions of Groovy and want to switch to version 2.1.1, for example, we can use the command gvm use groovy 2.1.1.

1.3   Test-Drive Using groovysh

We've installed Groovy and checked the version—it's time to take it for a test-drive. Using the command-line tool groovysh is one of the quickest ways to play with Groovy. Open a terminal window, and type groovysh; we'll see a shell, as shown next. Type some Groovy code to see how it works.

```
> groovysh
Groovy Shell (2.1.1, JVM: 1.7.0_04-ea)
Type 'help' or '\h' for help.
-----------------------------------------------
groovy:000> Math.sqrt(16)
===> 4.0
groovy:000> println 'Test drive Groovy'
Test drive Groovy
===> null
groovy:000> String.metaClass.isPalindrome = {
groovy:001>    delegate == delegate.reverse()
groovy:002> }
===> groovysh_evaluate$_run_closure1@64b99636
groovy:000> 'mom'.isPalindrome()
===> true
groovy:000> 'mom'.l

lastIndexOf(   leftShift(      length()
groovy:000> 'mom'.l
```

---

2.   http://gvmtool.net

groovysh is a good tool for interactively trying out small Groovy code examples. It is also useful for experimenting with some code while we're in the middle of coding. Be aware, however, that groovysh has some idiosyncrasies. If we run into problems with it, we can use the save command to save the code to a file and then try running from the command line using the groovy command to get around any tool-related issues. The groovysh command compiles and executes completed statements as soon as we press the Enter/Return key, and prints the result of that statement execution along with any output from the execution.

If we type Math.sqrt(16), for example, it prints the result, 4.0. However, if we type println 'Test drive Groovy', it prints the words in quotes followed by null, indicating that println() returned nothing.

We can also type code that spans multiple lines—simply use a semicolon at the end of the line if it complains, as in the line defining the dynamic method isPalindrome(). When we type a class, a method, or even an if statement, groovysh waits until we finish to execute that code. Next to the groovy: prompt it tells us how many lines it has accumulated for execution.

If we're not sure what command to type, we can type as much as we know and press the Tab key. The shell will print methods that are available to us, starting with the partial name we typed, as we can see in the previous snippet of the groovysh interactive shell. If we type only a dot (.) and Press the Tab key, it will ask if we want to display all methods that are available.

Type help to get a list of supported commands. We can use the up arrow to view commands we have already typed, which is useful for repeating statements or commands. It even remembers commands we typed in previous invocations.

When done, type exit to exit from the tool.

1.4 Using groovyConsole

Groovy has those of us who prefer to use a GUI covered—simply double-click groovyConsole.bat in Windows Explorer (look for it in the %GROOVY_HOME%\bin directory). Users of Unix-like systems can double-click the groovyConsole executable script using their favorite file/directory-browsing tool. We can also type groovyConsole on the command line to bring up the console GUI tool. A console GUI will pop up, as shown in the following figure.

Let's type some Groovy code in the top window of the console. When ready to execute the code, press Ctrl+R or Ctrl+Enter on a Windows system, or Command+R or Command+Enter on a Mac system.

We can also click the appropriate toolbar button to execute the script. The groovyConsole command has grown fancier over time—we can save the script, open existing scripts, and so on, so take some time to explore the tool.

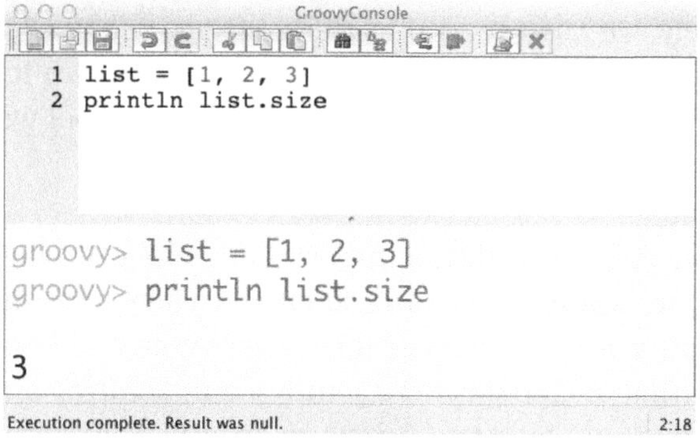

Figure 1—Using **groovyConsole**

1.5 Running Groovy on the Command Line

Of course, for some programmers nothing can give as much pleasure as getting into the command line and running the program from there. We can do that by typing the command groovy followed by the Groovy program filename, as shown next.

```
> cat Hello.groovy
println "Hello Groovy!"
> groovy Hello
Hello Groovy!
>
```

To try a couple of statements directly on the command line, use the -e option. Type groovy -e "println 'hello'" on the command line, and press Enter/Return. Groovy will output "hello."

Realistically, though, the groovy command is useful for executing large Groovy scripts and classes. It expects us to either have some executable code outside any class, or have a class with a static main(String[] args) method (the traditional Java main() method).

We can skip the main() method if our class extends GroovyTestCase (for more information see Section 18.2, *Unit Testing Java and Groovy Code*, on page 272) or if our class implements the Runnable interface. If the main() method is present in these cases, it takes precedence.

1.6   Using an IDE

As we start churning out more-complex Groovy code, we'll quickly graduate from these tools and want a full-featured integrated development environment (IDE). Fortunately, we have several to choose from. See http://groovy.codehaus.org/IDE+Support for some choices. We can edit Groovy code, run it from within an IDE, debug code, and a lot more, depending on which tool we pick.

IntelliJ IDEA

IntelliJ IDEA offers outstanding support for Groovy in the free-of-charge community edition.[3] Using it, we can edit Groovy code, take advantage of code completion, get support for Groovy builders, use syntax and error highlighting, use code formatting and inspection, jointly compile Java and Groovy code, refactor and debug both Java and Groovy code, and work with and build Java and Groovy code in the same project.

Eclipse Groovy Plug-In

Eclipse users can use the Groovy Eclipse plug-in.[4] We can edit Groovy classes and scripts with this plugin, take advantage of syntax highlighting, and compile and run the code and tests. Using the Eclipse debugger, we can step into Groovy code or debug unit tests. In addition, we can invoke the Groovy shell or Groovy console from within Eclipse to quickly experiment with Java and Groovy code.

TextMate Groovy Bundle

Programmers on the Mac use the Groovy bundle extensively in TextMate; see *TextMate: Power Editing for the Mac [Gra07]*.[5,6] (Windows users—take a look at E Text Editor.[7] Also, for editing small code snippets, we can use Notepad2.[8]) TextMate provides a number of time-saving snippets that allow code expansion for standard Groovy code, such as closures. We can take advantage of syntax highlighting and run Groovy code and tests quickly from within TextMate, as shown in the following figure. See my blog entry at http://blog.agiledeveloper.com/2007/10/tweaking-textmate-groovy-bundle.html for a minor tweak to quickly display results without a pop-up window.

---

3.   http://www.jetbrains.com/idea
4.   http://groovy.codehaus.org/Eclipse+Plugin
5.   http://docs.codehaus.org/display/GROOVY/TextMate
6.   http://macromates.com
7.   http://www.e-texteditor.com
8.   http://www.flos-freeware.ch/notepad2.html

Figure 2—Groovy code executed within TextMate

Many TextMate users are migrating to Sublime Text, the new kid on the block. To run Groovy code from within Sublime Text we need a build file. If it's not in the Tools > Build System menu, simply select the New Build System... menu item to create a file named groovy.sublime-build with a one-line command:

```
{ "cmd": ["/opt/groovy/bin/groovy", "$file"] }
```

This instructs the tool to run the groovy command in the specified path, sending it the Groovy code-source filename as the parameter. The results will be displayed in the output window. To run the code, either press F7 or Command+B. For more details on configuring the build in Sublime Text, refer to http://sublimetext.info/docs/en/reference/build_systems.html.

It's nice to have a choice of command-line and IDE tools. However, we need to decide which tool is right. I find it easiest to simply run Groovy code directly from within the editor or IDE, letting the groovy tool take care of compiling and executing the code behind the scene. That helps with my "rapid edit, code, and run my tests" cycle. At times, I find myself jumping over to groovysh to experiment with code snippets. But you don't have to do what I do. The right tool for you is the one you're most comfortable with. Start with a simple tool and the steps that work for you. Once you get comfortable, scale up to something more sophisticated when there's a need to do so.

In this chapter, we installed Groovy and took it for a quick test-drive. Along the way we looked at a few command-line tools and IDE support. That means we're all set to explore Groovy in the next chapter.

CHAPTER 2

Groovy for Java Eyes

Since Groovy supports Java syntax and preserves the Java semantics, we can intermix Java style and Groovy style at will. In this chapter we'll start on familiar ground and transition to a more Groovy style of coding. We'll begin with tasks we're used to doing in Java, and as we transition them to Groovy code we'll see how the Groovy versions are more concise and expressive. At the end of this chapter, we'll look at some "gotchas"—a few things that might catch us off guard if we aren't expecting them.

2.1 From Java to Groovy

Let's start with a piece of Java code with a simple loop. We'll first run it through Groovy. Then we'll refactor it from Java style to Groovy style. As we evolve the code, each version will do the same thing, but the code will be more expressive and concise. It will feel like our refactoring is on steroids. Let's begin.

Hello, Groovy

Let's start with a Java code example that's also Groovy code, saved in a file named Greetings.groovy.

```
// Java code
public class Greetings {
  public static void main(String[] args) {
    for(int i = 0; i < 3; i++) {
      System.out.print("ho ");
    }

    System.out.println("Merry Groovy!");
  }
}
```

Let's execute this code using the command groovy Greetings.groovy and take a look at the output:

```
ho ho ho Merry Groovy!
```

That's a lot of code for such a simple task. Still, Groovy obediently accepted and executed it.

Groovy has a higher signal-to-noise ratio than Java. Hence, less code, more result. In fact, we can get rid of most of the code from the previous program and still have it produce the same result. Let's start by removing the line-terminating semicolons. Losing the semicolons reduces noise and makes the code more fluent.

Now let's remove the class and method definitions. Groovy is still happy (or is it happier?).

Default Imports

We don't have to import all the common classes/packages when we write Groovy code. For example, Calendar readily refers to java.util.Calendar. Groovy automatically imports the following Java packages: java.lang, java.util, java.io, and java.net. It also imports the classes java.math.BigDecimal and java.math.BigInteger. In addition, the Groovy packages groovy.lang and groovy.util are imported.

GroovyForJavaEyes/LightGreetings.groovy
```
for(int i = 0; i < 3; i++) {
  System.out.print("ho ")
}

System.out.println("Merry Groovy!")
```

We can go even further. Groovy understands println() because it has been added on java.lang.Object. It also has a lighter form of the for loop that uses the Range object, and Groovy is lenient with parentheses. So, we can reduce the previous code to the following:

GroovyForJavaEyes/LighterGreetings.groovy
```
for(i in 0..2) { print 'ho ' }

println 'Merry Groovy!'
```

The output from the previous code is the same as the Java code we started with, but the code is a lot lighter. Simple things are simple to do in Groovy.

Ways to Loop

We're not restricted to the traditional for loop in Groovy. We already used the range 0..2 in the for loop. Groovy provides quite a number of elegant ways to iterate; let's look at a few.

Groovy has added a convenient upto() instance method to java.lang.Integer; let's use that to iterate.

```
GroovyForJavaEyes/WaysToLoop.groovy
0.upto(2) { print "$it "}
```

Here we called upto() on 0, which is an instance of Integer. The output should display each of the values in the range we picked.

```
0 1 2
```

So, what's that $it in the code block? In this context, it represents the index value through the loop. The upto() method accepts a closure as a parameter. If the closure expects only one parameter, we can use the default name it for it in Groovy. Keep that in mind, and move on for now; we'll discuss closures in more detail in Chapter 4, *Using Closures*, on page 71. The $ in front of the variable it tells the method print() to print the value of the variable instead of the characters "it"—using this feature we can embed expressions within strings, as you'll see in Chapter 5, *Working with Strings*, on page 97.

With the upto() method we can set both lower and upper limits. If we start at 0, we can also use the times() method, like in the next example.

```
GroovyForJavaEyes/WaysToLoop.groovy
3.times { print "$it "}
```

This version of code will produce the same output as the previous version, as we can see:

```
0  1  2
```

By using the step() method, we can skip values while looping.

```
GroovyForJavaEyes/WaysToLoop.groovy
0.step(10, 2) { print "$it "}
```

The output from the code will show select values in the range:

```
0  2  4  6  8
```

We can also iterate or traverse a collection of objects using similar methods, as you'll see later in Chapter 6, *Working with Collections*, on page 109.

To go further, we can rewrite the greetings example using the methods you learned earlier. Look at how short the following Groovy code is compared to the Java code we started with:

GroovyForJavaEyes/WaysToLoop.groovy
```
3.times { print 'ho ' }
println 'Merry Groovy!'
```

To confirm that this works, let's run the code and take a look at the output.

```
ho ho ho Merry Groovy!
```

A Quick Look at the GDK

One of the Java Platform's key strengths is its Java Development Kit (JDK). To program in Groovy, we're not forced to learn a new set of classes and libraries. Groovy extends the powerful JDK by adding convenience methods to various classes. These extensions are available in the library called the GDK, or the Groovy JDK (http://groovy.codehaus.org/groovy-jdk). We can leverage the JDK even further in Groovy by using the Groovy convenience methods. Let's whet our appetites by making use of a GDK convenience method for talking to an external process.

I spend part of my life maintaining version-control systems. Whenever a file is checked in, back-end hooks exercise some rules, execute processes, and send out notifications. In short, I have to create and interact with processes. Let's see how Groovy can help here.

In Java, we can use java.lang.Process to interact with a system-level process. Suppose we want to invoke Subversion's help from within our code; well, here's the Java code for that:

```
//Java code
import java.io.*;
public class ExecuteProcess {
  public static void main(String[] args) {
    try {
      Process proc = Runtime.getRuntime().exec("svn help");
      BufferedReader result = new BufferedReader(
        new InputStreamReader(proc.getInputStream()));
      String line;
      while((line = result.readLine()) != null) {
        System.out.println(line);
      }
    } catch(IOException ex) {
      ex.printStackTrace();
    }
  }
}
```

java.lang.Process is very helpful, but we had to jump through some hoops to use it in the previous code; in fact, all the exception-handling code and effort to get to the output can make us dizzy. The GDK makes this insanely simple by adding an execute() method on the java.lang.String class:

GroovyForJavaEyes/Execute.groovy
```
println "svn help".execute().text
```

Compare the two pieces of code. They remind me of the swordfight scene from the movie *Raiders of the Lost Ark*; the Java code is pulling a major stunt like the villain with the sword.[1] Groovy, on the other hand, like Indy, effortlessly gets the job done. Don't get me wrong—I am certainly not calling Java the villain. We're still using Process and the JDK in Groovy code. Our enemy is the unnecessary complexity that makes it harder and more time-consuming to utilize the power of the JDK and the Java platform.

In one of the Subversion hooks I maintain, a refactoring session helped reduce more than fifty lines of Java code to a mere three lines of Groovy code. Which of the previous two versions would we prefer? The short and sweet one-liner, of course (unless we're consultants who get paid by the number of lines of code we write…).

When we called the execute() method on the instance of String, Groovy created an instance that extends java.lang.Process, just like the exec() method of Runtime did in the Java code. We can verify this by using the following code:

GroovyForJavaEyes/Execute.groovy
```
println "svn help".execute().getClass().name
```

When run on a Unix-like machine, the code will report as follows:

```
java.lang.UNIXProcess
```

On a Windows machine, we'll get this:

```
java.lang.ProcessImpl
```

When we call text, we're calling the Groovy-added method getText() on the Process to read the process's entire standard output into a String. If we simply want to wait for a process to finish, either waitFor() or the Groovy-added method waitForOrKill() that takes a timeout in milliseconds will help. Go ahead—try the previous code.

Instead of using Subversion, we can try other commands; simply substitute svn help for some other program (such as groovy -v):

---

1. http://www.youtube.com/watch?v=anEuw8F8cpE

GroovyForJavaEyes/Execute.groovy

```
println "groovy -v".execute().text
```

The separate Groovy process we invoked from within our Groovy script will report the version of Groovy.

GroovyForJavaEyes/Execute.output

```
Groovy Version: 2.1.1 JVM: 1.7.0_04-ea Vendor: Oracle Corporation OS: Mac OS X
```

This code sample works on Unix-like systems and on Windows. Similarly, on a Unix-like system, to get the current-directory listing, we can call ls:

GroovyForJavaEyes/Execute.groovy

```
println "ls -l".execute().text
```

If we're on Windows, simply replacing ls with dir will not work. The reason is that although ls is a program we're executing on Unix-like systems, dir is not a program—it's a shell command. So, we have to do a little more than call dir. Specifically, we need to invoke cmd and ask it to execute the dir command:

GroovyForJavaEyes/Windows/ExecuteDir.groovy

```
println "cmd /C dir".execute().text
```

We've looked at how the GDK extensions can make our coding life much easier, but we've merely scratched the GDK's surface. We'll look at more GDK goodness in Chapter 7, *Exploring the GDK*, on page 127.

safe-navigation operator

Groovy has a number of little features that are exciting and help ease the development effort. You'll find them throughout this book. One such feature is the safe navigation operator (?.). It eliminates the mundane check for null, as in the next example:

GroovyForJavaEyes/Ease.groovy

```
def foo(str) {
  //if (str != null) { str.reverse() }
  str?.reverse()
}

println foo('evil')
println foo(null)
```

The ?. operator in the method foo() (programming books are required to have at least one method named "foo") calls the method or property only if the reference is not null. Let's run the code and look at the output:

```
live
null
```

The call to reverse() on the null reference using ?. resulted in a null instead of a NullPointerException—another way Groovy reduces noise and effort.

Exception Handling

Groovy has less ceremony than Java. That's crystal-clear in exception handling. Java forces us to handle checked exceptions. Consider a simple case: we want to call Thread's sleep() method. (Groovy provides an alternate sleep() method; see *Using sleep*, on page 130.) Java is adamant that we catch java.lang.InterruptedException. What does a Java developer do when forced? Finds a way around doing it. The result? Lots of empty catch blocks, right? Check this out:

GroovyForJavaEyes/Sleep.java
```java
// Java code
try {
  Thread.sleep(5000);
} catch(InterruptedException ex) {
  // eh? I'm losing sleep over what to do here.
}
```

Having an empty catch block is worse than not handling an exception. If we put in an empty catch block, we're suppressing the exception. If we don't handle it in the first place, it is propagated to the caller, who either can do something about it or can pass it yet again to its caller.

Groovy does not force us to handle exceptions that we don't want to handle or that are inappropriate at the current level of code. Any exception we don't handle is automatically passed on to a higher level. Here's an example of Groovy's answer to exception handling:

GroovyForJavaEyes/ExceptionHandling.groovy
```groovy
def openFile(fileName) {
  new FileInputStream(fileName)
}
```

The method openFile() does not handle the infamous FileNotFoundException. If the exception occurs, it's not suppressed. Instead, it's passed to the calling code, which can handle it, as in the next example:

GroovyForJavaEyes/ExceptionHandling.groovy
```groovy
try {
  openFile("nonexistentfile")
} catch(FileNotFoundException ex) {
  // Do whatever you like about this exception here
  println "Oops: " + ex
}
```

If we are interested in catching all Exceptions that may be thrown, we can simply omit the exception type in the catch statement:

GroovyForJavaEyes/ExceptionHandling.groovy
```groovy
try {
  openFile("nonexistentfile")
} catch(ex) {
  // Do whatever you like about this exception here
  println "Oops: " + ex
}
```

With the catch(ex) without any type in front of the variable ex, we can catch just about any exception thrown our way. Beware: this doesn't catch Errors or Throwables other than Exceptions. To catch *all* of them, use catch(Throwable throwable).

As we can see, Groovy lets us focus on getting our work done rather than on tackling annoying system-level details.

Groovy as Lightweight Java

Groovy has other features that make it lighter and easier to use. Here are some:

- The return statement is almost always optional (see Section 2.11, *Gotchas*, on page 46).

- The semicolon (;) is almost always optional, though we can use it to separate statements (see *The Semicolon Is Almost Always Optional*, on page 51).

- Methods and classes are public by default.

- The ?. operator dispatches calls only if the object reference is not null.

- We can initialize JavaBeans using named parameters (see Section 2.2, *JavaBeans*, on page 19).

- We're not forced to catch exceptions that we don't care to handle. They get passed to the caller of our code.

- We can use this within static methods to refer to the Class object. In the next example, the learn() method returns the class so we can chain calls:

  ```groovy
  class Wizard {
    def static learn(trick, action) {
      //...
      this
    }
  }
  ```

```
Wizard.learn('alohomora', {/*...*/})
  .learn('expelliarmus', {/*...*/})
  .learn('lumos', {/*...*/})
```

We've seen the expressive and concise nature of Groovy. Next we'll look at how Groovy reduces clutter in one of the most fundamental features of Java.

2.2 JavaBeans

It was exciting when the concept of JavaBeans was introduced—Java objects would be considered JavaBeans if they followed certain conventions to expose their *properties*. That raised a lot of hope, but we soon found that to access these properties, calls to mere getters and setters were required. The excitement came crashing down, and developers moved on to create thousands of silly methods in their applications.[2] If JavaBeans were human, they'd be on Prozac. To be fair, the intent of JavaBean is noble—it made component-based development, application assembly, and integration practical and paved the way for exceptional integrated development environment (IDE) and plug-in development.

Groovy treats JavaBeans with the respect they deserve. In Groovy, a JavaBean truly has properties. Let's start with Java code and reduce it to Groovy so we can see the difference.

GroovyForJavaEyes/Car.java
```java
//Java code
public class Car {
  private int miles;
  private final int year;

  public Car(int theYear) { year = theYear; }
  public int getMiles() { return miles; }
  public void setMiles(int theMiles) { miles = theMiles; }

  public int getYear() { return year; }

  public static void main(String[] args) {
    Car car = new Car(2008);

    System.out.println("Year: " + car.getYear());
    System.out.println("Miles: " + car.getMiles());
    System.out.println("Setting miles");
    car.setMiles(25);
    System.out.println("Miles: " + car.getMiles());
  }
}
```

---

2.   http://www.javaworld.com/javaworld/jw-09-2003/jw-0905-toolbox.html

That's all-too-familiar Java code, isn't it? Let's take a look at the output of the Car instance's properties:

```
Year: 2008
Miles: 0
Setting miles
Miles: 25
```

The previous Java code will run in Groovy, but we can reduce the clutter quite a bit if we rewrite it in Groovy:

GroovyForJavaEyes/GroovyCar.groovy
```
class Car {
  def miles = 0
  final year

  Car(theYear) { year = theYear }
}

Car car = new Car(2008)

println "Year: $car.year"
println "Miles: $car.miles"
println  'Setting miles'
car.miles = 25
println "Miles: $car.miles"
```

That code does the same thing (as we see in the following output), but it has less clutter and ceremony.

```
Year: 2008
Miles: 0
Setting miles
Miles: 25
```

def declared a *property* in this context. We can declare properties by either using def as in the example or giving the type (and optional value) as in int miles or int miles = 0. Groovy quietly created a getter and a setter method behind the scenes (just like how a constructor is created in Java if we don't write any constructor). When we call miles in our code, we're not referencing a field; instead, we're calling the getter method for the miles property. To make a property read-only, we declare it final, just like in Java. Optionally, we can add a type information to the declaration. Groovy provides a getter and no setter in this case. Any attempt to change the final field will result in an exception. We can mark fields as private, but Groovy does not honor that. So, if we want to make a variable private, we'd have to implement a setter that rejects any change. Let's verify these concepts with the following code:

GroovyForJavaEyes/GroovyCar2.groovy

```groovy
class Car {
  final year
  private miles = 0

  Car(theYear) { year = theYear }

  def getMiles() {
    println "getMiles called"
    miles
  }

  private void setMiles(miles) {
    throw new IllegalAccessException("you're not allowed to change miles")
  }

  def drive(dist) { if (dist > 0) miles += dist }
}
```

We declared year as final and miles as private. From within the drive() instance method we can't change year, but we can change miles. The setter prevents any change to the value of miles from outside the class. Let's use this Car class now.

GroovyForJavaEyes/GroovyCar2.groovy

```groovy
def car = new Car(2012)

println "Year: $car.year"
println "Miles: $car.miles"
println 'Driving'
car.drive(10)
println "Miles: $car.miles"

try {
  print 'Can I set the year? '
  car.year = 1900
} catch(groovy.lang.ReadOnlyPropertyException ex) {
  println ex.message
}

try {
  print 'Can I set the miles? '
  car.miles = 12
} catch(IllegalAccessException ex) {
  println ex.message
}
```

We can see in the following output that we're able to read the values for the two properties, but we're not allowed to set either of them.

```
Year: 2012
getMiles called
Miles: 0
Driving
getMiles called
Miles: 10
Can I set the year? Cannot set readonly property: year for class: Car
Can I set the miles? you're not allowed to change miles
```

If we want to access properties, we don't need to use getters or setters anymore in our call. The following code illustrates the elegance of this:

GroovyForJavaEyes/UsingProperties.groovy
```
Calendar.instance
// instead of Calendar.getInstance()
str = 'hello'

str.class.name
// instead of str.getClass().getName()
// Caution: Won't work for Maps, Builders,...
// use str.getClass().name to be safe
```

Use caution with the class property, however—some classes, like Map, and builders give special treatment to this property (see Section 6.5, *Using the Map Class*, on page 118, for example). As a result, in general, use getClass() instead of class to avoid any surprises.

2.3 Flexible Initialization and Named Arguments

Groovy gives us the flexibility to initialize a JavaBean class. When constructing an object, simply give values for properties as comma-separated name-value pairs. This is a post-construction operation if our class has a no-argument constructor. We can also design our methods so they can take named arguments. To take advantage of this feature, define the first parameter as a Map. Let's see these in action:

GroovyForJavaEyes/NamedParameters.groovy
```
class Robot {
  def type, height, width
  def access(location, weight, fragile) {
    println "Received fragile? $fragile, weight: $weight, loc: $location"
  }
}
robot = new Robot(type: 'arm', width: 10, height: 40)
println "$robot.type, $robot.height, $robot.width"

robot.access(x: 30, y: 20, z: 10, 50, true)
//You can change the order
robot.access(50, true, x: 30, y: 20, z: 10)
```

```
arm, 40, 10
Received fragile? true, weight: 50, loc: [x:30, y:20, z:10]
Received fragile? true, weight: 50, loc: [x:30, y:20, z:10]
```

The instance of Robot took type, height, and width parameters as name-value pairs. The flexible constructor the Groovy compiler created for us is used here.

The access() method receives three parameters, but if the first parameter is a Map we can float around the map's key-values in the argument list. In the first call to the access() method, we placed the values for the map, followed by the value for weight and the value for fragile. The arguments for the map can be moved further down in the arguments list if we desire, like in the second call to the access() method.

If the number of arguments we send is greater than the number of parameters the method expects and if the excess arguments are name-value pairs, then Groovy assumes the method's first parameter is a Map and groups all the name-value pairs in the arguments together as values for the first parameter. It then takes the rest of the arguments, in the presented order, as values for the remaining parameters, as we saw in the output.

Although the kind of flexibility in the Robot example is powerful, it can get confusing, so use it sparingly. If we desire named arguments, then it's better to simply accept one Map parameter and not mix different parameters. This feature also leads to a problem when we pass three integer arguments, as in our example. In this case, the arguments will be passed in order, no map is created from the arguments, and the result is not what we desire.

We can avoid confusion like this by explicitly naming the first parameter as a Map:

GroovyForJavaEyes/NamedParameters.groovy
```
def access(Map location, weight, fragile) {
  print "Received fragile? $fragile, weight: $weight, loc: $location"
}
```

Now, if our arguments do not contain two objects plus arbitrary name-value pairs, we will get an error.

As we can see, thanks to the makeover Groovy gave JavaBeans, they're quite vibrant in Groovy.

2.4 Optional Parameters

In Groovy we can make method and constructor parameters optional. In fact, we can make as many parameters optional as we like, but they have to be trailing. We can use this in evolutionary design to add new parameters to existing methods.

To define an optional parameter, simply give it a value in the parameter list. Here's an example of a log() function with optional base parameter. If we don't provide that argument, Groovy assumes a value of 10:

```
GroovyForJavaEyes/OptionalParameters.groovy
def log(x, base=10) {
  Math.log(x) / Math.log(base)
}


println log(1024)
println log(1024, 10)
println log(1024, 2)
```

Groovy fills the missing argument with the optional value, as we can see in the output:

```
3.0102999566398116
3.0102999566398116
10.0
```

Groovy also treats the trailing array parameter as optional. So, in the following example we can send zero or more values for the last parameter:

```
GroovyForJavaEyes/OptionalParameters.groovy
def task(name, String[] details) {
  println "$name - $details"
}


task 'Call', '123-456-7890'
task 'Call', '123-456-7890', '231-546-0987'
task 'Check Mail'
```

We can see from the output that Groovy gathers the trailing arguments into the array parameter:

```
Call - [123-456-7890]
Call - [123-456-7890, 231-546-0987]
Check Mail - []
```

Providing mundane arguments to methods can get tiring. Optional parameters reduce noise and allow for sensible defaults.

2.5   Using Multiple Assignments

Passing multiple arguments to methods is commonplace in many programming languages. Returning multiple results from functions, on the other hand, is not that common, though it can be quite convenient. We can return multiple results from functions and assign them to multiple variables in one shot. Simply return an array and use comma-separated variables wrapped in parentheses on the left side of the assignment.

In the next example, we have a function that splits a full name into first and last names. The split() function, as we'd expect, returns an array. We can assign the result of the splitName() function to a pair of variables: firstName and lastName. Groovy assigns the two values to the two variables, respectively.

GroovyForJavaEyes/MultipleAssignments.groovy

```groovy
def splitName(fullName) { fullName.split(' ') }

def (firstName, lastName) = splitName('James Bond')
println "$lastName, $firstName $lastName"
```

We didn't have to create temporary variables and write multiple assignment statements to set the result into the two variables, as the output shows:

```
Bond, James Bond
```

We can also use this feature to swap variables without having to create an intermediate variable to hold the values being swapped. Simply place the variables to be swapped within parentheses on the left and place them in reverse order within square brackets on the right.

GroovyForJavaEyes/MultipleAssignments.groovy

```groovy
def name1 = "Thomson"
def name2 = "Thompson"

println "$name1 and $name2"
(name1, name2) = [name2, name1]
println "$name1 and $name2"
```

The values of name1 and name2 were swapped, as we can see in the following output.

```
Thomson and Thompson
Thompson and Thomson
```

We've seen how Groovy takes care of multiple assignment when we have the proper number of variables on the left to receive the values on the right. Groovy can also deal with this gracefully when the number of variables and don't match. If we have excess variables, Groovy will set them to null, cess values will be discarded.

We can also specify types for individual variables being defined in the multiple assignment, as in the next example. To illustrate this, let's use the animals from a famous cartoon series.

GroovyForJavaEyes/MultipleAssignments.groovy
```
def (String cat, String mouse) = ['Tom', 'Jerry', 'Spike', 'Tyke']
println "$cat and $mouse"
```

On the left we only have two variables, and the dogs Spike and Tyke will be lost.

```
Tom and Jerry
```

In the next example we only have two values on the right, but more variables on the left.

GroovyForJavaEyes/MultipleAssignments.groovy
```
def (first, second, third) = ['Tom', 'Jerry']
println "$first, $second, and $third"
```

The value for the third variable is set to null.

```
Tom, Jerry, and null
```

If the excess variable is a primitive type, something that can't be set to null, then Groovy will throw an exception—this is a new behavior. int is treated as a primitive where possible, and not as an Integer in Groovy 2.x.

As you can see, Groovy makes it quite easy to send and receive multiple parameters.

2.6 Implementing Interfaces

In Groovy we can morph a map or a block of code into interfaces, which lets us implement interfaces with multiple methods quickly. In this section, you'll see a Java way of implementing interfaces, and then you'll learn how to take advantage of Groovy's facilities.

Here's the all-too-familiar Java code to register an event handler to a Swing JButton. The call to addActionListener() expects an instance that implements the ActionListener interface. We create an anonymous inner class that implements ActionListener, and we provide the required actionPerformed() method. This method insists on taking ActionEvent as an argument even though we have no use for it in this example.

```
// Java code
button.addActionListener(new ActionListener() {
  public void actionPerformed(ActionEvent ae) {
    JOptionPane.showMessageDialog(frame, "You clicked!");
  }
});
```

Groovy presents a charming idiomatic difference here—no need for that actionPerformed() method declaration or that explicit new anonymous inner class instance!

```
button.addActionListener(
  { JOptionPane.showMessageDialog(frame, "You clicked!") } as ActionListener
)
```

We call the addActionListener method and provide it with a block of code that morphs itself to implement the ActionListener interface because of the as operator.

That's it—Groovy takes care of the rest. It intercepts calls to any method on the interface (actionPerformed(), in this case) and routes it to the block of code we provided. To run this code we'll need to create the frame and its components; the full code listing is shown at the end of this section.

We don't have to do anything different if we plan to provide one single implementation for all the methods of a multimethod interface.

Suppose we want to display the location of the mouse pointer as the mouse is clicked and moved around in our application. In Java, we have to implement a total of seven methods of the MouseListener and MouseMotionListener interfaces. Since our implementation for all these methods is the same, Groovy makes our life easy.

```
displayMouseLocation = { positionLabel.setText("$it.x, $it.y") }
frame.addMouseListener(displayMouseLocation as MouseListener)
frame.addMouseMotionListener(displayMouseLocation as MouseMotionListener)
```

In this code, we created the variable displayMouseLocation that refers to a block of code. We then morphed it twice using the as operator—once for each of the interfaces, MouseListener and MouseMotionListener. Once again, Groovy takes care of the rest, and we can move on to focus on other things. It took three lines of code instead of...—sorry, I'm still counting—in Java.

In the previous example, we see the variable it again. it represents the method argument. If a method of the interface we're implementing takes multiple arguments, we can define them either as discrete arguments or as a parameter of type array—we'll discuss how in Chapter 4, *Using Closures*, on page 71.

Groovy does not force us to implement all the methods in an interface; we can define only the methods we care about and leave out the rest. If the methods left out are never called, then we didn't waste any effort implementing them. This technique is quite useful when implementing interfaces to mock up some behavior during unit testing.

OK, that was nice, but in most realistic situations, we'd want a different implementation for each method of an interface. No worries; Groovy can handle that. Simply create a map with each method name as a key and the method's body as the key's value—using the simple Groovy style—separate the method names from the code block using a colon (:). Also, we don't have to implement all the methods. We implement only those we really care about. If the methods we don't implement are never called, we didn't waste any effort implementing dummy stubs. Of course, if we fail to provide a method that's called, we'll get a NullPointerException. Let's put these to use in an example.

```
handleFocus = [
  focusGained : { msgLabel.setText("Good to see you!") },
  focusLost : { msgLabel.setText("Come back soon!") }
]
button.addFocusListener(handleFocus as FocusListener)
```

Whenever the button in this example gains focus, the first block of code associated with the key focusGained will be called. When the button loses focus, the block of code associated with focusLost is called. The keys in this case correspond to the methods of the FocusListener interface.

The as operator is good if we know the name of the interface we're implementing, but what if our application demands dynamic behavior and we'll know the interface name only at runtime? The asType() method comes to our rescue. We can use it to morph either a block of code or a map to an interface by sending the Class metaobject of the interface we want to implement as an argument to asType(). Let's look at an example.

Suppose we want to add an event handler for different events: WindowListener, ComponentListener... the list may be dynamic. Also suppose our handler will perform some common task to help with testing or debugging our application, such as logging or updating a status bar. We can dynamically add handlers for multiple events using a single block of code. Here's how:

```
events = ['WindowListener', 'ComponentListener']
// Above list may be dynamic and may come from some input
handler = { msgLabel.setText("$it") }
for (event in events) {
  handlerImpl = handler.asType(Class.forName("java.awt.event.${event}"))
  frame."add${event}"(handlerImpl)
}
```

The interfaces we want to implement—that is, the events we want to handle—are in the list events. This list is dynamic; suppose it will be populated with input during code execution. The common handler for the events is in the code block the variable handler refers to. We loop through the events, and for each event, we create an implementation of the interface using the asType() method. This method is called on the block of code and is given the Class metaobject of the interface obtained using the forName() method. Once we have the implementation of the listener interface on hand, we can register it by calling the appropriate add method (like addWindowListener()). The call to the add method itself is dynamic. You'll learn more about such methods later, in Section 11.2, *Querying Methods and Properties*, on page 180.

In the previous code, we used the asType() method. If we have different implementations for different methods, we'd have a map instead of a single block of code. In that case, we can call the asType() method on the map in a similar way. Finally, as promised, here is the full listing of the Groovy Swing code developed in this section:

GroovyForJavaEyes/Swing.groovy
```groovy
import javax.swing.*
import java.awt.*
import java.awt.event.*

frame = new JFrame(size: [300, 300],
  layout: new FlowLayout(),
  defaultCloseOperation: javax.swing.WindowConstants.EXIT_ON_CLOSE)
button = new JButton("click")
positionLabel = new JLabel("")
msgLabel = new JLabel("")
frame.contentPane.add button
frame.contentPane.add positionLabel
frame.contentPane.add msgLabel

button.addActionListener(
  { JOptionPane.showMessageDialog(frame, "You clicked!") } as ActionListener
)

displayMouseLocation = { positionLabel.setText("$it.x, $it.y") }
frame.addMouseListener(displayMouseLocation as MouseListener)
frame.addMouseMotionListener(displayMouseLocation as MouseMotionListener)

handleFocus = [
  focusGained : { msgLabel.setText("Good to see you!") },
  focusLost : { msgLabel.setText("Come back soon!") }
]
button.addFocusListener(handleFocus as FocusListener)
```

```
events = ['WindowListener', 'ComponentListener']
// Above list may be dynamic and may come from some input
handler = { msgLabel.setText("$it") }
for (event in events) {
  handlerImpl = handler.asType(Class.forName("java.awt.event.${event}"))
  frame."add${event}"(handlerImpl)
}
```

```
frame.show()
```

We've now covered the Groovy way to implement interfaces. It makes register-ing for events and passing anonymous implementations of interfaces really simple. The ability to morph blocks of code and maps into interface implemen-tations is a real time-saver.

2.7 Groovy Boolean Evaluation

Boolean evaluation in Groovy is different than in Java. Depending on the context, Groovy will automatically evaluate expressions as boolean.

Let's see a specific example. The following Java code will not work:

```
//Java code
String obj = "hello";
int val = 4;
if (obj) {} // ERROR
if(val) {} //ERROR
```

Java insists that we provide a boolean expression for the condition part of the if statement. It wants if(obj != null) and if(val > 0) in the previous example, for instance.

Groovy is not that picky. It tries to infer, so we need to know what Groovy is thinking.

If we place an object reference where a boolean expression is expected, Groovy checks whether the reference is null. It considers null as false, and true otherwise, as in the following code:

```
str = 'hello'
if (str) { println 'hello' }
```

Groovy evaluates the expression as Boolean, as we can see in the output:

```
hello
```

I must admit what I said about true earlier is not entirely true. If the object reference is not-null, then the truth depends on the type of the object. For example, if the object is a collection (like java.util.ArrayList), then Groovy checks whether the collection is empty. So, in this case, the expression if (obj) evaluates as true only if obj is not null and the collection has at least one element; look at the following code example:

```
lst0 = null
println lst0 ? 'lst0 true' : 'lst0 false'
lst1 = [1, 2, 3]
println lst1 ? 'lst1 true' : 'lst1 false'
lst2 = []
println lst2 ? 'lst2 true' : 'lst2 false'
```

We can check our understanding of how Groovy handles boolean for Collections with the following output:

```
lst0 false
lst1 true
lst2 false
```

Collections are not the only things that receive special boolean treatment. To see the types that get special treatment and how Groovy evaluates their truth, refer to the following table:

Type	Condition for Truth
Boolean	True
Collection	Not empty
Character	Value not 0
CharSequence	Length greater than 0
Enumeration	Has more elements
Iterator	Has next
Number	Double value not 0
Map	Not empty
Matcher	At least one match
Object[]	Length greater than 0
Any other type	Reference not null

Table 1—Types and Their Special Treatment for Boolean Evaluation

In addition to enjoying the built-in Groovy truth conventions, we can write our own boolean conversions easily by implementing an asBoolean() method in our classes.

2.8 Operator Overloading

We can use Groovy's support for operator overloading—judiciously—to create DSLs (see Chapter 19, *Creating DSLs in Groovy*, on page 295). When Java has no support for operator overloading, how does Groovy get away with that? It's really simple: each operator has a standard mapping to methods.[3] In Java we can use those methods, and on the Groovy side we can use either the operators or their corresponding methods.

Here's an example to show operator overloading in action:

GroovyForJavaEyes/OperatorOverloading.groovy
```
for(ch = 'a'; ch < 'd'; ch++) {
  println ch
}
```

We're looping through the characters *a* through *c* using the ++ operator. This operator maps to the next() method on the String class to produce this output:

```
a
b
c
```

We can use the concise for-each syntax in Groovy, but both implementations use the next() method of String:

GroovyForJavaEyes/OperatorOverloading.groovy
```
for (ch in 'a'..'c') {
  println ch
}
```

The String class has a number of operators overloaded, as you'll see in Section 5.4, *String Convenience Methods*, on page 105. Similarly, the collection classes—ArrayList and Map—have operators overloaded for convenience.

To add an element to a collection, we can use the << operator, which translates to the Groovy-added leftShift() method on Collection, as shown here:

GroovyForJavaEyes/OperatorOverloading.groovy
```
lst = ['hello']
lst << 'there'
println lst
```

We can see the full collection, after the append, in the output:

```
[hello, there]
```

We can provide operators for our own classes by adding the mapping methods, such as plus() for +.

Let's add an operator-overloaded method to a class:

---

3.   http://groovy.codehaus.org/Operator+Overloading

GroovyForJavaEyes/OperatorOverloading.groovy
```groovy
class ComplexNumber {
  def real, imaginary
  def plus(other) {
    new ComplexNumber(real: real + other.real,
         imaginary: imaginary + other.imaginary)
  }
  String toString() { "$real ${imaginary > 0 ? '+' : ''} ${imaginary}i"}
}
c1 = new ComplexNumber(real: 1, imaginary: 2)
c2 = new ComplexNumber(real: 4, imaginary: 1)
println c1 + c2
```

We overloaded the + operator on the ComplexNumber class. Complex numbers are useful for computing complex equations that involve the square root of negative numbers—they have real and imaginary parts, like our actual income and what we report on our tax returns. Because we added the plus() method on the ComplexNumber class, we can use + to add two complex numbers to get a resulting (more?) complex number:

```
5 + 3i
```

Operator overloading can make code expressive when used within a context. We should overload only operators that will make things very obvious. For example, overloading might not be a good choice if its not intuitive to someone with knowledge of context or domain.

When overloading, we must preserve the expected semantics. For instance, + must not change any of the operands in the operation. If an operation must be commutative, symmetric, or transitive, we have to make sure the implementation of the overloaded methods adhere to that.

2.9 Support of Java 5 Language Features

Java 5 language features like enums and annotations work in Groovy also. This means we can mix Java and Groovy quite fluently. To refresh, the Java 5 language features are as follows:

- Autoboxing
- for-each
- enum
- Varargs
- Annotation
- Static import
- Generics

Let's discuss the extent of the Groovy support for these features.

Autoboxing

Groovy, because of its dynamic typing, supports autoboxing from the get-go. In fact, Groovy automatically treats primitives as objects where necessary. For instance, execute the following code:

GroovyForJavaEyes/NotInt.groovy
```
int val = 5

println val.getClass().name
```

The type is reported as follows:

```
java.lang.Integer
```

In this code, we created an instance of java.lang.Integer and not a primitive int, even though we specified int. Groovy decides to store the instance as an int or Integer based on how we use it. Groovy's handling of autoboxing is a notch better than Java's. In Java, autoboxing and unboxing involve constant casting. Groovy, on the other hand, simply treats them as objects—so there's no repeated casting involved.

Prior to version 2.0 all primitive types were treated as objects in Groovy. To improve performance and use more-direct bytecode for operations on primitives, starting in version 2.0 Groovy does some optimization. Primitives are treated as objects only where necessary—for instance, if we invoke methods on them or pass them to object references. Otherwise, Groovy retains them as primitive types at the bytecode level.

for-each

Groovy's support for looping is superior to Java's (see *Ways to Loop*, on page 13). We can still use the traditional for loop (that is, for(int i = 0; i < 10; i++) {...}) in Groovy. Or, if we like the simpler form supported in Java 5, we can use that. In Java 5, objects that implement the Iterable interface can be used in a for-each loop, as in this example:

GroovyForJavaEyes/ForEach.java
```
// Java code
String[] greetings = {"Hello", "Hi", "Howdy"};

for(String greet : greetings) {
  System.out.println(greet);
}
```

We can rewrite it in Groovy like this:

GroovyForJavaEyes/ForEach.groovy
```groovy
String[] greetings = ["Hello", "Hi", "Howdy"]
for(String greet : greetings) {
  println greet
}
```

Groovy insists that we specify the type (String in the previous example) or def in the Java style for-each. If we don't want to specify the type, we use the in keyword instead of a colon (:), as in the next example:

GroovyForJavaEyes/ForEach.groovy
```groovy
for(greet in greetings) {
  println greet
}
```

In Groovy we prefer for with in over the Java-style for-each syntax. Alternatively, we can use the each() internal iterator (see Chapter 6, *Working with Collections*, on page 109).

enum

Groovy provides support for enum, which is the Java 5 feature that solves problems with enumerations. It's type-safe (we can distinguish between shirt sizes and days of the week, for example), printable, serializable, and so on.

Here's an example that defines different sizes of coffee drinks we can order:

GroovyForJavaEyes/UsingCoffeeSize.groovy
```groovy
enum CoffeeSize { SHORT, SMALL, MEDIUM, LARGE, MUG }
def orderCoffee(size) {
  print "Coffee order received for size $size: "
  switch(size) {
    case [CoffeeSize.SHORT, CoffeeSize.SMALL]:
      println "you're health conscious"
      break
    case CoffeeSize.MEDIUM..CoffeeSize.LARGE:
      println "you gotta be a programmer"
      break
    case CoffeeSize.MUG:
      println "you should try Caffeine IV"
      break
  }
}
orderCoffee(CoffeeSize.SMALL)
orderCoffee(CoffeeSize.LARGE)
orderCoffee(CoffeeSize.MUG)
print 'Available sizes are: '
for(size in CoffeeSize.values()) {
    print "$size "
}
```

The convenience of the switch statement and iteration on enums in the preceding code produces this output:

```
Coffee order received for size SMALL: you're health conscious
Coffee order received for size LARGE: you gotta be a programmer
Coffee order received for size MUG: you should try Caffeine IV
Available sizes are: SHORT SMALL MEDIUM LARGE MUG
```

We can use enum values in case statements. Specifically, we can use a single value, a list of values, or even a range of values. Examples of all these flavors are in the previous code.

We can define constructors and methods for Java 5 enum, and Groovy supports that too. See the next example:

GroovyForJavaEyes/AgileMethodologies.groovy
```
enum Methodologies {
    Evo(5),
    XP(21),
    Scrum(30);

    final int daysInIteration
    Methodologies(days) { daysInIteration = days }

    def iterationDetails() {
        println "${this} recommends $daysInIteration days for iteration"
    }
}

for(methodology in Methodologies.values()) {
    methodology.iterationDetails()
}
```

Take a look at the output from iterating over the values in our enum:

```
Evo recommends 5 days for iteration
XP recommends 21 days for iteration
Scrum recommends 30 days for iteration
```

varargs

Remember, with Java 5 varargs we can pass a variable number of arguments to methods, such as the printf() method. To use this feature in Java, we mark the trailing parameter type of a method with an ellipsis, as in public static Object max(Object... args). This is syntactic sugar—Java rolls all the arguments into an array at call time.

Groovy supports Java 5 varargs in two ways. In addition to supporting parameters marked with ellipses (...), we can pass variable arguments to methods that accept an array as a trailing parameter.

Let's look at a Groovy example for these two ways:

GroovyForJavaEyes/VarArgs.groovy
```groovy
def receiveVarArgs(int a, int... b) {
  println "You passed $a and $b"
}

def receiveArray(int a, int[] b) {
  println "You passed $a and $b"
}

receiveVarArgs(1, 2, 3, 4, 5)
receiveArray(1, 2, 3, 4, 5)
```

Both the versions received a variable number of arguments, as we see in the output:

```
You passed 1 and [2, 3, 4, 5]
You passed 1 and [2, 3, 4, 5]
```

We can send either an array or discrete values to methods that accept varargs or an array as trailing parameters, and Groovy figures out what to do.

We must use caution when we send an array instead of discrete values. Groovy treats the values wrapped in square brackets [] as an instance of ArrayList, not of the plain vanilla array. So if we simply send, for example, [2, 3, 4, 5], we'll get a MethodMissingException. To send an array, either define a reference of the array type or use the as operator.

GroovyForJavaEyes/VarArgs.groovy
```groovy
int[] values = [2, 3, 4, 5]
receiveVarArgs(1, values)
receiveVarArgs(1, [2, 3, 4, 5] as int[])
```

For the most part, Groovy makes typing optional, but here we see that specifying the type changes the semantics.

Annotations

We can use annotations in Java to express metadata, and Java 5 ships with a few predefined annotations, such as @Override, @Deprecated, and @SuppressWarnings.

We can define and use annotations in Groovy. The syntax for defining in Groovy is the same as in Java.

We use annotations most often for a framework or a tool to use; for example, JUnit 4.0 uses the @Test annotation. If we're using frameworks like Hibernate, JPA, Seam, Spring, and so on, we'll find Groovy's support for annotations quite helpful.

The Groovy compiler does not treat the Java compilation-related annotations the same way the Java compiler does. For example, groovyc ignores @Override.

Static Import

Static import in Java helps import static methods of a class into our namespace so we can refer to them without specifying the class name. For instance, if we place

```
import static Math.random;
```

in our Java code, then instead of Math.random(), we can call it like this:

```
double val = random();
```

Static import in Java improves job security. If we define several static imports or use * to import all static methods of a class, we're sure to confuse the heck out of programmers trying to figure out where these methods come from.

Groovy extends that luxury of job security to us in two forms. First, it implements static import. We can use it just like in Java. Feel free to lose the semicolon—that's optional in Groovy. Second, we can define aliases in Groovy—for both static methods and class names. To define an alias, use the as operator in the import statement:

```
import static Math.random as rand
import groovy.lang.ExpandoMetaClass as EMC

double value = rand()
def metaClass = new EMC(Integer)
assert metaClass.getClass().name == 'groovy.lang.ExpandoMetaClass'
```

In the previous code, we created rand() as an alias for the Math.random() method. We also created an alias EMC for the ExpandoMetaClass. Now we can use rand() and EMC instead of Math.random() and ExpandoMetaClass, respectively.

Generics

Groovy is a dynamically typed language with optional typing. Since it's a superset of Java, it supports Generics. However, the Groovy compiler does not perform type-checking the same way the Java compiler does (see *Compile-Time Type-Checking Is Off by Default*, on page 47); don't expect the Groovy compiler to reject at the outset code with type violations, like the Java compiler does. Groovy's dynamic typing will interplay here with generic types to get our code running, if possible. To see the stark difference between the two compilers, in the next example we'll add a few values of different types to an ArrayList of Integer.

Let's start with Java code:

```
GroovyForJavaEyes/Generics.java
// Java code
import java.util.ArrayList;

public class Generics {
  public static void main(String[] args) {
    ArrayList<Integer> list = new ArrayList<Integer>();
    list.add(1);
    list.add(2.0);
    list.add("hello");

    System.out.println("List populated");
    for(int element : list) { System.out.println(element); }
  }
}
```

When we compile that Java code using the Java compiler, we get a compilation error:

```
Generics.java:8: error: no suitable method found for add(double)
    list.add(2.0);
        ^
    method ArrayList.add(int,Integer) is not applicable
      (actual and formal argument lists differ in length)
    method ArrayList.add(Integer) is not applicable
      (actual argument double cannot be converted to Integer
         by method invocation conversion)
Generics.java:9: error: no suitable method found for add(String)
    list.add("hello");
        ^
    method ArrayList.add(int,Integer) is not applicable
      (actual and formal argument lists differ in length)
    method ArrayList.add(Integer) is not applicable
      (actual argument String cannot be converted to Integer
         by method invocation conversion)
2 errors
```

The Java compiler was not happy with us sending anything but an integer—or int, which will be autoboxed to Integer—to the add() method because we specified that the list will hold only Integers.

Let's see how Groovy deals with this. Copy the previous code to a file named Generics.groovy, and then run groovy Generics. Groovy will not prevent us from running the code:

```
List populated
1
2
Caught: org.codehaus.groovy.runtime.typehandling.GroovyCastException:
```

```
Cannot cast object 'hello' with class 'java.lang.String' to class 'int'
org.codehaus.groovy.runtime.typehandling.GroovyCastException:
Cannot cast object 'hello' with class 'java.lang.String' to class 'int'
        at Generics.main(Generics.java:12)
        at Generics.invokeMethod(Generics.java)
        at RunGenerics.run(RunGenerics.groovy:1)
```

Groovy took the type information more as a suggestion during the calls to the add() method. When we looped through the collection, Groovy tried to cast the elements as an int. A runtime failure results when such casting is not possible.

Groovy supports Generics while favoring dynamic behavior. The previous code example shows quite an interesting interplay of the two concepts. This dual nature of Groovy may be a surprise at first, but it will make sense when you learn the benefits of Groovy metaprogramming (see Part III, *MOPping Groovy*, on page 173).

The usefulness of Generics is not totally lost in Groovy. Groovy 2.x provides rigorous type-checking on parts of the code if we're willing to compromise metaprogramming capabilities—see Section 3.8, *Switching Off Dynamic Typing*, on page 65.

2.10 Using Groovy Code-Generation Transformations

Groovy tactfully eases the tension that language designers often face between a desire to evolve the language and a reluctance to modify the grammar due to its impact on performance, complexity, and semantic correctness. Rather than modifying the core syntax of the language, the Groovy compiler recognizes select annotations and generates appropriate code. In this section you'll learn about a few such annotations. Chapter 16, *Applying Compile-Time Metaprogramming*, on page 235, covers how to create our own annotations for custom transformations.

Groovy provides a number of code-generation annotations in the groovy.transform package and a few other packages. We'll talk about a few of these annotations in this section.

Using @Canonical

If we find ourselves writing a toString() method that simply displays select fields values as comma-separated, we can let the Grooovy compiler work for us by using the @Canonical transformation. By default it includes all the fields; however, we can ask it to include certain fields and exclude others, like in the next example.

GroovyForJavaEyes/Annotations.groovy
```groovy
import groovy.transform.*

@Canonical(excludes="lastName, age")
class Person {
  String firstName
  String lastName
  int age
}

def sara = new Person(firstName: "Sara", lastName: "Walker", age: 49)
println sara
```

Groovy excludes the fields we mentioned and prints the class name followed by the values for the remaining field(s), as we can see in the output.

```
Person(Sara)
```

Using @Delegate

Inheritance must be savored only where the derived class is truly substitutable and used in place of the base class. For most other purposes, delegation is better than inheritance from pure code-reuse point of view. Yet in Java we're reluctant to use delegation, as that leads to code duplication and more effort. Groovy makes delegation quite easy, so we can make the proper design choice.

To better understand delegation, let's start with a Worker class that has a few methods in it. Expert has one method with the same name and signature as the Worker class. Manager, as we'd expect, does nothing. But this manager is smart at delegating work, so the two fields are marked with the @Delegate annotation.

GroovyForJavaEyes/Annotations.groovy
```groovy
class Worker {
  def work() { println 'get work done' }
  def analyze() { println 'analyze...' }
  def writeReport() { println 'get report written' }
}
class Expert {
  def analyze() { println "expert analysis..." }
}
class Manager {
  @Delegate Expert expert = new Expert()
  @Delegate Worker worker = new Worker()
}
def bernie = new Manager()
bernie.analyze()
bernie.work()
bernie.writeReport()
```

At compile time, Groovy examines the Manager class and brings in methods from the delegated classes only if those methods don't already exist. As a result, it brings in the analyze() method of the Expert first. From the Worker class it brings in only the work() and writeReport() methods. At this time, since the analyze() method is present in the Manager, brought in from Expert, the one in Worker is ignored.

For each of the methods that are brought in, Groovy simply routes a call to the method on the instance, like so: public Object analyze() { expert.analyze() }. The delegating class responds to the newly acquired methods, as we can see in the following output.

```
expert analysis...
get work done
get report written
```

The Manager class is extensible thanks to the @Delegate annotation. If we add or remove methods to the Worker or the Expert class, we don't have to make any changes to Manager for the corresponding change to take effect. Simply recompile the code, and Groovy takes care of the rest.

Using @Immutable

Immutable objects are inherently thread-safe, and it is a good practice to mark fields as final. Groovy makes it easier to do the right thing by marking the fields as final and, as a bonus, creating some convenience methods for us if we mark a class with the @Immutable annotation.

Let's use this annotation in a CreditCard class.

```
GroovyForJavaEyes/Annotations.groovy
@Immutable
class CreditCard {
  String cardNumber
  int creditLimit
}

println new CreditCard("4000-1111-2222-3333", 1000)
```

Groovy rewards our gesture by providing us with a constructor where parameters appear in the order of the fields. The fields can't be changed after the construction time. In addition, Groovy adds the hashCode(), equals(), and toString() methods. Let's look at the output from exercising the provided constructor and the toString() method.

```
CreditCard(4000-1111-2222-3333, 1000)
```

We can use the @Immutable annotation to create lightweight immutable-value objects easily. These are ideal instances to pass as messages in the actor-based model in concurrent applications, where thread-safety is a big concern.

Using @Lazy

We want to defer the construction of time-consuming objects until we actually need them. We can be lazy and productive at the same time, write less code, and reap all the benefits of lazy initialization.

In the next example we want to postpone the creation of the instances of Heavy until they're needed. We can directly initialize instances at the point of declaration or we can wrap the logic for creation within a closure.

GroovyForJavaEyes/Annotations.groovy
```groovy
class Heavy {
  def size = 10
  Heavy() { println "Creating Heavy with $size" }
}

class AsNeeded {
  def value

  @Lazy Heavy heavy1 = new Heavy()
  @Lazy Heavy heavy2 = { new Heavy(size: value) }()

  AsNeeded() { println  "Created AsNeeded" }
}

def asNeeded = new AsNeeded(value: 1000)
println asNeeded.heavy1.size
println asNeeded.heavy1.size
println asNeeded.heavy2.size
```

Groovy not only defers the creation, but also marks the field as volatile and ensures thread safety during creation. The instances are created on the first access to the fields, as we can see in the output.

```
Created AsNeeded
Creating Heavy with 10
10
10
Creating Heavy with 10
1000
```

The @Lazy annotation provides a painless way to implement the virtual proxy pattern with thread safety as a bonus.

Using @Newify

In Groovy we often follow the traditional Java syntax of using new to create an instance. Losing this keyword will improve the fluency when creating DSLs, however. The @Newify annotation can help us create Ruby-like constructors where new is a method on the class. It can also help us create Python-like constructors (and Scala-like applicators) where we can do away with new entirely. To create the Python-like constructor, we must specify the list of types to the @Newify annotation. The Ruby-style constructor is created for us unless we set the value auto=false as a parameter to @Newify.

We can use the @Newify annotation in various scopes, such as classes or methods, as in the next example.

GroovyForJavaEyes/Annotations.groovy
```
@Newify([Person, CreditCard])
def fluentCreate() {
  println Person.new(firstName: "John", lastName: "Doe", age: 20)
  println Person(firstName: "John", lastName: "Doe", age: 20)
  println CreditCard("1234-5678-1234-5678", 2000)
}
```

```
fluentCreate()
```

The output indicates that with annotation we can create the instances using the Ruby and Python styles.

```
Person(John)
Person(John)
CreditCard(1234-5678-1234-5678, 2000)
```

The @Newify annotation is quite helpful when creating DSLs, making instance creation more of an implicit operation.

Using @Singleton

To implement the singleton pattern, normally we'd create a static field and a static method to initialize that field, then return that singleton instance. We have to ensure that this method is thread-safe and decide whether we want a lazy creation of the singleton. We can eliminate this effort entirely by using the @Singleton transformation, as in the following example.

GroovyForJavaEyes/Annotations.groovy
```
@Singleton(lazy = true)
class TheUnique {
  private TheUnique() { println 'Instance created' }

  def hello() { println 'hello' }
}
```

```
println "Accessing TheUnique"
TheUnique.instance.hello()
TheUnique.instance.hello()
```

When we run the code, the instance is created on the first call to the instance property, which maps to the getInstance() method.

```
Accessing TheUnique
Instance created
hello
hello
```

We marked the TheUnique class with the annotation to generate the static getInstance() method. Since we set the value for the lazy property to true, Groovy delays the creation of the instance until requested. We can examine the generated code by copying and pasting the previous code into groovyConsole and selecting the script | Inspect AST menu item.

```
public class TheUnique implements
  groovy.lang.GroovyObject extends java.lang.Object {

    private static volatile TheUnique instance
    //...

    private TheUnique() {
        metaClass = /*BytecodeExpression*/
        this.println('Instance created')
    }

    public java.lang.Object hello() {
        return this.println('hello')
    }

    public static TheUnique getInstance() {
        if ( instance != null) {
            return instance
        } else {
            synchronized (TheUnique) {
                if ( instance != null) {
                    return instance
                } else {
                    return instance = new TheUnique()
                }
            }
        }
    }
//...
```

Groovy not only delays the instance creation until the last responsible moment, but also makes the creation part thread-safe.

There's one caveat to using the @Singleton annotation. It makes the constructor of the target class private, as we'd expect, but since Groovy does not honor privacy, we can still create instances using the new keyword from within Groovy. We must take care to use the class properly and heed the warnings from code-analysis tools and integrated development environments.

In addition to what we've seen so far, Groovy provides an annotation that removes drudgery when extending classes with multiple constructors. Java forces us to mundanely implement the multiple constructors even if we merely want to route the calls back to the respective super constructors. If we annotate the class with @InheritConstructors, Groovy generates these constructors for us.

We've seen the beautiful side of Groovy, but as objective programmers, we must also acknowledge things that may trip us up. Learning those now will help us use caution where needed. We'll do that in the next section.

2.11 Gotchas

We'll see a number of nice Groovy capabilities throughout this book, but some "gotchas" do exist, ranging from minor annoyances to potential surprises. In the following sections, we'll explore a few of them.

Groovy's == Is Equal to Java's equals

== and equals() are a source of confusion in Java, and Groovy adds to the confusion. Groovy maps the == operator to the equals() method in Java. What if we want to actually perform the reference equals (the original ==, that is)? We have to use is() in Groovy for that. Let's understand the difference via an example:

GroovyForJavaEyes/Equals.groovy
```
str1 = 'hello'
str2 = str1
str3 = new String('hello')
str4 = 'Hello'

println "str1 == str2: ${str1 == str2}"
println "str1 == str3: ${str1 == str3}"
println "str1 == str4: ${str1 == str4}"

println "str1.is(str2): ${str1.is(str2)}"
println "str1.is(str3): ${str1.is(str3)}"
println "str1.is(str4): ${str1.is(str4)}"
```

Let's look at the behavior of the == operator in Groovy and the result of using the is method:

```
str1 == str2: true
str1 == str3: true
str1 == str4: false
str1.is(str2): true
str1.is(str3): false
str1.is(str4): false
```

The observation that Groovy == maps to equals() is only partially true—that mapping happens only if the class does not implement the Comparable interface. If it does, then it maps to the class's compareTo() method.

The following example shows this behavior:

GroovyForJavaEyes/WhatsEquals.groovy
```
class A {
  boolean equals(other) {
    println "equals called"
    false
  }
}

class B implements Comparable {
  boolean equals(other) {
    println "equals called"
    false
  }

  int compareTo(other) {
    println "compareTo called"
    0
  }
}

new A() == new A()
new B() == new B()
```

We can see Comparable taking precedence in the output:

```
equals called
compareTo called
```

In the output we see that the operator picks the compareTo() method over the equals() method for classes that implement the Comparable interface.

Use caution when comparing objects—first ask whether you're comparing references or values, and then ask whether you're using the correct operator.

Compile-Time Type-Checking Is Off by Default

Groovy is optionally typed; however, for the most part the Groovy compiler, groovyc, does not perform full type-checking. (Chapter 3, *Dynamic Typing*, on page 53, shows how Groovy allows selective type-checking.) Instead it performs casting when it encounters type definitions. Let's assign a string to a variable of the Integer type:

GroovyForJavaEyes/NoTypeCheck.groovy

```
Integer val = 4
val = 'hello'
```

The code will compile with no errors. When we try to run the Java bytecode created, we will receive a GroovyCastException exception, as we see in the output:

```
org.codehaus.groovy.runtime.typehandling.GroovyCastException:
Cannot cast object 'hello' with class 'java.lang.String'
to class 'java.lang.Integer'
```

The Groovy compiler, instead of verifying the type, simply cast it and left it to the runtime to deal with. We can verify this by digging into the generated bytecode (we can use the javap -c ClassFileName command to peek at the human-readable form of the bytecode):

```
...
35: ldc #71 // String hello
37: astore_3
38: aload_3
39: ldc #65 // class java/lang/Integer
41: invokestatic  #75 // Method ...castToType:(...)...
44: checkcast #65 // class java/lang/Integer
...
```

So, in Groovy, x = y is semantically equivalent to x = (ClassOfX)(y). Similarly, if we call a method that does not exist (such as the method call to the nonexistent method blah in the following example), we will get no compilation error:

GroovyForJavaEyes/NoTypeCheck.groovy

```
Integer val = 4
val.blah()
```

We will get a MissingMethodException at runtime, however:

```
groovy.lang.MissingMethodException:
No signature of method: java.lang.Integer.blah() is applicable
for argument types: () values: []
Possible solutions: each(groovy.lang.Closure), with(groovy.lang.Closure),
plus(java.lang.Character), plus(java.lang.String), plus(java.lang.Number),
wait()
```

This is actually an advantage, as you'll see in Chapter 13, *MOP Method Injection*, on page 193. Between when the code is compiled and when it is executed, we can inject missing methods dynamically.

The Groovy compiler may appear relaxed, but this behavior is necessary for the dynamic and metaprogramming strengths of Groovy.[4] In version 2.x we can turn this dynamic typing feature off and enhance compile-time type-checking, as we'll explore in Section 3.8, *Switching Off Dynamic Typing*, on page 65, and *Static Type-Checking*, on page 66.

Be Aware of New Keywords

def and in are among the new keywords in Groovy. def defines methods, properties, and local variables. in is used in for loops to specify the range for looping, as in for(i in 1..10).

Using these keywords as variable names or method names may lead to problems, especially when using existing Java code as Groovy code.

It is also not a smart idea to define a variable named it. Although Groovy will not complain, if we use a field by that name within a closure, the name refers to the closure parameter and not a field in our class—hiding variables is not going to help us pay our technical debt.[5]

No Code Block

The following is valid Java code:

GroovyForJavaEyes/Block.java
```
// Java code
public void method() {
  System.out.println("in method1");

  {
    System.out.println("in block");
  }
}
```

Code blocks in Java define a new scope, but Groovy gets confused. It thinks we're defining a closure and complains. We can't have arbitrary code blocks like this within methods in Groovy.

Closures—Anonymous-Inner-Classes Conflict

Groovy closures are defined using curly braces—{...}—which we also use to define the body for anonymous inner classes. We run into issues when our constructor accepts a closure as a parameter, as in the next example.

---

4. http://groovy.codehaus.org/Runtime+vs+Compile+time,+Static+vs+Dynamic
5. http://martinfowler.com/bliki/TechnicalDebt.html

GroovyForJavaEyes/Calibrator.groovy
```
class Calibrator {
  Calibrator(calculationBlock) {
    print "using..."
    calculationBlock()
  }
}
```

We normally pass a closure to functions by attaching a code block to the tail
end of the function call, like so: instance.method() {...}. Following that convention,
we can instantiate an instance of Calibrartor by passing a closure to its constructor, as in the next piece of code.

GroovyForJavaEyes/AnonymousConflict.groovy
```
def calibrator = new Calibrator() {
  println "the calculation provided"
}
```

In this example, we're calling the Calibrator class's constructor, which accepts
a closure as a parameter. Contrary to our expectations, Groovy assumes we're
creating an anonymous inner class and results in an error.

```
org.codehaus.groovy.control.MultipleCompilationErrorsException: startup failed:
.../code/GroovyForJavaEyes/AnonymousConflict.groovy:
2: unexpected token: println @ line 2, column 3.
     println "the calculation provided"
     ^

1 error
```

To work around this gotcha, we have to break away from the call convention
and place the closure within the constructor-call parentheses. We can still
define the closure at the point of call or pass a variable that refers to the
closure.

GroovyForJavaEyes/AnonymousConflictResolved.groovy
```
def calibrator1 = new Calibrator({
  println "the calculation provided"
})
def calculation = { println "another calculation provided" }
def calibrator2 = new Calibrator(calculation)
```

Let's run the code to verify this version does not confuse Groovy and produces
the desired result of passing the closure to the constructor.

```
using...the calculation provided
using...another calculation provided
```

This is a minor inconvenience; passing a reference to a closure is less noisy
than passing an inline closure.

The Semicolon Is Almost Always Optional

Programmers of C-derived languages who have subjected their pinky fingers to years of abuse will find relief in Groovy. We don't have to place a semicolon (;) at the end of statements. Losing semicolons is good—it helps in creating DSLs. Semicolons are optional but still useful for placing multiple statements on the same line. There's at least one place where the semicolon is not optional, though, as the following example illustrates:

GroovyForJavaEyes/SemiColon.groovy
```
class Semi {
  def val = 3

  {
    println "Instance Initializer called..."
  }
}

println new Semi()
```

We intend the code block to be an instance initializer for our class, but Groovy gets confused, treats the instance initializer as a closure, and gives the following error:

```
Caught: groovy.lang.MissingMethodException:
No signature of method: java.lang.Integer.call()
is applicable for argument types: (Semi$_closure1)
values: {Semi$_closure1@be513c}
  at Semi.<init>(SemiColon.groovy:3)
  at SemiColon.run(SemiColon.groovy:10)
  at SemiColon.main(SemiColon.groovy)
```

If we replace def val = 3 with def val = 3;, the code will run fine. Now Groovy recognizes the block of code as an instance initializer, not as being attached to the property definition.

If we have a static initializer instead of an instance initializer, we won't have this problem. If we have reason to use both static and instance initializers, we can avoid the semicolon by placing the static initializer before the instance initializer.

Different Syntax for Creating Primitive Arrays

To create a primitive array in Groovy, we can't use the notation we're accustomed to in Java.

In Java we can create an array of integers as follows:

```
int[] arr = new int[] {1, 2, 3, 4, 5};
```

In Groovy, that will result in a compilation error. The Groovy way to define a primitive array of int is as follows:

```
int[] arr = [1, 2, 3, 4, 5]

println arr
println "class is " + arr.getClass().name
```

The output shows that the instance type created is [I, which is the JVM representation for int[].

```
[1, 2, 3, 4, 5]
class is [I
```

If we omit the type int[] on the left side, then Groovy assumes we're creating an instance of ArrayList (see *varargs*, on page 36), so it's critical that we specify the type in this case. Alternatively, we could use the as operator to create an array:

```
def arr = [1, 2, 3, 4, 5] as int[]
println arr2
println "class is " + arr2.getClass().name
```

Groovy makes it easier to create instances of ArrayList, but we have to put some extra effort into creating an array.

We saw a few gotchas that can arise when programming in Groovy. Coming from a Java background, we can benefit from knowing ways in which Groovy is different from Java. Visit http://groovy.codehaus.org/Differences+from+Java for a nice list of Groovy-Java differences.

We've covered a lot in this chapter. You now know how to write classes in Groovy, you've picked up some Groovy idioms, and you know some Groovy ways to write code. You also know that we can fall back on Java syntax if necessary. You don't have to wait until you've finished this book to start experimenting and playing with Groovy. However, there is a lot of learning to come. The terms *dynamic typing* and *optional typing* have arisen a few times, so in the next chapter we'll cover those topics and how to take advantage of them in Groovy.

CHAPTER 3

Dynamic Typing

In dynamic typing, at runtime types are inferred and methods and their arguments are checked. With this ability, we can inject behavior into classes at runtime, making the code more extensible than with strict static typing.

In this chapter you'll learn the benefits of dynamic typing and how to use it in Groovy. With dynamic typing, as you'll see, we can create flexible design with less code than in Java. With the ability to defer arguments' type verification to runtime, polymorphism in Groovy is on steroids. With the *multimethods* tool, we can provide alternate behaviors to operations based on the arguments' runtime types. We'll cover how to keep these powerful features under control using the static compilation options in Groovy.

3.1 Typing in Java

We've all come to rely on the "safety" of compile-time type-checking. But, *safety* in *type safety* is as comforting as *security* in *Social Security*.

Suppose we have a class Car with a year and an Engine class, and we want to implement the ability to clone objects of this class. We'll ignore deeper issues with cloning in Java—see my article "Why Copying an Object Is a Terrible Thing to Do" in Appendix 1, *Web Resources*, on page 309. To clone, we implement the Cloneable interface and provide a public clone() method. Object's clone() can make a shallow copy of the object. However, we want different instances of Car to have different Engines. Therefore, we clone the Car using the base method but tweak it a little to have its own Engine, as in the following code.

TypesAndTyping/Car.java
```java
//Java code
public Object clone() {
  try {
    Car cloned = (Car) super.clone();
    cloned.engine = (Engine) engine.clone();
```

```
      return cloned;
  } catch(CloneNotSupportedException ex) {
      return null; // Will not happen, but we need to please the compiler
  }
```

That code is noisy—first, the compiler insists that we handle CloneNotSupport-edException, right in the very method that's implementing the clone. Second, when we're calling super.clone() within the Car class's instance method, we know we're asking for another Car. Yet the compiler is adamant that we must cast the result of that call. It's the same with the next statement, where we're cloning the Engine. Furthermore, when we're ready to call the clone() method on an instance of Car, we need to cast again to receive the result of that call into a Car reference. Sometimes the static type-checking amounts to mere annoyance and lowers our productivity. Good static type-checking should work like a good government—do the essential things and stay out of our way. However, the Java compiler is in our face most of the time.

Compile-time type-checking has its values. However, today's integrated development environments (IDEs) make developing code and running the tests so easy that we often do those things, and leave it to the IDE to save the relevant edited files and to compile the code as necessary. When our attempt to run the tests fails, we address those issues. Thus, while repeating our fast edit-run-test cycles, we don't distinguish much between compilation errors, runtime errors, and failures of the tests. Our focus is on getting the code working and having all the tests pass at all times.

3.2 Dynamic Typing

Dynamic typing relaxes the typing requirements. We let the language figure out the type based on the context.

What's the advantage of dynamic typing? Is it worth forgoing the benefit of type verification or confirmation at compile time or code-editing time? Dynamic typing provides two main advantages, and the benefits outweigh the costs.

We can write calls to methods on objects without nailing down the details at that moment. During runtime, objects dynamically respond to methods or messages. We can achieve this dynamic behavior to a certain extent using polymorphism in statically typed languages. However, most statically typed languages tie inheritance to polymorphism. They force us to conform to a structure rather than to actual behavior. True polymorphism does not care about types—send a message to an object, and at runtime it figures out the appropriate implementation to use. So, dynamic typing can help achieve a greater degree of polymorphism than traditional, statically typed languages allow.

The second advantage: we don't fight the compiler with excessive casting efforts, as in the examples from Section 3.1, *Typing in Java*, on page 53.

We feel like we're working with a language that's intelligent and follows along with us. We're more productive, partly because of less ceremony.

Working with static typing feels like having a nagging in-law standing next to us as we work—scrutinizing our every move. It doesn't give us the full flexibility to defer some implementation to a later time (before the code is executed). Working with dynamic typing, conversely, feels like having a kind grandfather standing next to us as we work—letting us experiment, figure things out, and be creative, but standing by to offer help when we need it.

The first advantage—true realization of polymorphism—significantly improves the way we design applications, as we'll discuss in Section 3.4, *Design by Capability*, on page 56.

3.3 Dynamic Typing != Weak Typing

In a statically typed language, we specify the types of variables, references, and so on at compile time—and many compilers insist that we do. Take C/C++ for example. We have to specify the variable type as a primitive type such as int or double, or a specific class type. However, what if we cast the variable to a wrong type? Will the compiler stop us? No. What's the fate of the program when we run? It depends. If we're lucky, the program will crash. If not, it may wait until that important demo to crash or misbehave. Depending on how the memory is laid out, whether our call is polymorphic, and how the v-table (some languages like C++ maintain a method dispatch table with addresses of polymorphic methods—see Margaret A. Ellis and Bjarne Stroustrup's *The Annotated C++ Reference Manual [ES90]*) is organized, things may behave quite unpredictably. If we listen closely we may hear the compiler laugh for our reliance on the type safety it pretends to provide. This is an example of static typing with weak typing at runtime.

In the following figure, we classify some common languages based on static versus dynamic and strong versus weak typing.

Java is a statically typed language, but it's strongly typed. The compiler checks for the types, but if we're coercing to a wrong type, the runtime is there to catch us.

Dynamically typed languages such as Groovy don't perform type-checking at code-editing time or compile time. However, if we treat an object as a wrong type, we'll hear about it in no uncertain terms at runtime. We postpone the actual verification until runtime; this helps us modify the structure of our program between the time we write/compile the code and the time it executes. The dynamically typed languages on the JVM show us that dynamic typing does not mean weak typing.

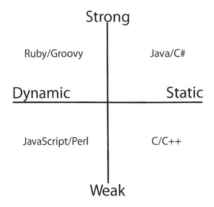

Figure 3—Classification of select languages: static vs. dynamic and strong vs. weak typing

3.4 Design by Capability

As Java programmers we rely heavily on *interfaces*. We value "design by contract," where interfaces define contracts for communication and classes implement and abide by these contracts—see Bertrand Meyer's *Object-Oriented Software Construction [Mey97]*.

Business contracts are good; they help ensure that certain expectations will be fulfilled. However, we don't want contracts to be too restrictive. We want the flexibility to meet and exceed the expectations in acceptable ways.

Software contracts must be similar. Interface-based programming, although very powerful, tends to be restrictive. Let's consider an example that highlights the differences between using static typing and dynamic typing.

Using Static Typing

Say we need to move some heavy stuff. We ask a willing and able man to help out. In Java, this would look like the following code:

```
TypesAndTyping/TakeHelp.java
public void takeHelp(Man man) {
  //...
  man.helpMoveThings();
  //...
}
```

Because of static typing, we ignored help from a willing and able woman nearby. Let's extend the code so we can seek the help of either a man or a woman by creating a Human abstract class with the helpMoveThings() method. Man and Woman will provide their own implementations for this method:

```
TypesAndTyping/Human.java
// Java code
public abstract class Human {
  public abstract void helpMoveThings();

  //...
}
```

Here's code that takes the help of a Human:

```
TypesAndTyping/TakeHelp.java
public void takeHelp(Human human) {
  //...
  human.helpMoveThings();
  //...
}
```

OK, now any human can help us move things. However, if we're rangers in the Serengeti, we'd fail to take advantage of that nice elephant who might be able to help. We depend on Human, and an elephant does not conform to that contract. It's time to extend again, this time with an interface Helper with the method helpMoveThings():

```
TypesAndTyping/Helper.java
// Java code
public interface Helper {
    public void helpMoveThings();
}
```

Then Human, Elephant, and any other helpers implement Helper. We now depend on Helper and can accept help from instances that implement that interface:

```
TypesAndTyping/TakeHelp.java
public void takeHelp(Helper helper) {
  //...
  helper.helpMoveThings();
  //...
}
```

Extending has required some effort so far. Using a wide variety of objects has meant creating interfaces and modifying the code to depend on them.

Using Dynamic Typing

Let's revisit the "take help" example using Groovy's dynamic typing capabilities:

TypesAndTyping/TakeHelp.groovy

```groovy
def takeHelp(helper) {
  //...
  helper.helpMoveThings()
  //...
}
```

The takeHelp() method accepts a helper but does not specify its type—it defaults to an Object. We call, among other things, the helpMoveThings() method on it. This is *design by capability*. Instead of asking the helper to conform to some explicit interface, we're making use of the object's capability—relying upon an implicit interface. This is called *duck typing*, and is based on the sentiment that "if it walks like a duck and quacks like a duck, it must be a duck."[1]

Classes that want that capability simply implement the method; we don't need to extend or implement anything. The result is low ceremony and high productivity. If a machine has that capability, we can use it without any change to the code. Let's look at a few classes with the capability we want.

TypesAndTyping/TakeHelp.groovy

```groovy
class Man {
  void helpMoveThings() {
    //...
    println "Man's helping"
  }
  //...
}

class Woman {
  void helpMoveThings() {
    //...
    println "Woman's helping"
  }
  //...
}

class Elephant {
  void helpMoveThings() {
    //...
    println "Elephant's helping"
  }
  void eatSugarcane() {
    //...
    println "I love sugarcanes..."
  }
  //...
}
```

---

1. http://c2.com/cgi/wiki?DuckTyping

Here is an example of calling the takeHelp() method:

TypesAndTyping/TakeHelp.groovy
```
takeHelp(new Man())
takeHelp(new Woman())
takeHelp(new Elephant())
```

Let's look at the effect of exercising each of the helpers:

```
Man's helping
Woman's helping
Elephant's helping
```

The classes don't extend from any common class or implement any common interface, but with the dynamic nature of Groovy we were able to use all of the classes in our takeHelp() method.

Coming from a Java background, we might have to expend some effort to get used to the dynamic nature of Groovy, but once we get comfortable we can put it to good use. For example, we can effortlessly substitute a credit-card processor with a mock object in an order-processing system for fast automated testing. We're not forced to make elaborate design decisions ahead of time. That means we can accommodate design afterthoughts without much effort, giving us more flexibility and power to create easily extensible code.

Dynamic Typing Needs Discipline

See how simple, elegant, and flexible the code is when we take advantage of dynamic typing? But is this risky business?

- We might mistype the method name when creating one of the helpers.

- Without the type information, how do we know what to send to the method?

- What if we send the method a nonhelper (an object that's not capable of moving stuff)?

These are valid concerns, but let's not turn them into fears. In this section we'll look at ways to address each of them.

We often introduce typos when we write code. Also, our minds constantly fool us; we tend to see what we want to see instead of what's really there. Therefore, we must ensure that the method names have the proper case and take proper parameters. The compiler in a statically typed language does this for us. In a dynamically typed language, either we don't have the compiler or the compiler does not check for these. We'll need to rely on unit testing (see Section 18.2, *Unit Testing Java and Groovy Code*, on page 272) to ensure that we have things correct. Writing unit tests only for this purpose is a rather outlandish ceremony. However, the fact that a compiler produces bytecode does not mean the code is right. We still need to verify that it meets our expectations—not just doing what we typed, but doing what we really meant.

I rely on unit testing heavily when I program, even in statically typed languages. The lack of compiler support (or of a compiler) to verify these doesn't bother me. Unit testing is a good practice, and dynamic typing requires that we do it with discipline. Programming with dynamic typing but not having the discipline of unit testing is playing with fire.

To a certain extent, typing helps us figure out what objects or values we need to send to a method. But that's only half the story. Knowing that we must send a double value to a method is hardly enough in practice (unless we want to end up on the news for crashing orbiters.[2] Disciplined unit testing and good naming conventions can help us a great deal.

If a method takes distance as a parameter, rather than naming the variable d, dist, or even distance, we can name it to be very expressive, such as distanceInMiles. Sure, we can create a type DistanceInMiles, but we don't need that much ceremony if we follow good conventions and testing practices.

Finally, what about conformance—what if someone sends an object that does not support the method we're expecting? There are two ways to look at it. We can assume that the callers take the responsibility to make sure they send only what's valid. If they send an invalid object, the code will fail, and an exception will be thrown their way. Even in compiled code we have to deal with precondition violations, and this is along the same lines, but broader. In special cases, where we want to deal with some alternative or optional behavior, we may ask the object whether it's capable of doing what we're expecting. Groovy's respondsTo() method can help here (see Section 11.2, *Querying Methods and Properties*, on page 180). Assume we own a sugarcane farm and want to share some sugarcane with our helper, but not all helpers may eat raw sugarcane. We can ask whether our helper likes sugarcane:

TypesAndTyping/TakeHelp.groovy
```
def takeHelpAndReward(helper) {
  //...
  helper.helpMoveThings()

  if (helper.metaClass.respondsTo(helper, 'eatSugarcane'))
  {
    helper.eatSugarcane()
```

---

2. http://www.cnn.com/TECH/space/9909/30/mars.metric.02/

```
    }
    //...
}
```

```
takeHelpAndReward(new Man())
takeHelpAndReward(new Woman())
takeHelpAndReward(new Elephant())
```

We're checking with the helper whether sugarcanes are OK, and if so, we share some, as we see in the output:

```
Man's helping
Woman's helping
Elephant's helping
I love sugarcanes...
```

When used with discipline, design by capability can help us create highly extensible and concise code. We will see less casting and noise in code, as well as shorter class hierarchies. It will begin to feel like the compiler is working for us rather than the other way around.

3.5   Optional Typing

Groovy is dynamically typed *and* optionally typed; we can adjust the dial of typing all the way to one extreme, where we do not specify any type and let Groovy figure things out, or we can move the dial all the way to the other extreme, where we will precisely specify the types of variables or references we use.

Remember that Groovy is a language that runs on top of the JVM. Optional typing can help integrate Groovy code with Java libraries, frameworks, and tools. Sometimes Groovy's dynamic type-mapping doesn't match what these libraries, frameworks, or tools expect. Such a situation is not a showstopper in Groovy—we can switch the typing mode readily and specify the type information to get moving. Optional typing is useful in other situations, such as when you need type information to generate database schema or to create validators in GORM/Grails.

Consider that you're writing a JUnit test using Groovy (see Section 18.2, *Unit Testing Java and Groovy Code*, on page 272). We can define methods using the def keyword to indicate an Object return type. Since JUnit expects test methods to be void, we'll get an error if we try to run a test defined using def. Instead, we'll have to define the method as void to satisfy JUnit. Groovy's optional typing is useful here.

Looking at Figure 3, *Classification of select languages: static vs. dynamic and strong vs. weak typing*, on page 56, we may wonder, if Groovy is optionally typed, why is it not in the middle between static and dynamic typing? That's because the Groovy compiler—groovyc—does not do full type checking (for details see *Compile-Time Type-Checking Is Off by Default*, on page 47). If we write X obj = 2, where X is a class, it simply places a cast like X obj = (X) 2 and lets the runtime dynamically determine whether that is valid. So, even though Groovy allows typing, it's still dynamically typed.

3.6 Multimethods

Dynamic typing and dynamic languages change how objects respond to method calls.

Groovy supports polymorphism, like Java does, but it goes far beyond simply dispatching methods based on the target object's type. Let's look at polymorphism in Java:

TypesAndTyping/Employee.java
```java
// Java code
public class Employee {
  public void raise(Number amount) {
    System.out.println("Employee got raise");
  }
}
```

The Employee class's raise() method simply reports that it was called. Now look at the Executive class:

TypesAndTyping/Executive.java
```java
// Java code
public class Executive extends Employee {
  public void raise(Number amount) {
    System.out.println("Executive got raise");
  }

  public void raise(java.math.BigDecimal amount) {
    System.out.println("Executive got outlandish raise");
  }
}
```

The executive has overloaded raise() methods—what else could we expect? The version that takes Number reports its call; the version that takes BigDecimal announces the outlandish raise.

Finally, here's Java code that puts these classes to use:

TypesAndTyping/GiveRaiseJava.java
```java
// Java code
import java.math.BigDecimal;
```

```
public class GiveRaiseJava {
  public static void giveRaise(Employee employee) {
    employee.raise(new BigDecimal(10000.00));
  }

  public static void main(String[] args) {
    giveRaise(new Employee());
    giveRaise(new Executive());
  }
}
```

We create an Employee and an Executive and send them to the same giveRaise()
method, which calls the raise() method on these objects. The output is quite
as expected in Java:

```
Employee got raise
Executive got raise
```

The raise() method in Employee is polymorphic, meaning that at runtime the
method invoked depends not on the target reference's type, but rather on the
type of the referenced object. There's one restriction, however. The method
called at runtime has to take Number as a parameter because that's what
Employee—the base—has defined. So, the compiler treats the instance of
BigDecimal as Number.

That's a standard, everyday operation in Java. Not a big deal, right? All that
changes when it comes to the dynamic nature of Groovy. Groovy knows that,
in the wise words of Tony Hoare, "premature optimization is the root of all
evil."

When we call the raise() method in Groovy, it does not go through the previous
sequence as in Java. Instead, it walks up to the object and asks—figuratively
speaking, that is—"Hey, do we have a raise() method that takes a
java.math.BigDecimal()?" An Employee would say, "No, but I can take a Number." On
the other hand, an Executive does have a raise() that takes a BigDecimal, and so
the call is routed to that implementation. Here's the code that illustrates this
behavior—we're still using the Java classes for Employee and Executive from
earlier, so there's no change to those:

TypesAndTyping/GiveRaise.groovy
```
void giveRaise(Employee employee) {
  employee.raise(new BigDecimal(10000.00))
  // same as
  //employee.raise(10000.00)
}

giveRaise new Employee()
giveRaise new Executive()
```

Groovy reports a different output than Java:

```
Employee got raise
Executive got outlandish raise
```

If we have overloaded methods in a class, Groovy smartly picks the correct implementation based not only on the target object—the object on which the method is invoked—but also on the parameter(s) we send to the call. Since the method-dispatching is based on multiple objects—the target plus the parameters—this is called *multiple dispatch* or *multimethods*.

Due to multimethods, Groovy does not suffer from the type-confusion problem that Java does—thanks to Neal Ford for this Java example. Take a look at the following Java code, which uses Generics. lst refers to an instance of ArrayList<String>, and col, which is of type Collection<String>, is referring to the same instance. We added three elements to lst and removed one. The removal got rid of the first element in the list. Now we intend the call col.remove(0) to remove another element. However, the remove() method in the Collection interface expects an Object, so Java boxes the 0 into an Integer. And since an instance of Integer is not part of the list, the method call did not remove anything.

TypesAndTyping/UsingCollection.java
```java
//Java code
import java.util.*;

public class UsingCollection {
  public static void main(String[] args) {
    ArrayList<String> lst = new ArrayList<String>();
    Collection<String> col = lst;

    lst.add("one");
    lst.add("two");
    lst.add("three");
    lst.remove(0);
    col.remove(0);

    System.out.println("Added three items, removed two, so 1 item to remain.");
    System.out.println("Number of elements is: " + lst.size());
    System.out.println("Number of elements is: " + col.size());
  }
}
```

The output shows the code's unpleasant behavior:

```
Added three items, removed two, so 1 item to remain.
Number of elements is: 2
Number of elements is: 2
```

Let's see how this code behaves in Groovy. Without making any change to the previous code, let's simply copy and paste it into a file named UsingCollection.groovy. Let's then run groovy UsingCollection and observe the output. We see that the Groovy execution produces a different output than the Java version:

```
Added three items, removed two, so 1 item to remain.
Number of elements is: 1
Number of elements is: 1
```

Groovy's dynamic and multimethod capabilities nicely handle this case. At runtime Groovy figures we meant to remove the first element and did not go into the unnecessary trouble of boxing that would lead to incorrect behavior here.

3.7 Dynamic: To Be or Not to Be?

Given that Groovy is a dynamically typed language that supports optional typing, should we specify the type or rely on dynamic typing? There are no real rules in this area, but we can certainly develop some preferences.

When programming in Groovy, I lean toward omitting the type and instead making the parameter/variable names very expressive. Not specifying the type has the added advantages of duck typing (Section 3.4, *Design by Capability*, on page 56) and the ease of applying mocks for testing (Section 18.2, *Unit Testing Java and Groovy Code*, on page 272).

I opt to specify the type if I am forced to, like when JUnit requires test methods to be void or when specificity provides a significant benefit, like when mapping types to databases in Grails object-relational mapping (GORM).

If we're developing an API that's intended for use by someone programming in a statically typed language, then we specify the parameter types for methods in the statically typed client-facing API.

From a usage point of view, the community has leaned toward always specifying types in method signatures. The benefit here is knowing the types for arguments during method calls and avoiding unnecessary runtime type-checking within methods.

3.8 Switching Off Dynamic Typing

All the capabilities of metaprogramming we'll see in this book rely on Groovy's dynamic typing, but it comes at a price. Mistakes that would otherwise be found at compile time are pushed to the runtime. In addition, the dynamic method-dispatch mechanism has overhead. Although Java 7 introduced the dynamic invocation feature to ease this performance concern, we'll still see a performance impact on Groovy running on older versions of the JVM.

We can ask the Groovy compiler to tighten its type-checking from its dynamic relaxed mode to the levels we'd expect from a statically typed compiler like javac. We can also trade in the benefits of dynamic typing and metaprogramming capabilities, and ask the Groovy compiler to statically compile code down to more-efficient bytecode.

In this section we'll look at two features, one to ask that Groovy perform more-rigorous checks at compile time and the other to ask that it create more-efficient statically compiled bytecode.

Static Type-Checking

We can use Groovy's dynamic nature to invoke methods and access properties that don't exist at compile time, with the assumption that these will be injected into the application at runtime. On one hand, this gives great flexibility to provide advanced capabilities in applications, as we'll see in the third part of this book. On the other hand, silly typos could slip by and result in annoying failures at runtime. Sure, these errors would surface quickly in our unit tests; however, this is an unnecessary burden in areas of our program where we're not making use of such dynamic capabilities.

We can ask Groovy to verify proper type and ensure that methods we call and properties we access are valid on the type. We can instruct Groovy to check for these kinds of errors with the special annotation @TypeChecked, which we can place on classes or individual methods. If we place it on a class, then type-checking is performed on all the methods, closures, and inner classes in the class. If we place it on a method, the type-checking is performed only on the members of the target method.

Let's use this annotation in an example. First we'll create a method with a lurking error and no compile-time safeguard.

TypesAndTyping/NoCompiletimeCheck.groovy

```groovy
def shout(String str) {
  println "Printing in uppercase"
  println str.toUpperCase()
  println "Printing again in uppercase"
  println str.toUppercase()
}
try {
  shout('hello')
} catch(ex) {
  println "Failed..."
}
```

The shout() method takes a parameter of type String and invokes the toUpperCase() method. In the second invocation of the method, there is a typo in the case. Groovy will report an error at runtime.

```
Printing in uppercase
HELLO
Printing again in uppercase
Failed...
```

This code is not making use of any metaprogramming, and can benefit from compile-time verification. Let's add the @TypeChecked annotation to the method.

```
@groovy.transform.TypeChecked
def shout(String str) {
//...
```

Once Groovy sees this annotation, it will perform rigorous checks on the targeted code. If we run this version of code, Groovy will not get as far as in the previous version; it will produce an error during compilation.

```
Static type checking] - Cannot find matching method java.lang.String#toUppercase().
Please check if the declared type is right and if the method exists.
 @ line 10, column 11.
     println str.toUppercase()
             ^


1 error
```

For code marked with the @TypeChecked annotation, at compile time the compiler will verify if the method/property used belongs to the class. This prevents us from using any metaprogramming capabilities. For example, in Groovy by default we can inject methods into classes:

```
TypesAndTyping/Inject.groovy
def shoutString(String str) {
  println str.shout()
}

str = 'hello'
str.metaClass.shout = {-> toUpperCase() }
shoutString(str)
```

We added the shout() method dynamically into the instance of String and were able to call it from the shoutString() method, as we see in the output:

```
HELLO
```

If we annotate the shoutString() method with @TypeChecked, then the compiler will prevent us from proceeding further.

```
@groovy.transform.TypeChecked
def shoutString(String str) {
  println str.shout() //Fails at compile time
}
```

Even though we can't directly invoke dynamic methods when static type-checking is in effect, there is a workaround; we can use a special invokeMethod() on Groovy objects, as we'll discuss in Section 10.6, *Calling Groovy Dynamic Methods from Java*, on page 165.

The static type-checking restricts us from using dynamic methods. However, it does not prevent us from using the methods that Groovy has added (see Chapter 7, *Exploring the GDK*, on page 127) to the JDK classes. The static type-checker checks for methods and properties in the class. It also checks a special DefaultGroovyMethods class, which contains some useful and fluent extension methods. Furthermore, it checks custom extensions that we as Groovy programmers can add, as we discuss in Section 7.3, *Custom Methods Using the Extension Modules*, on page 139. For example, we can freely call the Groovy-added reverse() method on String.

TypesAndTyping/Reverse.groovy
```
@groovy.transform.TypeChecked
def printInReverse(String str) {
  println str.reverse() //No problem
}
printInReverse 'hello'
```

To make use of the static type-checking, we have to specify the type of the parameters to methods and closures. The methods we can invoke on the parameters are restricted to the methods supported by the type known at compile time. Groovy will infer the return type of closures and perform type-checking accordingly, so we don't have to worry about specifying that detail.

Groovy's type-checking has one advantage over Java's. If we check for the type using instanceOf, then we don't have to perform a cast on that instance to use its specialized methods or properties, as the next example demonstrates.

TypesAndTyping/NoCast.groovy
```
@groovy.transform.TypeChecked
def use(Object instance) {
  if(instance instanceof String)
    println instance.length() //No need to cast
  else
    println instance
}
use('hello')
use(4)
```

We've covered how to ask Groovy to type-check at compile time. If we annotate an entire class for static type-checking, we can opt out specific methods from static type-checking using the SKIP parameter:

```
TypesAndTyping/Optout.groovy
import groovy.transform.TypeChecked
import groovy.transform.TypeCheckingMode

@TypeChecked
class Sample {
  //static type checking in effect here
  def method1() {
  }

  @TypeChecked(TypeCheckingMode.SKIP)
  def method2(String str) {
    str.shout()
  }
}
```

Static type-checking will be performed in the entire class except for the code within the method2(), which we opted out from compile-time checks.

The static type-checking is intended to help identify errors at compile time. If the code has no errors, the type-checked and the non-type-checked versions result in similar bytecode generated by the compiler. If we want efficient bytecode generation we'll have to use the static compilation option.

Static Compilation

Groovy metaprogramming and dynamic typing has significant benefits, but they come at a performance cost. The degradation in performance depends on the code, the number of methods invoked, and so on. The performance hit can be as high as ten percent compared to equivalent Java code when metaprogramming and dynamic capabilities are not needed. The Java 7 InvokeDynamic feature is intended to ease this pain, but for those of us using prior versions of Java, static compilation can be a useful feature.

We can turn off dynamic typing, prevent metaprogramming, forgo multimethods, and ask Groovy to generate efficient bytecode that can be as performant as Java's bytecode.

We can ask Groovy to perform static compilation by using the @CompileStatic annotation. The bytecode generated for the targeted code will be much like the bytecode generated by the javac compiler. For example, let's compile a sample code without this annotation.

TypesAndTyping/NoStaticCompile.groovy
```groovy
def shout1(String str) {
  println str.toUpperCase()
}
```

If we compile the previous code using groovyc and then perform javac -p NoStatic-Compile, we'll see that the call to the method toUpperCase() goes through the CallSite(), which takes care of Groovy's dynamic invocation mechanism.

```
...
14:  invokeinterface  #57, 2; //InterfaceMethod
org/codehaus/groovy/runtime/callsite/CallSite.call:...
19:  invokeinterface  #61, 3; //InterfaceMethod
org/codehaus/groovy/runtime/callsite/CallSite.callCurrent:...
...
```

Let's mark the method with the @CompileStatic annotation.

TypesAndTyping/StaticCompile.groovy
```groovy
@groovy.transform.CompileStatic
def shout1(String str) {
  println str.toUpperCase()
}
```

Now the Groovy compiler generates a call to invokeVirtual, like the Java compiler does.

```
...
2: invokevirtual       #63; //Method java/lang/String.toUpperCase:()...
5: invokevirtual       #67; //Method groovy/lang/Script.println:...
...
```

Static compilation is a good option for areas of code that deserve performance comparable to Java's. We can skip this for areas of code where performance is not critical and in places where we want to gain from metaprogramming.

In this chapter we journeyed through the typing-related issues, benefits, and features of Groovy. We saw how Groovy's dynamic typing makes typing implicit when we don't care to specify. We also saw how easily we can use the optional typing to reach for the type declaration when we need it. We learned that method-dispatching is quite different and powerful in Groovy, how to enjoy true polymorphism, and how to take advantage of design by capability. Finally, we saw how in Groovy we can selectively turn off dynamic typing and invoke the benefits of static typing in areas of code where we desire more compiler checks or better performance. In the next chapter, we'll walk through one of the most interesting features in Groovy—closures.

CHAPTER 4

Using Closures

We create anonymous inner classes in Java, where we define method arguments to register event handlers and provide short local glue code. Back when introduced in Java 1.1, anonymous inner classes seemed like a nice idea, but soon we realized that they become verbose, especially for really short implementations of single-method interfaces. Closures in Groovy are short anonymous methods that remove that verbosity.

Closures are lightweight, short, concise, and one of the features we'll employ the most in Groovy. Where we used to pass instances of anonymous classes, now we can pass closures.

Closures are derived from the lambda expressions from functional programming, and "a lambda expression specifies the parameter and the mapping of a function"—see Robert Sebesta's *Concepts of Programming Languages [Seb04]*. Closures are one of the most powerful features in Groovy, yet they are syntactically elegant. Or as the computer scientist and functional-programming pioneer Peter J. Landin put it, "A little bit of syntax sugar helps you to swallow the λ calculus."

We'll use closures extensively through the Groovy JDK (GDK), which has extended the Java Development Kit (JDK) with fluent and convenient methods that take closures. Rather than being forced to create interfaces and a number of small classes, we can design applications with small chunks of low-ceremony code. This means less code, less clutter, and more reuse.

In this chapter you'll learn to create and use closures. We'll cover how to use them to elegantly implement some design patterns. You'll learn that closures don't simply stand in as anonymous methods, but can turn into a versatile tool to solve problems with high memory demands. So let's roll up our sleeves and get down to some code.

4.1 The Convenience of Closures

Closures in Groovy totally remove verbosity in code and help create lightweight reusable pieces of code. To understand the convenience they offer, let's contrast them with familiar traditional solutions for common tasks.

The Traditional Way

Let's consider a simple example—assume we want to find the sum of even values from 1 to a certain number, n.

Here is the traditional approach:

UsingClosures/UsingEvenNumbers.groovy
```
def sum(n) {
  total = 0
  for(int i = 2; i <= n; i += 2) {
    total += i
  }
  total
}
println "Sum of even numbers from 1 to 10 is ${sum(10)}"
```

In the method sum(), we're running a for loop that iterates over even numbers and sums them. Now, suppose instead of that we want to find the product of even numbers from 1 to n.

UsingClosures/UsingEvenNumbers.groovy
```
def product(n) {
  prod = 1
  for(int i = 2; i <= n; i += 2) {
    prod *= i
  }
  prod
}
println "Product of even numbers from 1 to 10 is ${product(10)}"
```

We again iterate over even numbers, this time computing their product. Now, what if we want to get a collection of squares of these values? The code that returns an array of squared values might look like the following:

UsingClosures/UsingEvenNumbers.groovy
```
def sqr(n) {
  squared = []
  for(int i = 2; i <= n; i += 2) {
    squared << i ** 2
  }
  squared
}
println "Squares of even numbers from 1 to 10 is ${sqr(10)}"
```

The code that does the looping is the same (and duplicated) in each of the previous code examples. What's different is the part dealing with the sum, product, or squares. If we want to perform some other operation over the even numbers, we'd be duplicating the code that traverses the numbers. Let's find ways to remove that duplication.

The Groovy Way

Each of the previous three examples produced different results, but all three of them have a common task—picking even numbers from a given collection. Let's start with a function for that common task. Instead of returning a list of even numbers, let's write the function so that when an even number is picked, the function immediately sends it to a code block for processing. Let the code block simply print that number for now:

UsingClosures/PickEven.groovy
```
def pickEven(n, block) {
  for(int i = 2; i <= n; i += 2) {
    block(i)
  }
}
```

```
pickEven(10, { println it } )
```

The pickEven() method is a *higher-order function*—a function that takes functions as arguments or returns a function as a result.[1] The method is iterating over values (like before), but this time it yields, or sends, the value over to a block of code. In Groovy we refer to the anonymous code block as a *closure*—Groovy programmers use a relaxed definition of the term.[2]

The variable block holds a reference to a closure. Much like the way we can pass objects around, we can pass closures around. The variable name does not have to be named block; it can be any legal variable name. When calling the method pickEven(), we can now send a code block as shown in the earlier code. The block of code (the code within {}) is passed for the parameter block, like the value 10 for the variable n. In Groovy, we can pass as many closures as we want. So, the first, third, and last arguments for a method call, for example, may be closures. If a closure is the last argument, there is an elegant syntax, as we see here:

UsingClosures/PickEven.groovy
```
pickEven(10) { println it }
```

---

1. See http://c2.com/cgi/wiki?HigherOrderFunction.
2. See http://groovy.codehaus.org/Closures+-+Formal+Definition.

If the closure is the last argument to a method call, we can attach the closure to the method call. The code block, in this case, appears like a parasite to the method call. Unlike Java code blocks, Groovy closures can't stand alone; they're either attached to a method or assigned to a variable.

What's that it in the block? If we're passing only one parameter to the code block, then we can refer to it with a special variable name it. We can give an alternate name for that variable if we like, as in the next example:

UsingClosures/PickEven.groovy
```
pickEven(10) { evenNumber -> println evenNumber }
```

The variable evenNumber now refers to the argument that's passed to this closure from within the pickEven() method.

Now let's revisit the computations on even numbers. We can use pickEven() to compute the sum, like so:

UsingClosures/PickEven.groovy
```
total = 0
pickEven(10) { total += it }
println "Sum of even numbers from 1 to 10 is ${total}"
```

We started out simply printing the even numbers generated by pickEven(), but now we're totaling those values, without any change to the function. Rather than duplicating the code, as in the traditional-way examples, we have concise code with greater reuse. The function is not limited to totaling the values; we can use it, for example, to compute the product, as in the next code:

UsingClosures/PickEven.groovy
```
product = 1
pickEven(10) { product *= it }
println "Product of even numbers from 1 to 10 is ${product}"
```

Other than the syntactic elegance, closures provide a simple and easy way for a function to delegate part of its implementation logic.

The block of code in the previous example does something more than the block of code we saw earlier. It stretches its hands and reaches out to the variable product in the scope of the caller of pickEven(). This is an interesting characteristic of closures. A closure is a function with variables bound to a context or environment in which it executes.

We know how to create closures; next let's discuss how to use them in applications.

4.2 Programming with Closures

We're talking about the power and elegance of closures in this chapter, but first let's discuss how to approach them in our projects. We need to decide whether we want to implement a certain functionality or task as a regular function/method or whether we should use a closure.

Closures augment, refine, or enhance another piece of code. For example, a closure may be useful to express a predicate or condition that will refine the selection of objects. We can use closures to take advantage of coroutines such as the control flow like in iterators or loops.

Closures are very helpful in two specific areas. They can help manage resource cleanup (see Section 4.5, *Using Closures for Resource Cleanup*, on page 78) and they can help create internal domain-specific languages (DSLs)—see Chapter 19, *Creating DSLs in Groovy*, on page 295.

To implement a certain well-identified task, a regular function is better than a closure. A good time to introduce closures is during refactoring.

Once we get the code working, we can revisit it to see whether closures would make it better and more elegant. Let a closure emerge from this effort rather than forcing a use to begin with.

We should keep closures small and cohesive. These are intended to be small chunks of code, only a few lines, that are attached to method calls. When writing a method that uses a closure, it's better not to overuse dynamic properties of closures, like determining the number and types of parameters at runtime. It must be very simple and obvious to implement a closure when calling methods.

We saw the convenience and benefits of using closures. Next, let's look at a couple of different ways to use closures.

4.3 Ways to Use Closures

We covered how to create a closure just in time, at the point of defining arguments in a method call. We can also assign them to variables and reuse them, as we'll do here.

In the following example, totalSelectValues() accepts a closure to help decide the set of values used in a computation:

UsingClosures/Strategy.groovy
```groovy
def totalSelectValues(n, closure) {
  total = 0
  for(i in 1..n) {
    if (closure(i)) { total += i }
  }
  total
}
print "Total of even numbers from 1 to 10 is "
println totalSelectValues(10) { it % 2 == 0 }

def isOdd = { it % 2 != 0}
print "Total of odd numbers from 1 to 10 is "
println totalSelectValues(10, isOdd)
```

The method totalSelectValues() iterates from 1 to n. For each value it calls the closure to determine whether the value must be used in the computation, and it delegates the selection process to the closure.

return is optional even in closures; the value of the last expression (possibly null) is automatically returned to the caller if we don't have an explicit return.

We've defined inline the closure attached to the first call to totalSelectValues(), and it selects only even numbers. On the other hand, we've predefined the closure passed to the second call. This closure, referred by the variable isOdd, selects only odd numbers. Unlike the just-in-time-created closures, this pre-defined closure can be used in multiple calls. As an aside, in this example we effortlessly implemented the Strategy pattern.[3]

We went from just-in-time creation of closures to predefining closures. This approach can be useful for caching closures for later use, as we'll see next.

Assume we're creating a simulator that allows us to plug in different calculations for equipment. We want to perform some computation but want to use the appropriate calculator. Here's an example of how to do that:

UsingClosures/Simulate.groovy
```groovy
class Equipment {
  def calculator
  Equipment(calc) { calculator = calc }
  def simulate() {
    println "Running simulation"
    calculator() // We may send parameters as well
  }
}
```

---

3. See *Design Patterns: Elements of Reusable Object-Oriented Software [GHJV95]* for details about the pattern.

```
def eq1 = new Equipment({ println "Calculator 1" })
def aCalculator = { println "Calculator 2" }
def eq2 = new Equipment(aCalculator)
def eq3 = new Equipment(aCalculator)

eq1.simulate()
eq2.simulate()
eq3.simulate()
```

Equipment's constructor takes a closure as a parameter and caches that in a property called calculator. In the simulate() method, we call the closure to perform the calculations. When an instance eq1 of Equipment is created, a calculator is provided to it inline as a closure (see *Closures—Anonymous-Inner-Classes Conflict*, on page 49, for limitations on the syntax). What if we need to reuse that code block? We can save the closure into a variable—like the aCalculator in the previous code. We've used this in the creation of two other instances of Equipment—namely, eq2 and eq3. The output shows the equipment using the cached calculators:

```
Running simulation
Calculator 1
Running simulation
Calculator 2
Running simulation
Calculator 2
```

The Collections classes, which make extensive use of closures, are a great place to look for closure examples. For details refer to Section 6.2, *Iterating Over an ArrayList*, on page 111.

We covered how to create and reuse closures; next we'll see how to pass parameters to closures.

4.4 Passing Parameters to Closures

In the previous sections, we saw how to define and use closures. In this section, we'll talk about how to send multiple parameters to closures.

it is the default name for a single parameter passed to a closure. We can use it as long as we know that only one parameter is passed in. If we have more than one parameter passed, we need to list those by name, as in this example:

UsingClosures/ClosureWithTwoParameters.groovy
```
def tellFortune(closure) {
  closure new Date("09/20/2012"), "Your day is filled with ceremony"
}
tellFortune() { date, fortune ->
  println "Fortune for ${date} is '${fortune}'"
}
```

The method tellFortune() calls its closure with two parameters, namely an instance of Date and a fortune message String. The closure refers to these two with the names date and fortune. The symbol -> separates the closure's parameter declarations from its body. Let's exercise this code and take a look at the output:

```
Fortune for Thu Sep 20 00:00:00 MST 2012 is 'Your day is filled with ceremony'
```

Since Groovy supports optional typing, we can define the types of parameters in the closure, as in the next example:

```
UsingClosures/ClosureWithTwoParameters.groovy
tellFortune() { Date date, fortune ->
  println "Fortune for ${date} is '${fortune}'"
}
```

We can generally avoid defining the types if we use expressive names for parameters. In metaprogramming, as we'll see later, we can use closures to override or replace methods, and in that situation the type information is quite important to ensure proper implementation.

4.5 Using Closures for Resource Cleanup

Java's automatic garbage collection is a mixed blessing. We don't have to worry about resource deallocation, provided we release references. But there's no guarantee of when the resource will actually be cleaned up, because it's at the discretion of the garbage collector. In certain situations, we might want the cleanup to happen straightaway. This is the reason we see methods such as close() and destroy() on resource-intensive classes.

One problem, though, is that the users of our class may forget to call these methods. Closures can help ensure that the methods get called. In the following code we create a FileWriter and write some data, but ignore the call to close() on it. If we run this code, the file output.txt will not have the data or characters we wrote.

```
UsingClosures/FileClose.groovy
writer = new FileWriter('output.txt')
writer.write('!')
// forgot to call writer.close()
```

Let's rewrite this code using the Groovy-added withWriter() method. withWriter() flushes and closes the stream automatically when we return from the closure.

```
UsingClosures/FileClose.groovy
new FileWriter('output.txt').withWriter { writer ->
  writer.write('a')
} // no need to close()
```

Now we don't have to worry about closing the stream; we can focus on getting our work done. We can implement such convenience methods for our own classes also, making our class's users happy and productive. For example, suppose we expect users of our class Resource to call open() before calling any other instance methods, and then call close() when done.

Here is an example of the Resource class:

UsingClosures/ResourceCleanup.groovy

```groovy
class Resource {
  def open() { print "opened..." }
  def close() { print "closed" }
  def read() { print "read..." }
  def write() { print "write..." }
  //...
```

Here is a usage of this class:

UsingClosures/ResourceCleanup.groovy

```groovy
def resource = new Resource()
resource.open()
resource.read()
resource.write()
```

Sadly, our class's user failed to use the close(), and the resource was not closed, as we can see in the following output:

```
opened...read...write...
```

Closures can help here—we can use the Execute Around Method pattern (see *Execute Around Method*, on page 80) to tackle this problem.

Let's create a static method named use():

UsingClosures/ResourceCleanup.groovy

```groovy
def static use(closure) {
  def r = new Resource()
  try {
    r.open()
    closure(r)
  } finally {
    r.close()
  }
}
```

In the static method, we create an instance of Resource, call open() on it, invoke the closure, and, finally, call close(). We guard the call with a try-finally, so we'll close() even if the closure call throws an exception.

Execute Around Method

If we have a pair of actions that have to be performed together—such as open and close—we can use the Execute Around Method pattern, a Smalltalk pattern discussed in Kent Beck's *Smalltalk Best Practice Patterns [Bec96]*. We write an "execute around" method that takes a block as a parameter. In the method, we sandwich the call to the block in between calls to the pair of methods; that is, call the first method, then invoke the block, and finally call the second method. Users of our method don't have to worry about the pair of actions; they're called automatically. We can even take care of exceptions within the "execute around" method.

Let's look at how our class's users can use it:

UsingClosures/ResourceCleanup.groovy

```
Resource.use { res ->
  res.read()
  res.write()
}
```

Here's the output from invoking the use() method, with the closure happening automatically:

```
opened...read...write...closed
```

Thanks to the closure, now the call to close() is automatic, deterministic, and right on time. We can focus on the application domain and its inherent complexities and let the libraries handle system-level tasks such as guaranteed cleanup in file I/O, and so on.

We've learned how to create closures and pass them around to functions and classes. Next let's look at how functions and closures interact.

4.6 Closures and Coroutines

Calling a function or method creates a new scope in a program's execution sequence. We enter the function at one entry point (top). After we complete the method, we return to the caller's scope.

Coroutines, on the other hand, support multiple entry points, each following the place of the last suspended call. We can enter a function, execute part of it, suspend, and go back to execute some code in the context or scope of the caller. We can then resume execution of the function from where we suspended. As Donald E. Knuth says, "In contrast to the unsymmetric relationship between a main routine and a subroutine, there is complete symmetry between coroutines, which call on each other."[4]

---

4. *The Art of Computer Programming: Fundamental Algorithms [Knu97]*

Coroutines are handy for implementing some special logic or algorithms, such as in a producer-consumer problem. A producer receives some input, does initial processing on it, and notifies a consumer to take that processed value for further computation and output or storage. The consumer does its part and, when done, notifies the producer to get more input.

In Java, wait() and notify() help implement coroutines when combined with multithreading. Closures give the impression (or illusion) of coroutines in a single thread.

For example, take a look at this:

```
UsingClosures/Coroutine.groovy
def iterate(n, closure) {
  1.upto(n) {
    println "In iterate with value ${it}"
    closure(it)
  }
}

println "Calling iterate"
total = 0
iterate(4) {
  total += it
  println "In closure total so far is ${total}"
  }
println "Done"
```

In this code, the control transfers back and forth between the iterate() method and the closure:

```
Calling iterate
In iterate with value 1
In closure total so far is 1
In iterate with value 2
In closure total so far is 3
In iterate with value 3
In closure total so far is 6
In iterate with value 4
In closure total so far is 10
Done
```

In each call to the closure, we're resuming with the value of total from the previous call. The execution sequence feels like the one shown in Figure 4, *Execution sequence of a coroutine*, on page 82—we're switching between two functions' context.

We've looked at how functions and closures interact. Next we'll look at how we can morph closures and transform their parameters.

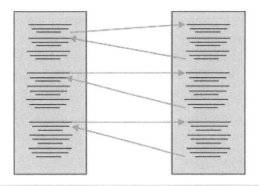

Figure 4—Execution sequence of a coroutine

4.7 Curried Closure

Closures may receive zero or more parameters. Each time we call a closure, we're expected to pass arguments for each of these parameters. However, this can get tedious if one or more arguments are the same between multiple calls to a closure. We can ease this pain by prebinding some closure parameters.

Closures with prebound parameters are called *curried closures*—despite the name, it has nothing to do with my favorite Indian dish. (The term *curry* comes from the name Haskell B. Curry, famed mathematician who contributed to lambda calculus, and was coined by Christopher Strachey, Moses Schönfinkel, and Friedrich Ludwig. Gottlob Frege invented the concept.) When we curry() a closure, we're asking the parameters to be prebound. Once we prebind a parameter, we don't have to send it repeatedly to calls on closures. The method call can now take fewer parameters, as illustrated in Figure 5, *Currying a closure*, on page 83. This can help remove redundancy or duplication in method calls, as we can see in the next example.

```
UsingClosures/Currying.groovy
def tellFortunes(closure) {
  Date date = new Date("09/20/2012")
  //closure date, "Your day is filled with ceremony"
  //closure date, "They're features, not bugs"
  // We can curry to avoid sending date repeatedly
  postFortune = closure.curry(date)
  postFortune "Your day is filled with ceremony"
  postFortune "They're features, not bugs"
}
tellFortunes() { date, fortune ->
  println "Fortune for ${date} is '${fortune}'"
}
```

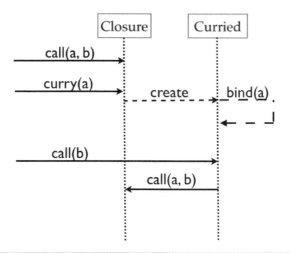

Figure 5—Currying a closure

The tellFortunes() method calls a closure multiple times. The closure takes two parameters. So, tellFortunes() would have to send the first parameter date in each call. Alternatively, we can curry that parameter using a call to the curry() method with date as an argument. postFortune holds a reference to the curried closure, which prebinds the value of date.

We can now call the curried closure and pass only the second parameter (fortune) that's intended for the original closure. The curried closure takes care of sending fortune along with the prebound parameter date to the original closure:

```
Fortune for Thu Sep 20 00:00:00 MST 2012 is 'Your day is filled with ceremony'
Fortune for Thu Sep 20 00:00:00 MST 2012 is 'They're features, not bugs'
```

We can curry any number of parameters, but we can curry only leading parameters using the curry() method. So if we have n parameters, we can curry any of the first k parameters, where 0 <= k <= n.

If we'd like to curry the trailing parameters, we can use the rcurry() method. If we need to curry values in the middle of the parameter list, we can use the ncurry() method that takes the order of the parameter we'd like to curry, along with the value.

Currying is a transformation from a function that takes multiple parameters to a function that takes fewer (typically one). The curry function on the function f(X,Y) -> Z is defined as curry(f): X -> (Y -> Z). Currying helps reduce and simplify methods for mathematical proofs. For our purpose, in Groovy, curry-ing can reduce the noise in code.

Continuing on the topic of parameters, next we'll see how to explore a closure's presence, and the number and types of parameters a closure may receive.

4.8 Dynamic Closures

We can determine whether a closure has been provided to us. Otherwise, we may decide to use a default implementation for, say, an algorithm in place of a specialized implementation the caller failed to provide. Here's an example to figure out whether a closure is present:

UsingClosures/MissingClosure.groovy
```
def doSomeThing(closure) {
  if (closure) {
    closure()
  } else {
    println "Using default implementation"
  }
}

doSomeThing() { println "Use specialized implementation" }

doSomeThing()
```

The code determines if a closure is provided and responds accordingly:

```
Use specialized implementation
Using default implementation
```

We also have quite a bit of flexibility in passing parameters. We can dynami-cally determine the number and types of parameters a closure expects. Assume we use a closure to compute the tax for a sale. The tax amount depends on the sale amount and the tax rate. Also assume that the closure may or may not need us to provide the tax rate. Here's an example to examine the number of parameters:

UsingClosures/QueryingClosures.groovy
```
def completeOrder(amount, taxComputer) {
  tax = 0
  if (taxComputer.maximumNumberOfParameters == 2) {// expects tax rate
    tax = taxComputer(amount, 6.05)
  } else {// uses a default rate
    tax = taxComputer(amount)
  }
  println "Sales tax is ${tax}"
}
completeOrder(100) { it * 0.0825 }
completeOrder(100) { amount, rate -> amount * (rate/100) }
```

The maximumNumberOfParameters property (or getMaximumNumberOfParameters() method) tells us the number of parameters the given closure accepts. Using this method, in the computeOrder() method we determine the number of parameters the given closure takes, using this to decide whether to send the tax rate. This helps us invoke the given closure with exactly the number of parameters it expects, as we see in the output:

```
Sales tax is 8.2500
Sales tax is 6.0500
```

In addition to the number of parameters, we can find the types of these parameters using the parameterTypes property (or the getParameterTypes() method). Here is an example examining the parameters of the closures provided:

UsingClosures/ClosuresParameterTypes.groovy
```
def examine(closure) {
  println "$closure.maximumNumberOfParameters parameter(s) given:"
  for(aParameter in closure.parameterTypes) { println aParameter.name }

  println "--"
}

examine() { }
examine() { it }
examine() {-> }
examine() { val1 -> }
examine() {Date val1 -> }
examine() {Date val1, val2 -> }
examine() {Date val1, String val2 -> }
```

Let's run the code and take a look at the number of parameters and their reported types:

```
1 parameter(s) given:
java.lang.Object
--
1 parameter(s) given:
java.lang.Object
--
0 parameter(s) given:
--
1 parameter(s) given:
java.lang.Object
--
1 parameter(s) given:
java.util.Date
--
2 parameter(s) given:
java.util.Date
java.lang.Object
```

```
--
2 parameter(s) given:
java.util.Date
java.lang.String
--
```

Even when a closure is not using any parameters, as in {} or { it }, it takes one parameter (whose name defaults to it). If the caller does not pass any values to the closure, then the first parameter (it) refers to null. If we want our closure to take absolutely no parameters, then we have to use the syntax {-> }—the lack of a parameter before -> indicates that our closure takes 0 parameters.

Using the maximumNumberOfParameters and parameterTypes properties, we can examine the given closures dynamically and implement logic with greater flexibility.

Speaking of examining objects, what does this mean within a closure? We will look at that next.

4.9   Closure Delegation

Closures in Groovy go far beyond being simple anonymous methods; they have some powerful capabilities, as we'll see in the rest of this chapter. Groovy closures support method delegation, and provide capabilities for method-dispatching—much like JavaScript's support for prototypal inheritance. Let's understand the magic behind this and how to put this to good use.

Three properties of a closure—this, owner, and delegate—determine which object handles a method call from within a closure. Generally, the delegate is set to owner, but changing it lets us exploit Groovy for some really good metaprogramming capabilities. Let's examine these properties for closures:

UsingClosures/ThisOwnerDelegate.groovy
```
def examiningClosure(closure) {
  closure()
}

examiningClosure() {
  println "In First Closure:"
  println "class is " + getClass().name
  println "this is " + this + ", super:" + this.getClass().superclass.name
  println "owner is " + owner + ", super:" + owner.getClass().superclass.name
  println "delegate is " + delegate +
            ", super:" + delegate.getClass().superclass.name

  examiningClosure() {
    println "In Closure within the First Closure:"
```

```
    println "class is " + getClass().name
    println "this is " + this + ", super:" + this.getClass().superclass.name
    println "owner is " + owner + ", super:" + owner.getClass().superclass.name
    println "delegate is " + delegate +
            ", super:" + delegate.getClass().superclass.name
  }
}
```

Within the first closure, we fetch the details about the closure, finding out what this, owner, and delegate refer to. Then within the first closure, we call the examiningClosure() method and send it another closure defined within the first closure, making the first closure the owner of the second closure. Within this second closure, we print those details again. Here's the output from the code:

```
In First Closure:
class is ThisOwnerDelegate$_run_closure1
this is ThisOwnerDelegate@55e6cb2a, super:groovy.lang.Script
owner is ThisOwnerDelegate@55e6cb2a, super:groovy.lang.Script
delegate is ThisOwnerDelegate@55e6cb2a, super:groovy.lang.Script
In Closure within the First Closure:
class is ThisOwnerDelegate$_run_closure1_closure2
this is ThisOwnerDelegate@55e6cb2a, super:groovy.lang.Script
owner is ThisOwnerDelegate$_run_closure1@15c330aa, super:groovy.lang.Closure
delegate is ThisOwnerDelegate$_run_closure1@15c330aa, super:groovy.lang.Closure
```

The previous code example and the corresponding output show that closures are created as inner classes. They also show that the delegate is set to owner. Certain Groovy functions—such as with()—modify delegate to perform dynamic routing. this within a closure refers to the object to which the closure is bound (the executing context). Variables and methods referred to within the closure are bound to this—it has dibs on handling any methods calls or access to any properties or variables. The owner stands in next, followed by the delegate. This sequence is illustrated in the following figure.

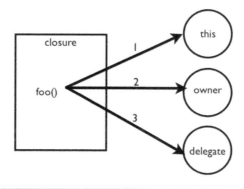

Figure 6—Order of method resolution on method calls from closures

Let's examine the method resolution further with an example:

UsingClosures/MethodRouting.groovy

```groovy
class Handler {
  def f1() { println "f1 of Handler called ..."}
  def f2() { println "f2 of Handler called ..."}
}

class Example {
  def f1() { println "f1 of Example called ..."}
  def f2() { println "f2 of Example called ..."}

  def foo(closure) {
    closure.delegate = new Handler()
    closure()
  }
}

def f1() { println "f1 of Script called..." }

new Example().foo {
  f1()
  f2()
}
```

In this code, calls to methods within the closure are first routed to the context object—this—for the closure. If they're not found, they're routed to the delegate:

```
f1 of Script called...
f2 of Handler called ...
```

In the previous example we set the delegate property on a closure. This has side effects, especially if the closure can be used in other functions or in other threads. If we're absolutely sure that the closure is not used elsewhere, we can set the delegate. If it is used elsewhere, avoid the side effect—clone the closure, set the delegate on the clone, and use the clone. Groovy provides a convenient method to achieve this. Rather than performing

```
def clone = closure.clone()
clone.delegate = handler
clone()
```

we can perform those three steps in one shot using a special with() method:

```
handler.with closure
```

Section 19.7, *Closures and DSLs*, on page 301, covers how the concepts from this section are used to build DSLs. Also refer to Section 7.1, *Using Object Extensions*, on page 128, and Section 13.2, *Injecting Methods Using*

ExpandoMetaClass, on page 198. ExpandoMetaClass uses delegate to proxy methods of classes.

Groovy closures go beyond being just glue code. In addition to dynamic method-dispatching abilities, Groovy closures have some interesting convenience methods, as we'll see next.

4.10 Programming with Tail Recursion

Closures in Groovy provide a way to reap the benefits of recursion and at the same time avoid some of the common problems we run into when using recursions.

With recursion, we solve a problem using solutions to its subproblems. Recursive solutions have charm—they're concise, and how cool is it that we can compose the solution using the solutions to the same problem but with smaller input size. In spite of these benefits, programmers often shy away from recursive solutions. The threat of a potential StackOverflowError for large input size can dissuade even the geekiest programmers among us.

Here's the all-too-familiar overly simplified factorial function implemented as a simple recursion.

UsingClosures/simpleFactorial.groovy
```groovy
def factorial(BigInteger number) {
  if (number == 1) 1 else number * factorial(number - 1)
}

try {
  println "factorial of 5 is ${factorial(5)}"
  println "Number of bits in the result is ${factorial(5000).bitCount()}"
} catch(Throwable ex) {
  println "Caught ${ex.class.name}"
}
```

The factorial for 5 is a small value, but the factorial for 5000 is a large number. If the computation is successful, we should see the result of 120 and the number of bits in the large factorial for 5000. When we run the program we'll notice that the JVM chokes on the large number of recursive calls:

```
factorial of 5 is 120
Caught java.lang.StackOverflowError
```

If we write the function as an iteration, then we won't run into resource constraints like this. But recursions are so cool and expressive! If only they were kind on resource utilization....

In the wonderful book *Structure and Interpretation of Computer Programs* *[AS96]*, the authors discuss an elegant way to deal with this. They suggest via compiler-optimization techniques and language support, recursive programs can be translated into iterative processes. Using such transformations, we can write highly expressive elegant code and reap the efficiency benefits of simple iteration. The Groovy language offers this technique through a special trampoline() method on closures.

To use this feature, we'll first have to implement the factorial function as a closure:

UsingClosures/trampolineFactorial.groovy

```
def factorial

factorial = { int number, BigInteger theFactorial ->
  number == 1 ? theFactorial :
    factorial.trampoline(number - 1, number * theFactorial)
}.trampoline()

println "factorial of 5 is ${factorial(5, 1)}"
println "Number of bits in the result is ${factorial(5000, 1).bitCount()}"
```

We define a variable named factorial and assign it to a closure that takes two parameters—the number, which is a candidate for which we want to determine the factorial—and theFactorial, which stands for the partial result being computed through the recursion. In the closure, if the given number is 1, we return the value of theFactorial as the result. Otherwise, we invoke the closure recursively using a call to the trampoline() method. To this method we pass as the first parameter one less than the given number, narrowing down the computation range. The second parameter is the partial factorial result computed so far.

The factorial variable itself is assigned the result of a call to the method trampoline() on the closure.

The implementation of tail recursion in Groovy is just brilliant, done without any change to the language itself. When we invoke the trampoline() method, the closure immediately returns an instance of a special class TrampolineClosure. When we pass parameters to this instance, like in factorial(5, 1), we invoke this instance's call() method. This method uses a simple for loop to invoke the call method on closure until it no longer yields an instance of TrampolineClosure. This simple technique turns our recursive invocation into a simple iteration under the hood.

This kind of recursion is called *tail recursion* because the last expression in the method either terminates the recursion or calls itself back. In contrast, in the straight recursion for computing the factorial, for example, the last expression was a call to *, the multiplication operation.

Let's exercise the new tail-recursive version of factorial() to see that it does not have the drawbacks of the straight recursion:

```
factorial of 5 is 120
Number of bits in the result is 24654
```

The trampoline() method helps us enjoy the power of recursion without the associated drawbacks. It is a significant step forward, but we also lost simplicity in the process. Rather than a simple call to the method, such as factorial(5), we're forced to send an additional argument, such as factorial(5, 1). In addition to the added burden, this is error-prone if we pass some value other than 1 to the second parameter.

As a quick fix to this problem, we can define a default value to the closure's second parameter, like so: BigInteger theFactorial = 1. The caller can now skip the second parameter, but this does not prevent sending a wrong value. We can eliminate this problem by encapsulating the closure within a function.

UsingClosures/trampoline.groovy
```
def factorial(int factorialFor) {
  def tailFactorial
  tailFactorial = { int number, BigInteger theFactorial = 1 ->
    number == 1 ? theFactorial :
      tailFactorial.trampoline(number - 1, number * theFactorial)
  }.trampoline()
  tailFactorial(factorialFor)
}
println "factorial of 5 is ${factorial(5)}"
println "Number of bits in the result is ${factorial(5000).bitCount()}"
```

We defined a function factorial() and defined the tail-recursive closure within that function. Finally we invoked the trampoline() closure, passing it the number for which we want to compute the factorial. The default value of 1 is passed to the closure's second parameter.

Unlike some languages, where tail-call optimization is realized through compilation techniques, Groovy realizes it through a simple convenience method on closure. The entire impact on the language and its grammar is avoided this way, providing programming elegance while reducing the memory footprint. There's one catch, however, in using the trampoline() feature—it is slower performancewise than the simple recursion or pure iteration. For a large input size, this could be a huge limitation. (An implementation without any compiler tricks is nice to see, but not with a performance impact.) For trampoline() to be useful for large a input size, either the implementation has to significantly improve in performance or we need a compiler transformation to improve efficiency.

In the next section we'll see how closures impact the runtime of a specialized type of recursive algorithms.

4.11 Improving Performance Using Memoization

I once attended a bird show where a performer challenged a teenager to compete against a parrot in arithmetic. To the chagrin of the young fellow and the amusement of the viewers, the parrot swiftly replied to "what's 200 times 50?" After the parrot aced the next few questions, the performer revealed the secret—the parrot simply repeated memorized answers to scripted questions. In this section we'll use a similar technique, but rather than calling it memorization, we'll term it *memoization*, continuing the tradition in our field of giving odd names to concepts.

In the previous section you learned a technique to make recursive calls memory-efficient. Recursion in essence is a way to solve a problem using solutions to its subproblems. In a variation of this technique, oddly named *dynamic programming*, we break the problem into parts that are redundantly solved several times over. During execution, we save results of the subproblems, and when the redundant computation is invoked, we simply use the saved result—avoiding the rerun and thus greatly reducing the computation time. Memoization can reduce some algorithms' computational time complexity from exponential ($O(k^n)$) to mere linear order ($O(n)$) on the input size (n).

To help understand this concept and the memoization facility in Groovy, let's get into the business of selling rods. Rods of different length are sold at retail for different prices. We are in the business of buying wholesale rods of a particular length—for example, 27 inches—and selling them in pieces of various length to maximize our revenue.

We will first use simple recursion to solve this problem. Then we'll use memoization to solve it again. Since memoization is about reducing computation time, we need a way to measure the time taken; let's start with a little function that will help with that.

UsingClosures/rodCutting.groovy
```groovy
def timeIt(length, closure) {
  long start = System.nanoTime()
  println "Max revenue for $length is ${closure(length)}"
  long end = System.nanoTime()
  println "Time taken ${(end - start)/1.0e9} seconds"
}
```

The timeIt() method reports the time the given closure takes to run, and reports the maximum revenue we can expect to receive for the given length of rod, as reported by the closure.

Define a sample of retail prices for various lengths of rods, from 0 inches to 30 inches in an array—the size 0 is included to offset the zero-based array indexing:

UsingClosures/rodCutting.groovy

```groovy
def rodPrices = [0, 1, 3, 4, 5, 8, 9, 11, 12, 14,
  15, 15, 16, 18, 19, 15, 20, 21, 22, 24,
  25, 24, 26, 28, 29, 35, 37, 38, 39, 40]

def desiredLength = 27
```

The rodPrices variable refers to a list with the prices for various lengths, and the variable desiredLength holds the length of rod we're interested in selling to maximize the revenue.

Based on the given retail prices, if we sell a rod of 27 inches as is, we'd make $38. If we cut it into two pieces of lengths 1 and 26 inches, we'd make the same amount, so that's really not worth it. We'd lose money if we split it into two pieces of 4 and 23 inches. We can make more than $38 for the 27-inch rod if we split it into six pieces—five pieces of 5 inches each, and the last piece of 2 inches will bring a total of $43. Figuring that out manually will take an awfully long time. If we're given an arbitrary length and prices, we'd want a program that quickly computes an optimal split that maximizes our revenue.

The code we'll create next will tell us both the maximum revenue for a given length and the lengths into which to cut the rod for maximum revenue.

Let's start with a class RevenueDetails to hold the price and the pieces' lengths.

UsingClosures/rodCutting.groovy

```groovy
@groovy.transform.Immutable
class RevenueDetails {
  int revenue
  ArrayList splits
}
```

Finding an optimal maximum revenue requires trying out various combinations. The maximum revenue for a given length is the maximum of the revenues of splitting it various ways. For example, we can start by splitting the rod into a 2-inch piece and a 25-inch piece. The maximum revenue this split can produce is not the total of the price for these two lengths, however. It's the total of maximum revenue for the 2 inches and the maximum revenue for the 25 inches. We can see the recursive structure emerge in the solution.

To determine the maximum revenue for the 25 inches, we'd split that into smaller pieces, and in turn have to repeatedly compute maximum revenues for smaller pieces, such as 2 inches. This is the redundancy we can memoize to save time, as we'll see soon.

First let's implement the simple recursion for the rod-cutting problem.

```
UsingClosures/rodCutting.groovy
def cutRod(prices, length) {
  if(length == 0)
    new RevenueDetails(0, [])
  else {
    def maxRevenueDetails = new RevenueDetails(Integer.MIN_VALUE, [])
    for(rodSize in 1..length) {
      def revenueFromSecondHalf = cutRod(prices, length - rodSize)
      def potentialRevenue = new RevenueDetails(
        prices[rodSize] + revenueFromSecondHalf.revenue,
        revenueFromSecondHalf.splits + rodSize)
      if(potentialRevenue.revenue > maxRevenueDetails.revenue)
        maxRevenueDetails = potentialRevenue
    }
    maxRevenueDetails
  }
}

timeIt desiredLength, { length -> cutRod(rodPrices, length) }
```

The cutRod() method takes two parameters, prices and length, and returns an instance of RevenueDetails with the maximum revenue for the given length and a possible lengths of pieces. If the length is 0, the recursion ends. Given a length, we try as many combinations as possible of split: 1 and length - 1, 2 and length - 2, 3 and length - 3, and so on, and pick the maximum value from those combinations. For each length pair, we recursively invoke the cutRod() method.

This is a simple recursion and each call to the method will do the entire calculation. Repeated calls to the method for the same length will redundantly recalculate the results. Run the code for a rod length of 27 inches and note the maximum revenue, optimal split lengths, and the time the code takes to arrive at the results.

```
Max revenue for 27 is RevenueDetails(43, [5, 5, 5, 5, 5, 2])
Time taken 162.89431500 seconds
```

For a maximum profit of $43 we'd have to split our rod into six pieces. The program took well over two minutes to figure that out. We can improve this speed using memoization. Surprisingly we'll have to make only a few changes to realize this—we convert the function into a closure and invoke the memoize() method on it:

```
UsingClosures/rodCutting.groovy
def cutRod
cutRod = { prices, length ->
  if(length == 0)
    new RevenueDetails(0, [])
  else {
    def maxRevenueDetails = new RevenueDetails(Integer.MIN_VALUE, [])
    for(rodSize in 1..length) {
      def revenueFromSecondHalf = cutRod(prices, length - rodSize)
      def potentialRevenue = new RevenueDetails(
        prices[rodSize] + revenueFromSecondHalf.revenue,
        revenueFromSecondHalf.splits + rodSize)
      if(potentialRevenue.revenue > maxRevenueDetails.revenue)
        maxRevenueDetails = potentialRevenue
    }
    maxRevenueDetails
  }
}.memoize()

timeIt desiredLength, { length -> cutRod(rodPrices, length) }
```

After converting the function and invoking the memoize() method on it, we saved the result to the cutRod variable. Using these steps we created a specialized instance of a Memoize class. This has a reference to the closure we provided, and a cache of results. When we invoke the closure, this instance will cache the response before returning the result. Subsequent calls will return the appropriate cached values based on the parameters, if present.

Let's run the modified version of this code and ensure the maximum revenue and the pieces' lengths are the same as in the previous version. This version should take a lot less time:

```
Max revenue for 27 is RevenueDetails(43, [5, 5, 5, 5, 5, 2])
Time taken 0.01171600 seconds
```

The memoized version produces the same results but takes only *1/100* of a second compared to more than two minutes the simple recursion took.

The memoization technique trades space for speed. We saw the speed improve. The amount of space this takes depends on the number of times the recursive method is called with unique parameters. For a large problem size, the memory demand can drastically increase. Groovy is quite sensitive to this and gives us a few options. A simple call to memoize() uses an unlimited cache. We can limit the cache size by instead using the memoizeAtMost() method. This method limits the size of the cache and when the limit is reached, the least-recently used values are removed from the cache to accommodate new values.

We can also use variations such as memoizeAtLeast() to set a lower limit on the cache size, and memoizeAtLeastBetween() to set a lower and an upper limit.

In addition to managing the cache, the implementations of the memoize() functions provide thread safety; we can safely access the cache from multiple threads.

We've seen how Groovy, which is dynamically typed, makes dynamic programming trivial to implement.

In this chapter we covered one of the most important concepts in Groovy—one that we'll use repeatedly. We now know how to work with closures in a dynamic context. We also understand how closures dispatch method calls. In the following chapters, we'll see several examples where closures stand out, so we'll have plenty of opportunity to appreciate their charm.

Strings are commonplace in programming and Groovy provides great convenience and flexibility to work with them. In the next chapter we'll discuss the facilities that Groovy provides, from creating strings to formatting expressions with them.

Working with Strings

We all know it's a pain to work with strings in Java. As fundamental as strings are in programming, we would think it would be easier. But no, it takes effort to do basic string manipulation, to evaluate multiple variables or expressions into a string representation, and even to do something as simple as create a string that spans multiple lines. Groovy to the rescue! Groovy takes away the pain of dealing with strings on these fronts. It also makes pattern-matching of strings with regular expressions much easier by providing special operators. We'll go through the basics of Groovy strings in this chapter.

5.1 Literals and Expressions

We can create literals in Groovy using single quotes—like 'hello'. In Java, 'a' is a char, while "a" is a String. Groovy makes no such distinction; both of these are instances of String in Groovy. If we want to explicitly create a character, we simply type 'a' as char. Of course, Groovy may implicitly create Character objects if any method calls demand it.

Groovy is also flexible about what we can put into a literal. For example, we can have double quotes in our string if we want:

WorkingWithStrings/Literals.groovy
```
println 'He said, "That is Groovy"'
```

Groovy handled that fairly well, as we can see in the output:

```
He said, "That is Groovy"
```

Let's examine the type of the object that was created using the single quotes:

WorkingWithStrings/Literals.groovy
```
str = 'A string'
println str.getClass().name
```

From the output we can see the object is the popular String:

```
java.lang.String
```

Groovy treats a String created using single quotes as a pure literal. So, if we put any expressions in it, Groovy won't expand them; instead, it will use them literally as we provided them. We'll have to use double quotes to evaluate the expressions in a String, as we'll see soon.

WorkingWithStrings/Literals.groovy
```
value = 25
println 'The value is ${value}'
```

From the output we can see that Groovy did not evaluate or expand the value:

```
The value is ${value}
```

Java Strings are immutable, and Groovy honors that immutability. Once we create an instance of String, we can't modify its content by calling setters and so on. We can read a character using the [] operator; however, we can't modify it, as we can see from the following code:

WorkingWithStrings/Literals.groovy
```
str = 'hello'
println str[2]
try {
  str[2] = '!'
} catch(Exception ex) {
  println ex
}
```

Our effort to modify the String results in an error:

```
l
groovy.lang.MissingMethodException: No signature of method:
  java.lang.String.putAt() is applicable for argument types:
  (java.lang.Integer, java.lang.String) values: [2, !]
...
```

We can create an expression with either double quotes ("") or slashes (//). However, double quotes are often used to define string expressions, and forward slashes are used for regular expressions. Here's an example for creating an expression:

WorkingWithStrings/Expressions.groovy
```
value = 12
println "He paid \$${value} for that."
```

Groovy evaluates the expression, as we can see in the output:

```
He paid $12 for that.
```

The variable value was expanded within the string. We use the escape character (\) to print the $ symbol because Groovy uses that symbol for embedding expressions. We don't have to escape the $ if we use slashes instead of double quotes to define the string. The {} around expressions are optional if the expression is a simple variable name like value or a simple accessor to a property. So, we could write the statement println "He paid \$${value} for that." as println "He paid \$$value for that." or println (/He paid $$value for that/). Try leaving out the {} in expressions and see whether Groovy complains. We can always add it if needed.

We can store an expression in a string and print it later—Groovy uses lazy evaluation. Let's look at an example:

WorkingWithStrings/Expressions.groovy
```
what = new StringBuilder('fence')
text = "The cow jumped over the $what"
println text

what.replace(0, 5, "moon")
println text
```

Let's look at the output to see how Groovy resolved that expression:

```
The cow jumped over the fence
The cow jumped over the moon
```

When we print the string expression in text, the current value in the object that what refers to is used. So, the first time we printed text, we got "The cow jumped over the fence." Then, after changing the value in the StringBuilder when we reprinted the string expression—we did not modify the content of text—we got a different output, this time the phrase "The cow jumped over the moon" from the popular rhyme "Hey Diddle Diddle."

From this behavior we see that strings created using single quotes are different from those created using double quotes or slashes. Strings created using single quotes are regular java.lang.Strings. However, those created using double quotes and slashes are special. The authors of Groovy have a weird sense of humor—they called them GStrings, short for *Groovy strings*. Let's look at the types of the objects created using different string syntax:

WorkingWithStrings/Expressions.groovy
```
def printClassInfo(obj) {
  println "class: ${obj.getClass().name}"
  println "superclass: ${obj.getClass().superclass.name}"
}

val = 125
```

```
printClassInfo ("The Stock closed at ${val}")
printClassInfo (/The Stock closed at ${val}/)
printClassInfo ("This is a simple String")
```

From the output we can see the types of the objects created:

```
class: org.codehaus.groovy.runtime.GStringImpl
superclass: groovy.lang.GString
class: org.codehaus.groovy.runtime.GStringImpl
superclass: groovy.lang.GString
class: java.lang.String
superclass: java.lang.Object
```

Groovy does not readily create an instance of GString simply because we use double quotes or slashes. It intelligently analyzes the string to determine whether it can get away with a simple regular String. In the example, the argument to the last call of printClassInfo() is an instance of String even though we used double quotes to create it.

It's easy to get too comfortable with the seamless interplay of different string types in Groovy. As we'll see in the next section, we must use some caution when working with them.

5.2 GString Lazy-Evaluation Problem

The result we get from GString expressions depends on whether we use values or references in the expression. The result may lead to some surprises if we're not careful how we compose the expression. Learning this now will help avoid stumbling like your humble author did when learning about string manipulation in Groovy. Here's the example that worked well in the previous section:

WorkingWithStrings/LazyEval.groovy
```
what = new StringBuilder('fence')
text = "The cow jumped over the $what"
println text

what.replace(0, 5, "moon")
println text
```

The output from the code looks pretty reasonable:

```
The cow jumped over the fence
The cow jumped over the moon
```

The GString (text) contains the variable what. The expression is evaluated just in time each time we print it—when the toString() method is called on it. If we change the value in the StringBuilder object that what refers to, the expression reflects it when printed. That seems reasonable, right?

Unfortunately, this is not the behavior we'll see if we modify the reference what instead of changing the referenced object's properties—that's what we'd naturally do if the object were immutable. Here's an example that shows the problem:

WorkingWithStrings/LazyEval.groovy
```groovy
price = 684.71
company = 'Google'
quote = "Today $company stock closed at $price"
println quote

stocks = [Apple : 663.01, Microsoft : 30.95]

stocks.each { key, value ->
  company = key
  price = value
  println quote
}
```

We stored an expression in the variable quote with the embedded variables company and price. When we print it the first time, it correctly prints Google and its stock price. We have the stocks of a few other companies, and we want to use the expression we created before to print the quote for these companies as well. To do that, we iterate over the stocks map—within the closure we have the company as the key and the price as the value. However, when we print the quote, the result (shown next) is not what we expect. We have to fix this problem before our colleagues start another "Google has taken over the world" debate.

```
Today Google stock closed at 684.71
Today Google stock closed at 684.71
Today Google stock closed at 684.71
```

First let's figure out why it did not work as expected, and then we can figure out a solution. When we defined the GString—quote—we bound the variables company and price to a String holding the value Google and an Integer holding that obscene stock price, respectively. We can change the company and price references all we want (both of these are referring to immutable objects) to refer to other objects, but we're not changing what the GString instance has been bound to.

"The cow jumping over..." example worked because we modified the object that the GString was bound to; however, in this example we don't. We can't because of immutability. The solution? We need to ask the GString to reevaluate the reference—after all, as computer scientist David Wheeler said, "Any problem in computer science can be solved with another level of indirection."

Before we fix the problem, let's take a moment to understand how GString expressions are evaluated. When evaluating a GString, if we have a variable, its value is simply printed to a writer, typically a StringWriter. However, if we have a closure instead of a variable, the closure is invoked. If our closure takes a parameter, then GString sends the Writer object as an argument to the closure. If our closure takes no parameters at all, then GString simply calls our closure and prints the result we return to the writer. If our closure takes more than one parameter, then the call fails with an exception; let's not go there.

Let's put that knowledge to use to solve our expression-evaluation problem. Here's the first attempt:

WorkingWithStrings/LazyEval.groovy
```
companyClosure = { it.write(company) }
priceClosure = { it.write("$price") }
quote = "Today ${companyClosure} stock closed at ${priceClosure}"
stocks.each { key, value ->
  company = key
  price = value
  println quote
}
```

Let's run the code to see the output:

```
Today Apple stock closed at 663.01
Today Microsoft stock closed at 30.95
```

We got the output we desire, but the code does not look very groovy. Even though we don't want to implement our final code this way, seeing this example will help in two ways. First, we can see what's really going on—the GString is calling our closure at the time when the expression needs to be evaluated/printed. Second, if we need to do some computations that are more than merely displaying a property's value, we know how to do that.

Let's get rid of that it parameter. Like we discussed earlier, if our closure has no parameters, then GString uses what we return. We know how to create a closure with no parameters—define it with the syntax {-> . So, let's refactor the previous code:

WorkingWithStrings/LazyEval.groovy
```
companyClosure = {-> company }
priceClosure = {-> price }
quote = "Today ${companyClosure} stock closed at ${priceClosure}"
stocks.each { key, value ->
  company = key
  price = value
  println quote
}
```

Here's the output of the refactored version:

```
Today Apple stock closed at 663.01
Today Microsoft stock closed at 30.95
```

That's a notch better, but we don't want to define the closures separately. Instead, we want our code to be self-contained for simple cases, and we're willing to write a separate closure if we have more code to compute the values. Here's the self-contained code that solves the problem (we'll call it the "Google and Apple trying to take over the world" problem):

```
WorkingWithStrings/LazyEval.groovy
quote = "Today ${-> company } stock closed at ${-> price }"

stocks.each { key, value ->
  company = key
  price = value
  println quote
}
```

This concise version produces the same output as the previous version:

```
Today Apple stock closed at 663.01
Today Microsoft stock closed at 30.95
```

GString's lazy evaluation is a very powerful concept. However, use caution not to trip over that string. If we expect our references used in expressions to change and we want their current value to be used in the lazy evaluation, we must remember not to place them directly in the expressions, but rather within a no-parameter closure.

We've seen the elegance of Groovy's string manipulation and formatting, but we've merely scratched the surface of this capability. In the next section we'll discuss ways in which Groovy simplifies the dreadful and cumbersome process of creating multiline strings in Java.

5.3 Multiline Strings

When we want to create a multiline string in Java, we have to use code like str += …, concatenated multiple lines using the + operator, or multiple calls to the append() method of StringBuilder or StringBuffer.

We'd have to use a lot of escape characters, and that usually is followed by a complaint that "there's gotta be a better way to do that." In Groovy there is. We can define a multiline literal by enclosing the string within three single quotes ('''...''')—that's Groovy's support of here documents, or *heredocs*:

WorkingWithStrings/MultilineStrings.groovy

```
memo = '''Several of you raised concerns about long meetings.
To discuss this, we will be holding a 3 hour meeting starting
at 9AM tomorrow. All getting this memo are required to attend.
If you can't make it, please have a meeting with your manager to explain.
'''

println memo
```

Here's the multiline string created from the code:

```
Several of you raised concerns about long meetings.
To discuss this, we will be holding a 3 hour meeting starting
at 9AM tomorrow. All getting this memo are required to attend.
If you can't make it, please have a meeting with your manager to explain.
```

Just as we can create GStrings that can hold expressions using double-quoted strings, we can create multiline expressions using three double quotes.

WorkingWithStrings/MultilineStrings.groovy

```
price = 251.12

message = """We're very pleased to announce
that our stock price hit a high of \$${price} per share
on December 24th. Great news in time for..."""
println message
```

Groovy evaluates the expression in the multiline string, as we see in the output:

```
We're very pleased to announce
that our stock price hit a high of $251.12 per share
on December 24th. Great news in time for...
```

I write a monthly newsletter, and a couple of years ago I decided to convert to Groovy the program I use to send email notifications. Groovy's ability to create multiline strings with embedded values came in handy. Groovy even makes it easy to spam! (Just kidding.)

Let's look at an example using the feature we just covered. Assume we have a map of languages and authors and want to create an XML representation of it. Here is a way to do that:

WorkingWithStrings/CreateXML.groovy

```
langs = ['C++' : 'Stroustrup', 'Java' : 'Gosling', 'Lisp' : 'McCarthy']

content = ''
langs.each { language, author ->
  fragment = """
```

```
    <language name="${language}">
      <author>${author}</author>
    </language>
  """
```

```
  content += fragment
}
xml = "<languages>${content}</languages>"
println xml
```

This is impressive, but wait until we see the XML builders in Section 17.1, *Building XML*, on page 253! Here's the XML output produced using the multiline string expressions:

```
<languages>
  <language name="C++">
    <author>Stroustrup</author>
  </language>

  <language name="Java">
    <author>Gosling</author>
  </language>

  <language name="Lisp">
    <author>McCarthy</author>
  </language>
</languages>
```

We're using the multiline string with embedded expressions to create the desired content. The content is generated by iterating over the map that contains the data.

We've seen ways to create strings, and in the next section we'll talk about the convenience functions Groovy provides to manipulate strings.

5.4 String Convenience Methods

We already praised String's execute method. In fact, it helped us create a Process object so we can execute system-level processes with only a couple of lines of code; see *A Quick Look at the GDK*, on page 14.

We can get fancier with String using other methods. For example, take a look at the following code, which uses an overloaded operator of String:

```
WorkingWithStrings/StringConvenience.groovy
str = "It's a rainy day in Seattle"
println str

str -= "rainy "
println str
```

The output shows the effect of the overloaded operator:

```
It's a rainy day in Seattle
It's a day in Seattle
```

The -= operator is useful for manipulating a string, it removes part of the left-side string that matches the string on the right side. The Groovy-added minus() method on the String class makes this possible (see Section 2.8, *Operator Overloading*, on page 31). Groovy adds other convenience methods to String: plus() (+), multiply() (*), next() (++), replaceAll(), and tokenize(), to mention a few.[1]

We can iterate over a range of Strings as well, as shown here:

WorkingWithStrings/StringRange.groovy
```
for(str in 'held'..'helm') {
  print "${str} "
}
println ""
```

The sequence generated by the code is as follows:

```
held hele helf helg helh heli helj helk hell helm
```

Here we're still using the same java.lang.String; however, all these added facilities help us get our work done quickly.

Now we know how to extract parts of a string. Hardcore programmers often reach out to regular expressions, and Groovy makes that easy, as well, as we'll see next.

5.5 Regular Expressions

The JDK package java.util.regex contains the API for pattern-matching with regular expressions (RegEx). For a detailed discussion of RegEx, refer to Jeffrey Friedl's *Mastering Regular Expressions [Fri97]*. String's replaceFirst() and replaceAll() methods, among other methods, make good use of RegEx pattern-matching. Groovy adds operators and symbols to make it easier to program with RegEx.

Groovy provides the operator ~ to easily create a RegEx pattern. This operator maps to String's negate() method:

WorkingWithStrings/RegEx.groovy
```
obj = ~"hello"
println obj.getClass().name
```

The output shows the type of the instance created:

```
java.util.regex.Pattern
```

1.　http://groovy.codehaus.org/groovy-jdk/java/lang/String.html

The previous example shows that ~ applied to String creates an instance of Pattern. We can use slashes or single or double quotes to create a RegEx. The slashes have an advantage: we don't have to escape backslashes. So, /\d*\w*/ is an equivalent and elegant cousin of "\\d*\\w*".

Groovy provides a couple of operators to facilitate matching regular expressions: =~ and ==~. Let's explore the differences between and capabilities of these operators:

```
WorkingWithStrings/RegEx.groovy
pattern = ~"(G|g)roovy"
text = 'Groovy is Hip'
if (text =~ pattern)
  println "match"
else
  println "no match"

if (text ==~ pattern)
  println "match"
else
  println "no match"
```

Let's run the code and see the difference between the two operators.

```
match
no match
```

The =~ performs a RegEx partial match, whereas the ==~ performs a RegEx exact match. So, in the previous code example, the first pattern match reports a "match," while the second one reports a "no match."

The =~ operator returns a Matcher object, which is an instance of java.util.regex.Matcher. Groovy handles boolean evaluation of Matcher differently than Java; it returns true if there's at least one match (see Section 2.7, *Groovy Boolean Evaluation*, on page 30). If the match results in multiple matches, then the matcher contains an array of the matches. This helps quickly get access to parts of the text that match the given RegEx.

```
WorkingWithStrings/RegEx.groovy
matcher = 'Groovy is groovy' =~ /(G|g)roovy/
print "Size of matcher is ${matcher.size()} "
println "with elements ${matcher[0]} and ${matcher[1]}."
```

The previous code reports the details of the Matcher, as follows:

```
Size of matcher is 2 with elements [Groovy, G] and [groovy, g].
```

We can replace matching text easily using the replaceFirst() method (for replacing only the first match, as the name indicates) or the replaceAll() method (for replacing all matches).

```
str = 'Groovy is groovy, really groovy'
println str
result = (str =~ /groovy/).replaceAll('hip')
println result
```

The original text and the replaced text are as follows:

```
Groovy is groovy, really groovy
Groovy is hip, really hip
```

To summarize, here are the Groovy operators related to RegEx:

- To create a pattern from a string, use the ~ operator.
- To define a RegEx, use forward slashes, as in /[G|g]roovy/.
- To determine whether there's a match, use =~.
- For an exact match, use ==~.

In this chapter, we saw how Groovy makes creating and using strings so much easier than in Java. It is a breeze to create multiline strings, as well as strings with expressions. We also saw how Groovy simplifies the effort required to work with RegEx. Groovy strings will make us feel turbocharged when we get down to regular string manipulations and working with regular expressions.

Collections of objects are as fundamental in programming as working with strings is. Groovy has enhanced the JDK collections API with the convenience and fluency closures offer, as we'll see in the next chapter.

CHAPTER 6

Working with Collections

We use collections extensively when programming. The Java Development Kit (JDK) has a number of useful collections, and Groovy extends those collections, making them more convenient to use. For example, we can use internal iterators, which are concise, easier to use, and less error-prone than the traditional for loop. We can use a different specialized iterator, find, to pick an element from a collection. To pick several matching elements we simply change find to findAll, and the rest of the code remains the same—concise, no extra baggage of the new collection to carry around. Once we get used to the collections in Groovy, it's pretty hard to go back and use the Java API for these collections. You've been warned!

In this chapter we'll use the JDK collections, but will learn to use the lightweight, fluent methods available in Groovy. We will start by looking at various iterators and convenience methods on List, which are ordered collections. After that we'll look at similar methods provided for the Maps, the associative collections with key-value pairs.

6.1 Using List

Creating an instance of java.util.ArrayList is easier in Groovy than in Java. We don't have to use new or specify the class name. We can simply list the initial values we want in the List, as shown here:

WorkingWithCollections/CreatingArrayList.groovy
```
lst = [1, 3, 4, 1, 8, 9, 2, 6]
println lst
println lst.getClass().name
```

Let's look at the ArrayList's contents and its type, as reported by Groovy:

```
[1, 3, 4, 1, 8, 9, 2, 6]
java.util.ArrayList
```

When we declare a list in Groovy, the reference lst refers to an instance of java.util.ArrayList, as we can see from the previous output.

We can fetch the elements of the List by using the [] operator, as shown in the next example:

WorkingWithCollections/CreatingArrayList.groovy
```
println lst[0]
println lst[lst.size() - 1]
```

The output shows the values of the first and last elements in the list:

```
1
6
```

But we don't have to jump through that many hoops to get to the last element of the list—Groovy has a simpler way. We can use negative index values, and Groovy will traverse from the right instead of the left:

WorkingWithCollections/CreatingArrayList.groovy
```
println lst[-1]
println lst[-2]
```

The previous code gets the last two elements of the list, as we see in the output:

```
6
2
```

We can even get contiguous values from the collection using the Range object:

WorkingWithCollections/CreatingArrayList.groovy
```
println lst[2..5]
```

The four contiguous values in the list, starting from the element at position 2, are as follows:

```
[4, 1, 8, 9]
```

We can even use a negative index in the range, as in the following code, which produces the same result as the previous code:

WorkingWithCollections/CreatingArrayList.groovy
```
println lst[-6..-3]
```

Let's quickly examine what lst[2..5] actually returned:

WorkingWithCollections/CreatingArrayList.groovy
```
subLst = lst[2..5]
println subLst.dump()
subLst[0] = 55
println "After  subLst[0]=55 lst = $lst"
```

We can see the instance's details as reported by the dump() method and the list after the change:

```
<java.util.ArrayList$SubList@fedbf parent=[1, 3, 4, 1, 8, 9, 2, 6]
  parentOffset=2 offset=2 size=4 this$0=[1, 3, 4, 1, 8, 9, 2, 6] modCount=1>
After  subLst[0]=55 lst = [1, 3, 55, 1, 8, 9, 2, 6]
```

If we use a range like 2..5 as the index, java.util.ArrayList returns an instance that refers to part of the the original list. So be aware—we did not get a copy; if we change an element using one list, we're affecting the other.

We can see how Groovy has made the application programming interface (API) for List much simpler. We are using the same, good old ArrayList, but when seen through our Groovy eyes, it looks a lot prettier and lighter.

The convenience Groovy offers continues far beyond creating lists, as we'll see in the next section.

6.2 Iterating Over an ArrayList

We often navigate or iterate over a list of values. Groovy provides elegant ways to iterate, and to perform operations on the values as we iterate over lists.

Using List's each Method

As we saw in Chapter 4, *Using Closures*, on page 71, Groovy provides convenient ways to iterate collections. This iterator, the method named each(), is also known as an *internal iterator*. For more information, see *Internal vs. External Iterators*, on page 112.

Let's create an ArrayList and iterate over it using the each() method.

WorkingWithCollections/IteratingArrayList.groovy
```
lst = [1, 3, 4, 1, 8, 9, 2, 6]

lst.each { println it }
```

We printed each element as we iterated over it, as we can see in the output:

```
1
3
4
1
8
9
2
6
```

Internal vs. External Iterators

We're used to external iterators in languages like C++ and Java. These iterators allow their user or client to control the iteration. We have to check whether we're at the end of iteration and explicitly move to the next element.

Internal iterators are popular in languages that support closures—the iterator's user or client does not control the iteration, but rather sends a block of code that will be executed for each element in the collection.

Internal iterators are easier to use—we don't have to control the iteration. External iterators are more flexible—we can take control of the iteration sequence, skip elements, terminate, restart iteration, and so on more easily.

Let's not let this apparent lack of flexibility dissuade us. Implementors of internal iteration often take extra effort to provide us with more flexibility and convenience. In the case of a List, the flexibility to control iteration comes in the form of different convenience methods we'll see in this chapter.

We can use the reverseEach() to iterate elements in the reverse order. To keep a tab of the count or index during iteration, we can use the eachWithIndex() method.

We can do other operations (see Section 4.3, *Ways to Use Closures*, on page 75), such as summing the elements of the collection, as we see here:

WorkingWithCollections/IteratingArrayList.groovy
```
total = 0
lst.each { total += it }
println "Total is $total"
```

The following is the result of executing the code:

```
Total is 34
```

Suppose we want to double each element of the collection. Let's take a stab at it using the each() method:

WorkingWithCollections/IteratingArrayList.groovy
```
doubled = []
lst.each { doubled << it * 2 }

println doubled
```

Here is the result:

```
[2, 6, 8, 2, 16, 18, 4, 12]
```

We create an empty ArrayList named doubled to hold the result. While iterating through the collection, we double each element and push the value into the result using the << operator (leftShift()).

If we want to perform some operations on each element in a collection, the each() method is our friend, but if we want the operation to yield some result, we can turn to other methods.

Using List's collect Method

Groovy provides a simple solution when we want to operate on each element in a collection and return a resulting collection—it's the collect() method, which we see here:

```
WorkingWithCollections/IteratingArrayList.groovy
println lst.collect { it * 2 }
```

The collect() method, like each(), invokes the closure for each element of the collection. However, it *collects* the return value from the closure into a collection and finally returns that resulting collection. The closure in the previous example is returning double the value it's given—there's an implicit return in the closure. We get back an ArrayList with the input values doubled, as we see in the output:

```
[2, 6, 8, 2, 16, 18, 4, 12]
```

If we want to perform operations on each element of a collection, we use each(); however, if we want a collection of the result of such a computation, we use the collect() method.

We're not limited to these two internal iterators, as we'll see next.

6.3 Using Finder Methods

We know how to iterate over a collection and perform operations on each element. However, if we want to search for a particular element, each() or collect() is not convenient. Instead, we should use find(), like so:

```
WorkingWithCollections/Find.groovy
lst = [4, 3, 1, 2, 4, 1, 8, 9, 2, 6]

println lst.find { it == 2 }
```

The code picks up the first element, which equals 2, as we see from the output:

```
2
```

In this code, we're looking for an object that matches value 2 in the collection. find() gets the first occurrence of the matching object. In this case, it returns the object at position 3. Just like the each() method, the find() method iterates over the collection, but only until the closure returns a true. On receiving a true, find() breaks from the iteration and returns the current element. If it never receives a true, then find() returns a null.

We can specify any condition in the closure we attach to find(). For example, here's how we'd look for the first element greater than 4:

WorkingWithCollections/Find.groovy
```
println lst.find { it > 4 }
```

The code reports the first number in the list that's greater than 4:

```
8
```

We can also find all occurrences of 2. Just as the find() method behaves like each(), the findAll() method behaves like collect():

WorkingWithCollections/Find.groovy
```
println lst.findAll { it == 2 }
```

We can see all the 2s that were found in the list:

```
[2, 2]
```

In this example, we looked for 2s, and the findAll() method is returning the objects and not the positions. If we want to find the position of the first matching object, we can use the findIndexOf() method.

In the simplest case, picking all 2s does not sound very useful. However, in general if we're looking for objects that match some criteria, we will get those objects. For example, if we look for all cities with populations greater than a certain number, the result will be a list of the appropriate cities. Returning to the previous example, if we want all numbers that are greater than 4, here's how to get them:

WorkingWithCollections/Find.groovy
```
println lst.findAll { it > 4 }
```

All elements greater than 4 are reported:

```
[8, 9, 6]
```

You learned how to iterate and to select elements from collections. Because things we can do with collections go far beyond these operations, Groovy extends its fluency with more convenience methods, as we'll see next.

6.4 Other Convenience Methods on Lists

Groovy adds a number of convenience methods to Collections. (For a list, refer to http://groovy.codehaus.org/groovy-jdk/java/util/Collection.html.) Let's implement an example using the method we're already familiar with—each(). Then we'll refactor that example using methods that will make our code self-contained and expressive. Along the way, we'll see how Groovy treats code blocks as first-class citizens, like functional programming languages do.

Suppose we have a collection of strings and want to count the total number of characters. Here's a way to do that using the each() method:

WorkingWithCollections/CollectionsConvenienceMethods.groovy
```
lst = ['Programming', 'In', 'Groovy']

count = 0
lst.each { count += it.size() }
println count
```

The number of characters found is as follows:

```
19
```

Groovy often gives us more than one way to accomplish a task. Here's another way using collect() and sum() (both are Groovy-added methods on Collections):

WorkingWithCollections/CollectionsConvenienceMethods.groovy
```
println lst.collect { it.size() }.sum()
```

We're calling the sum() method on the Collection the collect() method returns, and the code produces the same output as the previous version:

```
19
```

The code is a bit terse, but is self-contained: each() is useful to work on every individual element of a collection and get a cumulative result. However, collect() is useful if we want to apply some computation on each element of a collection but retain the result as a collection. We can take advantage of this to apply other operations (such as the sum() method) that can cascade down on the collection.

We can do the same using the inject() method:

WorkingWithCollections/CollectionsConvenienceMethods.groovy
```
println lst.inject(0) { carryOver, element ->  carryOver + element.size() }
```

The output is as follows:

```
19
```

inject() calls the closure for each element of the collection. The element is represented, in this example, by the element parameter. inject() takes as a parameter an initial value that it will inject, through the carryOver parameter, into the first call to the closure. It then injects the result from the closure into the subsequent call to the closure. We'll prefer the inject() method over the collect() method if we want a cumulative result of applying a computation on each element of a collection.

Suppose we want to concatenate the elements of the collection into a sentence. We can do that easily with join():

WorkingWithCollections/CollectionsConvenienceMethods.groovy
```
println lst.join(' ')
```

Here is the result of joining the elements:

```
Programming In Groovy
```

join() iterates over each element, concatenating every element with the character given as the input parameter. In this example, the whitespace character is given as the input parameter, so join() returns the string "Programming In Groovy." The join() method comes in handy when we want to concatenate a collection of paths—for instance, using a colon (:) to form a classpath—using one simple call.

We can replace an element of a List by assigning it to an index. In the following code, we're setting ['Be', 'Productive'] to element 0:

WorkingWithCollections/CollectionsConvenienceMethods.groovy
```
lst[0] = ['Be', 'Productive']
println lst
```

This results in a List within the collection, as we see here:

```
[[Be, Productive], In, Groovy]
```

If that's not what we want, we can flatten the List with the flatten() method:

WorkingWithCollections/CollectionsConvenienceMethods.groovy
```
lst = lst.flatten()
println lst
```

The result is a flattened single List of objects:

```
[Be, Productive, In, Groovy]
```

We can also use the - operator (minus() method) on List, like so:

WorkingWithCollections/CollectionsConvenienceMethods.groovy
```
println lst - ['Productive', 'In']
```

The elements in the right operand are removed from the collection on the left. If we provide a nonexistent element, no worries—it's simply ignored. The - operator is flexible, so we can provide either a list or a single value for the right operand. The list that results from the minus operation is as follows:

```
[Be, Groovy]
```

We can use the reverse() method to get a copy of the list with the elements in reverse order.

Here's another convenience in Groovy: we can easily perform an operation on each element without explicitly using an iterator:

WorkingWithCollections/CollectionsConvenienceMethods.groovy
```
println lst.size()
println lst*.size()
```

The code prints the number of elements and the size of each element:

```
4
[2, 10, 2, 6]
```

The first call to size() is on the list, so it returns 4, the current number of elements in the list. The second call—known as the *spread* operator because of the influence of *—is on each element (String in this example) of the list, so it returns a List with each element holding the size of corresponding elements in the original collection. The effect of lst*.size() is the same as lst.collect { it.size() }.

Finally, let's see how to use an ArrayList in method calls. If a method takes a number of parameters, instead of sending individual arguments, we can explode an ArrayList as arguments; that is, split the collection into individual objects using the * operator (the spread operator), as we'll see next. For this to work correctly, the size of the ArrayList must be the same as the number of parameters the method expects.

WorkingWithCollections/CollectionsConvenienceMethods.groovy
```
def words(a, b, c, d) {
  println "$a $b $c $d"
}

words(*lst)
```

The following is the result of using the spread operator:

```
Be Productive In Groovy
```

We've explored the Groovy facilities to work with a List of objects. Next we'll see how to use a Map in Groovy.

6.5 Using the Map Class

Java's java.util.Map is useful when we want to work with an associative set of key and value pairs. Groovy makes working with Maps simple and elegant with the use of closures. Creating an instance of Map is also simple, because we don't need to use new or specify any class names. Simply create pairs of values:

WorkingWithCollections/UsingMap.groovy
```
langs = ['C++' : 'Stroustrup', 'Java' : 'Gosling', 'Lisp' : 'McCarthy']

println langs.getClass().name
```

Let's confirm in the output the class of the collection we created:

```
java.util.LinkedHashMap
```

This example creates a hash map of some languages as keys, and their authors as values. The keys are separated from their values using a colon (:), and the entire map is placed in a []. This simple Groovy syntax creates an instance of java.util.LinkedHashMap. We can see that by calling getClass() and getting its name property. We used the verbose call to the getClass() method instead of favoring the JavaBean convention and directly accessing the class property. Read further to see the reason for that little gotcha.

We can access the value for a key using the [] operator, as in the following code:

WorkingWithCollections/UsingMap.groovy
```
println langs['Java']
println langs['C++']
```

The following are the values for the two keys we requested:

```
Gosling
Stroustrup
```

If we're expecting something fancier here, Groovy is sure not going to let us down. We can access the values by using the key as if it were a property of the Map:

WorkingWithCollections/UsingMap.groovy
```
println langs.Java
```

Groovy will return the value for the key used as a property:

```
Gosling
```

That is neat—it's convenient to send a key as if it were a property of the object, and the Map smartly returns the value. Of course, an experienced programmer immediately asks, "What's the catch?" We already saw a catch or gotcha:

we're not able to call the class property on the Map; the Map assumes that the name class refers to a (nonexistent) key and returns a null value. The subsequent call to the name property on null fails, obviously. Instances of Map and a few other classes don't return the Class metaobject when we call the class property. To avoid surprises, always use the getClass() method instead of the class property on instances.

So, we had to call the getClass() method. But what about the key *C++*? Let's try that:

WorkingWithCollections/UsingMap.groovy
```
println langs.C++ // Invalid code
```

Here's the output we get:

```
java.lang.NullPointerException: Cannot invoke method next() on null object
```

What the...? We may discard this example code by saying C++ is always a problem, no matter where we go.

But this problem is actually because of interference from another Groovy feature—operator overloading (see Section 2.8, *Operator Overloading*, on page 31). Groovy took the previous request as a get with key "C," which doesn't exist. Therefore, it returned a null and then tried to call the next() method (the operator ++ maps to it). Luckily, there is a workaround for special cases like this. Simply present the key with offending characters as a String.

WorkingWithCollections/UsingMap.groovy
```
println langs.'C++'
```

Now we can celebrate—we get the proper output:

```
Stroustrup
```

Groovy adds another convenience to creating maps. When defining a Map, we can skip the quotes around well-behaved key names. For instance, let's rewrite the map of languages and their authors without the quotes around the keys:

WorkingWithCollections/UsingMap.groovy
```
langs = ['C++' : 'Stroustrup', Java : 'Gosling', Lisp : 'McCarthy']
```

We know how to create a map and access individual values in the collection. Next we'll see how to iterate over collections.

6.6   Iterating Over Map

Groovy has added quite a few convenience methods to maps.[1] We can iterate over a Map, just like how we iterated over an ArrayList (see Section 6.2, *Iterating Over an ArrayList*, on page 111).

Map has a flavor of the each() and collect() methods.

Map's each Method

Let's look at an example of using the each() method:

WorkingWithCollections/NavigatingMap.groovy
```
langs = ['C++' : 'Stroustrup', 'Java' : 'Gosling', 'Lisp' : 'McCarthy']

langs.each { entry ->
  println "Language $entry.key was authored by $entry.value"
}
```

The output from the previous code is as follows:

```
Language C++ was authored by Stroustrup
Language Java was authored by Gosling
Language Lisp was authored by McCarthy
```

If the closure we attach to each() takes only one parameter, then each() sends an instance of MapEntry for that parameter. If we want to get the key and the value separately, we simply provide two parameters in the closure, as in the following example:

WorkingWithCollections/NavigatingMap.groovy
```
langs.each { language, author ->
  println "Language $language was authored by $author"
}
```

Here is the output from iterating over the map using two-parameter closure:

```
Language C++ was authored by Stroustrup
Language Java was authored by Gosling
Language Lisp was authored by McCarthy
```

This code example iterates over the langs collection using the each() method, which calls the closure with a key and value. We refer to these two parameters in the closure using the variable names language and author, respectively.

Similarly, for other methods—such as collect(), find(), and so on—we use one parameter if we want only the MapEntry and two parameters if we want the key and the value separately.

---

1.   http://groovy.codehaus.org/groovy-jdk/java/util/Map.html

Map's collect Method

Let's next examine the collect() method in Map. First, it's similar to the method in ArrayList in that both methods return a list. However, if we want Map's collect() to send our closure a MapEntry, we define one parameter; otherwise, we define two parameters, one for the key and one for the value, respectively, as shown here:

WorkingWithCollections/NavigatingMap.groovy
```
println langs.collect { language, author ->
  language.replaceAll("[+]", "P")
}
```

The code returns the following list:

```
[CPP, Java, Lisp]
```

In the previous code, we created a list of keys with all occurrences of + replaced with the character P.

We can easily transform the data in a Map into other representations. For example, in Section 17.1, *Building XML*, on page 253, we'll see how easy it is to create an XML representation.

Map's find and findAll Methods

Groovy also adds the find() and findAll() methods to Map. Let's look at an example:

WorkingWithCollections/NavigatingMap.groovy
```
println "Looking for the first language with name greater than 3 characters"
entry = langs.find { language, author ->
  language.size() > 3
}
println "Found $entry.key written by $entry.value"
```

The output from using the find() method is as follows:

```
Looking for the first language with name greater than 3 characters
Found Java written by Gosling
```

The find() method accepts a closure that takes the key and value (again, use a single parameter to receive a MapEntry). Similar to its counterpart in ArrayList, it breaks from the iteration if the closure returns true. In the previous example code, we're finding the first language with more than three characters in its name. The method returns null if the closure never returns a true. Otherwise, it returns an instance of a matching entry in the Map.

We can use the findAll() method to get all elements that match the condition we're looking for, as in the following example:

```
WorkingWithCollections/NavigatingMap.groovy
println "Looking for all languages with name greater than 3 characters"
selected = langs.findAll { language, author ->
  language.size() > 3
}
selected.each { key, value ->
  println "Found $key written by $value"
}
```

The code reports all languages that satisfy the given condition:

```
Looking for all languages with name greater than 3 characters
Found Java written by Gosling
Found Lisp written by McCarthy
```

In addition to the internal iterators, Groovy provides powerful convenience functions to select and group elements in a map, as we'll see next.

6.7 Other Convenience Methods on Maps

Let's wrap up our discussion of collections by looking at a few convenience methods of Map.

We saw how the find() method is useful for fetching an element that satisfies a given condition. However, instead of getting the element, if we're simply interested in determining whether any elements in the collection satisfy some condition, we can use the any() method.

Let's continue with the example of languages and authors from Section 6.6, *Iterating Over Map*, on page 120. We can use the any() method to determine whether any language name has a nonalphabetic character:

```
WorkingWithCollections/NavigatingMap.groovy
print "Does any language name have a nonalphabetic character? "
println langs.any { language, author ->
  language =~ "[^A-Za-z]"
}
```

With *C++* among the key values, our code reports the following:

```
Does any language name have a nonalphabetic character? true
```

any() takes a closure with two parameters, just like the other methods of Map we've discussed. The closure in this example uses a regular-expression comparison (see Section 5.5, *Regular Expressions*, on page 106) to determine whether the language name has a nonalphabetic character.

While the method any() looks for at least one element of the Map to satisfy the given condition (predicate), the every() method checks whether *all* elements satisfy the condition:

WorkingWithCollections/NavigatingMap.groovy

```
print "Do all language names have a nonalphabetic character? "
println langs.every { language, author ->
  language =~ "[^A-Za-z]"
}
```

The output tells us if all elements satisfy the given condition:

```
Do all language names have a nonalphabetic character? false
```

If we want to group the elements of a map based on some criteria, we don't bother iterating or looping through the map—groupBy() does that. We only have to specify our criteria as a closure. Here's an example: friends refers to a map of some friends (many of whom have the same first name). If we want to group friends by first name, we can do that with just one call to groupBy(), as shown in the following code. In the closure attached to groupBy(), we specify what we like to group—in this example, we strip out the first name from the full name and return it. In general, we can simply return the property we're interested in grouping by. For example, if we store friends' names in a Person object with the properties firstName and lastName instead of a simple String, we can write the closure as { it.firstName }. In the following code, groupByFirstname is a map with the first names as the keys, and the value for each key is itself another map of first names and the corresponding full names. Finally, we iterate over the result and print the values.

WorkingWithCollections/NavigatingMap.groovy

```
friends = [ briang : 'Brian Goetz', brians : 'Brian Sletten',
        davidb : 'David Bock', davidg : 'David Geary',
        scottd : 'Scott Davis', scottl : 'Scott Leberknight',
        stuarth : 'Stuart Halloway']

groupByFirstName = friends.groupBy { it.value.split(' ')[0] }

groupByFirstName.each { firstName, buddies ->
  println "$firstName : ${buddies.collect { key, fullName -> fullName }.join(', ')}"
}
```

Here is the result in each group:

```
Brian : Brian Goetz, Brian Sletten
David : David Bock, David Geary
Scott : Scott Davis, Scott Leberknight
Stuart : Stuart Halloway
```

We have two final conveniences to remember: Groovy's use of Map for named parameters—we discussed this in Section 2.2, *JavaBeans*, on page 19—and the use of Maps to implement interfaces (see Section 2.6, *Implementing Interfaces*, on page 26).

In this chapter, we saw the power of closures mixed into the Java collections API. As we apply these concepts on our projects, we'll find that working with collections is easier and faster, our code is shorter, and it's fun. Yes, the Groovy way brings excitement into what otherwise is a mundane task of traversing and manipulating collections.

We've taken a tour of the Groovy language capabilities and the fluency Groovy adds to different APIs. We're ready to move beyond the basic features of the language. In the next part we'll cover how to put this language to good use for operations such as processing XML and accessing databases.

Part II

Using Groovy

CHAPTER 7

Exploring the GDK

Groovy not only brings the strength of dynamic languages onto the Java Virtual Machine (JVM), but also enhances the good old Java Development Kit (JDK). When programming with Groovy, we're productive because we enjoy a better, lighter, and fancier Java API.

We've seen already in this book that Groovy enhances the JDK with convenience methods, quite a few of which make extensive use of closures. This extension is called the Groovy Java Development Kit (Groovy JDK) or the GDK.[1]

Let's look at the relationship between the JDK and the GDK in the following figure. The GDK sits on top of the JDK, so when we pass objects between our Java code and Groovy code, we are not dealing with any conversions. It's the same object on both sides of the languages when we're within the same JVM. However, what we see on the Groovy side is an object that looks hip, thanks to the methods Groovy adds to make it convenient to use and to make us more productive.

Figure 7—The JDK and the GDK

---

1. http://groovy.codehaus.org/groovy-jdk

We'll find extensions to several classes from the JDK. We discuss a number of these in various chapters in this book. In this chapter, we'll focus on two areas—extensions to the java.lang.Object class and various other extensions to popular classes.

7.1 Using Object Extensions

In this section, we'll explore some additions to the mother of all classes, the java.lang.Object class. In Chapter 6, *Working with Collections*, on page 109, we saw Groovy-added methods on Collections: each(), collect(), find(), findAll(), any(), and every(). These are not only available on Collections; we can also use these methods on any object. This gives us a consistent API to work with individual objects and collections alike—one of the benefits elicited in the Composite pattern (see *Design Patterns: Elements of Reusable Object-Oriented Software [GHJV95]*). Groovy has added non-collections-related convenience methods to Object, as well. We won't go over all of those in this section—we don't want this chapter to turn into a complete reference to the GDK library. Instead, we'll focus on methods that are likely to pique our interest and those that we'll find useful for our everyday tasks.

Using the dump and inspect Methods

If we're curious about what makes an instance of our class, we can easily find that at runtime using the dump() method:

ExploringGDK/ObjectExtensions.groovy
```
str = 'hello'

println str
println str.dump()
```

Let's look at the details of the object the code prints:

```
hello
<java.lang.String@5e918d2 value=hello offset=0 count=5 hash=99162322>
```

dump() lets us take a peek into an object. We can use it for debugging, logging, and learning. It tells us about the class of the target instance, its hash code, and its fields.

Groovy also adds another method, inspect(), to Object. This method is intended to tell what input would be needed to create an object. If unimplemented on a class, the method simply returns what toString() returns. If our object takes extensive input, this method will help our class's users figure out at runtime what input they should provide.

Using the Context with() Method

JavaScript and VBScript have a nice feature called with that lets us create a *context*. Any method called within the scope of with is directed to the context object, removing redundant references to the instance. In Groovy the Object's with() method provides the same capability. (The with() method in Groovy was introduced as a synonym to identity(), so we can use them interchangeably.) It accepts a closure as a parameter. Any method call we make within the closure is automatically resolved to the context object. Let's look at an example, starting with code that does not make use of this conciseness:

ExploringGDK/Identity.groovy
```
lst = [1, 2]
lst.add(3)
lst.add(4)
println lst.size()
println lst.contains(2)
```

In the preceding code we're calling methods on lst, which refers to an instance of ArrayList. There's no implicit context, and we're repeatedly (redundantly) using the object reference lst. In Groovy we can set a context using the with() method, so we can change the code to the following:

ExploringGDK/Identity.groovy
```
lst = [1, 2]
lst.with {
  add(3)
  add(4)
  println size()
  println contains(2)
}
```

The code is less noisy and produces the following output:

```
4
true
```

How does the with() method *know* to route calls within the closure to the context object? The magic happens because of the closure's delegate property (for more information, see Section 4.9, *Closure Delegation*, on page 86). Let's examine the delegate property along with the this and owner properties within the closure attached to with():

ExploringGDK/Identity.groovy
```
lst.with {
  println "this is ${this},"
  println "owner is ${owner},"
  println "delegate is ${delegate}."
}
```

The output shows the details of the references we're curious about:

```
this is Identity@ce56f8,
owner is Identity@ce56f8,
delegate is [1, 2, 3, 4].
```

When we invoke the with() method, it sets the closure's delegate property to the object on which with() is called. As discussed in Section 4.9, *Closure Delegation*, on page 86, the delegate has dibs on methods that this doesn't pick up.

We can benefit from the with() method if we need to call multiple methods on an object. Take advantage of the context and reduce clutter. We'll find this method very useful when building domain-specific languages (DSLs). We can implement scriptlike calls to be implicitly routed to our instance behind the scenes, as we'll see in Chapter 19, *Creating DSLs in Groovy*, on page 295.

Using sleep

The sleep() method added to Object should be called *soundSleep*, as it ignores interrupts while sleeping for the given number of milliseconds (approximately).

Let's look at an example of the sleep() method:

```
ExploringGDK/Sleep.groovy
thread = Thread.start {
  println "Thread started"
  startTime = System.nanoTime()
  new Object().sleep(2000)
  endTime = System.nanoTime()
  println "Thread done in ${(endTime - startTime)/10**9} seconds"
}
new Object().sleep(100)
println "Let's interrupt that thread"
thread.interrupt()
thread.join()
```

The output shows that the thread ignored the interrupts and completes:

```
Thread started
Let's interrupt that thread
Thread done in 2.000272 seconds
```

We're using the Groovy-added Thread.start() method here. It's a convenient way to execute a piece of code in a different thread. The difference between calling sleep() on Object and using the Java-provided Thread.sleep() is that the former suppresses the InterruptedException if it's ever raised. If we do care to be interrupted, we don't have to endure try-catch. Instead, we can use a variation on the previous sleep() method that accepts a closure to handle the interruption:

```
ExploringGDK/Sleep.groovy
def playWithSleep(flag)
{
  thread = Thread.start {
    println "Thread started"
    startTime = System.nanoTime()
    new Object().sleep(2000) {
      println "Interrupted... " + it
      flag
    }
    endTime = System.nanoTime()
    println "Thread done in ${(endTime - startTime)/10**9} seconds"
  }

  thread.interrupt()
  thread.join()
}

playWithSleep(true)
playWithSleep(false)
```

We see in the output how the closure handles the interruption:

```
Thread started
Interrupted... java.lang.InterruptedException: sleep interrupted
Thread done in 0.00437 seconds
Thread started
Interrupted... java.lang.InterruptedException: sleep interrupted
Thread done in 1.999077 seconds
```

Within the interrupt handler, we can take any appropriate actions. If we need to access the InterruptedException, we can—it is available as a parameter to our closure. If we return a false value from within the closure, sleep() will continue as if uninterrupted, as we can see in the second call to playWithSleep() in the previous example.

Accessing Properties Indirectly

We know that Groovy makes it easy to access properties. For example, to get the property miles of a Car class's car instance, we can simply call car.miles. However, this syntax is not helpful if we don't know the property name at coding time, such as if the property name depends on user input and we don't want to hard-code a branch for all possible input. We can use the [] operator—the Groovy-added getAt() method maps to this operator—to access properties dynamically. If we use this operator on the left side of an assignment, then it maps to the putAt() method.

Let's see an example:

```
ExploringGDK/IndirectProperty.groovy
class Car {
  int miles, fuelLevel
}

car = new Car(fuelLevel: 80, miles: 25)

properties = ['miles', 'fuelLevel']
// the above list may be populated from some input or
// may come from a dynamic form in a web app

properties.each { name ->
  println "$name = ${car[name]}"
}

car[properties[1]] = 100

println "fuelLevel now is ${car.fuelLevel}"
```

We're able to interact with the instance indirectly, as the output shows:

```
miles = 25
fuelLevel = 80
fuelLevel now is 100
```

Here we're accessing the miles and fuelLevel properties using the [] operator. We can use this approach if we receive property names as input; we can dynamically create and populate web forms, for example. We can easily write a high-level function that takes a list of property names and an instance and outputs the names and values in XML, HTML, or any other format we desire. We can get a list of all an object's properties by using its properties property; namely, the getProperties() method.

Invoking Methods Indirectly

If we receive the method name as a String and we want to call that method, we know how to use reflection to do that—we have to first fetch the Class metaobject from the instance, call getMethod() to get the Method instance, and, finally, call the invoke() method on it. And, oh yeah—don't forget those exceptions we'll be forced to handle.

No, we don't have to do all that in Groovy; we simply have to call the invokeMethod() method. All objects support this method in Groovy. Here's an example:

```
ExploringGDK/IndirectMethod.groovy
class Person {
  def walk() { println "Walking..." }
  def walk(int miles) { println "Walking $miles miles..." }
```

```
    def walk(int miles, String where) { println "Walking $miles miles $where..." }
}

peter = new Person()

peter.invokeMethod("walk", null)
peter.invokeMethod("walk", 10)
peter.invokeMethod("walk", [2, 'uphill'] as Object[])
```

Here's the output of calling the methods indirectly:

```
Walking...
Walking 10 miles...
Walking 2 miles uphill...
```

So if we don't know the method names at coding time but we receive the names at runtime, we can turn that into a dynamic call on our instance with a single line of code.

Groovy also provides getMetaClass() to get the metaclass object, which is a key object for taking advantage of dynamic capabilities in Groovy, as we'll see in later chapters.

Groovy's extension API reaches far beyond the most fundamental class in the JDK, the Object class, as we'll see next.

7.2 Other Extensions

The GDK extensions go beyond the Object class. Several other JDK classes and interfaces have been enhanced in the GDK. Again, the list is vast and we'll look at only a subset of extensions in this section. These are the extensions we're likely to put to regular use.

Array Extensions

We can use the Range object as an index on all the array types (for the syntax for creating arrays, see *Different Syntax for Creating Primitive Arrays*, on page 51), such as int[], double[], and char[]. Here's how we can access contiguous values in an int array using the range of index:

ExploringGDK/Array.groovy
```
int[] arr = [1, 2, 3, 4, 5, 6]

println arr[2..4]
```

The output shows the values in the given range:

```
[3, 4, 5]
```

We're already familiar with a number of convenience methods that the GDK added to Lists, Collections, and Maps (see Chapter 6, *Working with Collections*, on page 109).

Using java.lang Extensions

One of the noticeable additions to the primitive type wrappers like Character, Integer, and so on is the overloaded operator-mapping methods. These are methods such as plus() for operator +, next() for operator ++, and so on. We'll find these methods—*operators*, we should say—useful when creating DSLs.

Number (which Integer and Double extend) has picked up the iterator methods upto() and downto(). It also has the step() method (see *Ways to Loop*, on page 13). These help iterate over a range of values.

We looked at a few examples to interact with system-level processes in *A Quick Look at the GDK*, on page 14. The Process class has convenience methods to access the stdin, stdout, and stderr commands—the out, in, and err properties, respectively. It also has the text property that can give us the entire standard output or response from the process. If we want to read the entire standard error in one shot, we can use err.text on the process instance. We can use the << operator to pipe into a process. (A pipe—|—on Unix-like systems is used to chain the output from one process into the input of another process.) Here's an example to illustrate communicating with a process—the wc program is a popular utility on Unix-like systems that prints to the standard output the number of words, lines, and characters it finds in its standard input:

ExploringGDK/UsingProcess.groovy
```
process = "wc".execute()

process.out.withWriter {
  // Send input to process
  it << "Let the World know...\n"
  it << "Groovy Rocks!\n"
}

// Read output from process
println process.in.text
// or
//println process.text
```

The output from the preceding code is the result returned by wc—two lines, six words, and thirty-six characters:

```
2     6     36
```

In this code, first we obtain an instance of the process by calling String's execute() method. We want to write to wc's standard input, so we need an OutputStream from our program. We can obtain that from the process by calling the out property.

To write content, we can use the << operator. However, once we write to the stream, we want to flush and close it. We can handle both with one method: withWriter(). This method attaches an OutputStreamWriter to the OutputStream and hands it to the closure. When we return from the closure, it flushes and closes the stream automatically (see Section 4.5, *Using Closures for Resource Cleanup*, on page 78).

Try implementing the previous code using Java, and appreciate not only the time savings but also the elegance Groovy provides.

If we want to send command-line parameters to the process, we have two options. We can format the parameters as one string or create a String array of parameters. String[] supports the execute() method, as well; the first element is treated as the command to execute, and the remaining elements are considered command-line arguments to that command. Instead, we can use List's execute() method.

Here's an example of passing command-line parameters to the groovy command:

```
ExploringGDK/ProcessParameters.groovy
String[] command = ['groovy', '-e', '"print \'Groovy\'"']
println  "Calling ${command.join(' ')}"
println command.execute().text
```

The preceding code's executed command and output are as follows:

```
Calling groovy -e "print 'Groovy'"
Groovy
```

We can start a process, send parameters, and interact with the process fairly easily in Groovy. It takes only a couple of lines of code.

If we have to create threads and assign tasks to execute in those separate threads, Groovy will save us quite a bit of typing. We can start a Thread and provide it a closure that will be run in a separate thread using the start() method. If we want that thread to be a daemon thread, we can use the startDaemon() method instead. A daemon thread quits if there are no active nondaemon threads currently running—kind of like employees who work only when the boss is around. Let's take a look at an example that shows these two methods in action:

ExploringGDK/ThreadStart.groovy

```groovy
def printThreadInfo(msg) {
  def currentThread = Thread.currentThread()
  println "$msg Thread is ${currentThread}. Daemon? ${currentThread.isDaemon()}"
}

printThreadInfo 'Main'

Thread.start {
  printThreadInfo "Started"
  sleep(3000) { println "Interrupted" }
  println "Finished Started"
}

sleep(1000)

Thread.startDaemon {
  printThreadInfo "Started Daemon"
  sleep(5000) { println "Interrupted" }
  println "Finished Started Daemon" // Will not get here
}
```

Here's the output showing thread information:

```
Main Thread is Thread[main,5,main]. Daemon? false
Started Thread is Thread[Thread-1,5,main]. Daemon? false
Started Daemon Thread is Thread[Thread-2,5,main]. Daemon? true
Finished Started
```

The daemon thread in the previous example was aborted as soon as the main thread and the nondaemon thread we created quit. We can see that to create threads in Groovy, we don't need to work with instances of Thread or Runnable. It's very simple and easy to get going with thread creation.

Using java.io Extensions

A lot of methods have been added to the File class in the java.io package. It has methods such as eachFile() and eachDir() (and variations of these) that accept closures and provide easy navigation or iteration through directories and files.

Suppose we want to read the contents of a file. Here's the Java code for that:

```java
// Java code
import java.io.*;
public class ReadFile {
  public static void main(String[] args) {
    try {
      BufferedReader reader = new BufferedReader(
                  new FileReader("thoreau.txt"));
```

```
    String line = null;
    while((line = reader.readLine()) != null) {
      System.out.println(line);
    }
  } catch(FileNotFoundException ex) {
    ex.printStackTrace();
  } catch(IOException ex) {
    ex.printStackTrace();
  }
}
}
```

That's quite an effort to read a file. Groovy makes this much simpler by adding a text property to BufferedReader, InputStream, and File so we can read the entire content of the reader into a String. This is useful if we want to take the entire output for processing or printing. Here's the previous code rewritten in Groovy:

ExploringGDK/ReadFile.groovy
```
println new File('thoreau.txt').text
```

The output from the previous code—the content of my file thoreau.txt—is as follows:

```
"I went to the woods because I wished to live deliberately,
to front only the essential facts of life, and see if I could
not learn what it had to teach, and not, when I came to die,
to discover that I had not lived..."
- Henry David Thoreau
```

Instead of reading the entire file in one shot, if we want to read and process one line at a time, we can use the eachLine() method, which calls a closure for each line of text read:

ExploringGDK/ReadFile.groovy
```
new File('thoreau.txt').eachLine { line ->
  println line // or do whatever you like with that line here
}
```

If we want to fetch only those lines of text that meet a certain condition, we can use filterLine(), as shown here:

ExploringGDK/ReadFile.groovy
```
println new File('thoreau.txt').filterLine { it =~ /life/ }
```

The filtered lines of text extracted by the previous code look like this:

```
to front only the essential facts of life, and see if I could
```

We filtered only the line(s) in the input file that contained the word "life."

If we want to automatically flush and close an input stream when we're done using it, we can use the withStream() method. This method calls the closure it accepts as a parameter and sends the instance of InputStream as a parameter. It then flushes and closes the stream as soon as we return from the closure. The Writer has a similar method, named withWriter(); we saw an example of this earlier in this section.

InputStream's withReader() method creates a BufferedReader that's attached to the input stream and sends it to the closure that it accepts as a parameter. We can also obtain a new instance of BufferedReader by calling the newReader() method.

We can iterate over the stream of input in InputStream and DataInputStream using an Iterator we obtain by calling the iterator() method. Speaking of iterating, we can conveniently iterate over objects in an ObjectInputStream, as well.

If we want to use a Reader instead, we can. The convenience methods added to InputStream are still available on it.

We can easily write contents to a file or stream in Groovy. The OutputStream, ObjectOutputStream, and Writer classes have received a face-lift via the leftShift() method (the << operator). The following code example uses that operator to write to a file:

ExploringGDK/ShiftOperator.groovy
```groovy
new File("output.txt").withWriter{ file ->
  file << "some data..."
}
```

Several other extensions to classes in the java.io package make our life easier and coding time shorter.

Using java.util Extensions

We discussed Groovy extensions to the collection classes in Chapter 6, *Working with Collections*, on page 109. In this section, we'll check out a few other extensions to classes in the java.util package.

List, Set, SortedMap, and SortedSet have gained the method asImmutable() to obtain an immutable instance of their respective instances. They also have a method asSynchronized() to create an instance that is thread-safe.

The Iterator supports the inject() method we discussed in Section 6.4, *Other Convenience Methods on Lists*, on page 115.

A runAfter() method has been added to the java.util.Timer class. The syntax is easier to use because this method accepts a closure that will run after a given delay, in milliseconds.

As we've discussed in this chapter, Groovy adds a number of methods at the java.lang.Object level. There are methods that let us peek into an object for debugging, logging, or informational purposes, and methods that let us treat a single object and a collection of objects using a consistent interface, such as the Composite pattern.

Object also supports methods for metaprogramming to dynamically access properties and invoke methods. The high level of abstraction that these methods have collectively built reduces our application-code size and the time we need for routine tasks.

We also can use specialized methods on different classes—Groovy enhances the API for several classes and interfaces—Matcher, Writer, Reader, List, Map, Socket...the list goes on. The GDK has extensions for several JDK classes and interfaces. The GDK is far too large for us to cover entirely in this book; visit http://groovy.codehaus.org/groovy-jdk for a comprehensive and updated list of the GDK API.

When we're programming in Groovy, we need to refer to both the JDK and the GDK. If we don't find what we're looking for in the JDK, we must remember to check the GDK to see if it supports the feature.

7.3 Custom Methods Using the Extension Modules

Groovy 2.x helps us move quickly beyond the privilege of using methods added to the GDK. Using the extension-modules feature, we can add our own instance or static methods to existing classes at compile time and use them throughout the application at runtime. Let's take a look at the simple steps we have to follow for this using an example.

We need two things for this feature to work: First, a method we want to add must be defined in an extension-module class. Second, we need a descriptor file in the manifest file to tell the Groovy compiler what extension-module classes to look for.

Let's create two extension methods—an instance method and a static method—both on the String class, to get the price for a given stock. Once we introduce these extension methods, anyone who includes, in their classpath, the jar file containing these classes can invoke these methods as if they were provided in the JDK or the GDK.

Both types of extension methods have to be defined as static, and the first parameter should be of the type on which the method is expected to be added. The definition provides as additional parameters any arguments the extension method is expected to take.

Here's an instance extension method on the String class, written in a extension helper class PriceExtension (here we write it as a Groovy class, but it could be in any JVM language, including Java).

Extension/com/agiledeveloper/PriceExtension.groovy
```
package com.agiledeveloper;

class PriceExtension {
  public static double getPrice(String self) {
      def url = "http://ichart.finance.yahoo.com/table.csv?s=$self".toURL()

      def data = url.readLines()[1].split(",")
      Double.parseDouble(data[-1])
    }
}
```

The getPrice() method is defined as static, and the first parameter tells to which class this method will be added. The code does not quite tell what type of method this will be added as, instance or static; that information goes in the manifest declaration, as we'll see soon.

Let's define a static extension method for the same purpose.

Extension/com/agiledeveloper/PriceStaticExtension.groovy
```
package com.agiledeveloper;

class PriceStaticExtension {
  public static double getPrice(String selfType, String ticker) {
      def url = "http://ichart.finance.yahoo.com/table.csv?s=$ticker".toURL()

      def data = url.readLines()[1].split(",")
      Double.parseDouble(data[-1])
    }
}
```

This getPrice() method takes two parameters, the first one to tell which class this method will be added to, and the second for the actual value of the stock to get the price for. In the first version of the method the stock was implicitly contained in the instance; however, in this version it has to be passed in as a parameter since the method will be run in the static context of the String class.

We have the helper classes with the extension methods ready. We need to declare their presence and bundle that declaration into a jar file along with the compiled classes. Here's the declaration, in the file named org.code-haus.groovy.runtime.ExtensionModule, under the directory META-INF/services:

```
Extension/manifest/META-INF/services/org.codehaus.groovy.runtime.ExtensionModule
moduleName=price-module
moduleVersion=1.0-test
extensionClasses=com.agiledeveloper.PriceExtension
staticExtensionClasses=com.agiledeveloper.PriceStaticExtension
```

The declaration file contains four key-value pairs of information. moduleName is a logical name we give for the module. moduleVersion is useful to check if the version is already loaded. extensionClasses is a comma-separated name of the helper classes with instance extension methods. Finally, staticExtensionClass is a comma-separated name of the helper classes with static extension methods.

Let's use the following command to compile the two helper classes and create the necessary jar file:

```
$ groovyc -d classes com/agiledeveloper/*.groovy
$ jar -cf priceExtensions.jar -C classes com -C manifest .
```

The priceExtensions.jar file contains the compiled helper classes along with the manifest file.

Let's create an example Groovy file to use these extension methods:

```
Extension/FindPrice.groovy
def ticker = "ORCL"

println "Price for $ticker using instance method is ${String.getPrice(ticker)}"
println "Price for $ticker using static method is ${ticker.getPrice()}"
```

We invoke both the instance and the static extension methods. To bring these in we have to include the priceExtensions.jar file in the classpath, like in the command below:

```
$ groovy -classpath priceExtensions.jar FindPrice.groovy
```

Groovy will seamlessly bring in the extension methods, based on the information we provided in the manifest. The following output shows the result of calling these extension methods:

```
Price for ORCL using instance method is 34.75
Price for ORCL using static method is 34.75
```

We saw the Groovy extensions to the JDK methods and how to add custom extensions. Groovy also offers its own powerful set of libraries for various tasks. In the next chapter you'll learn how Groovy elegantly handles the otherwise-mundane task of processing XML.

CHAPTER 8

Working with XML

Working with XML can be tedious. Working with traditional Java APIs and libraries to create and parse XML documents tends to lower our spirits. And navigating the document hierarchy using the DOM API is sure to drive us insane.

Groovy brings relief for both parsing and creating XML documents. We already saw a few ways to create XML documents. We'll revisit that topic in this chapter and learn to use three different facilities to parse XML documents, with varying degrees of convenience and efficiency. We will also browse Groovy's support for creating XML documents.

8.1 Parsing XML

In Groovy we can use the Java-based parsing approaches and tools we are already familiar with if we have some special need or reasons to depend on the older APIs or have legacy code that already uses them. If we have working Java code to parse XML documents, we can reuse those readily in Groovy. Groovy does not force us to duplicate our efforts.

If we're creating new code to parse XML, though, we can benefit from the Groovy facilities.

On a recent project, I had to populate an application with data from some 400 XML documents. At first glance, that task was intimidating; the sheer volume of files to deal with was enough to dissuade me. After quickly browsing through several files, I decided to use Groovy to process the files, parse the XML documents, and populate the application. The XmlSlurper class, along with about 30 lines of Groovy code, was enough to get the job done.

Groovy parsers are fairly powerful, they're convenient to use, and they support namespaces, as we'll see in this section.

For the examples in the rest of this chapter, we'll work with an XML document (shown next) with a list of languages and authors:

WorkingWithXML/languages.xml

```xml
<languages>
  <language name="C++">
    <author>Stroustrup</author>
  </language>
  <language name="Java">
    <author>Gosling</author>
  </language>
  <language name="Lisp">
    <author>McCarthy</author>
  </language>
  <language name="Modula-2">
    <author>Wirth</author>
  </language>
  <language name="Oberon-2">
    <author>Wirth</author>
  </language>
  <language name="Pascal">
    <author>Wirth</author>
  </language>
</languages>
```

Using DOMCategory

We can use Groovy categories to define dynamic methods on classes. We'll discuss categories in detail in Section 13.1, *Injecting Methods Using Categories*, on page 193. Groovy provides a category for working with the Document Object Model (DOM)—DOMCategory. Groovy simplifies the DOM application programming interface (API) by adding convenience methods.

We can use DOMCategory to navigate the DOM structure using GPath-like notation.

We can access all child elements simply using the child name. For example, instead of calling getElementsByTagName('name'), use the property name to get it, as in rootElement.language. That is, given the root element, languages, a simple call rootElement.language will get all the language elements. The DOM parser gives the rootElement; in the following example, we'll use the DOMBuilder's parse() method to get the document loaded in memory.

We can obtain the value for an attribute by placing an @ before the attribute name, as in language.@name.

In the following code, we use DOMCategory to fetch language names and authors from the document:

What's GPath?

Much like how XPath helps navigate the hierarchy of an XML document, GPath helps navigate the hierarchy of objects (plain old Java objects and plain old Groovy objects —POJOs and POGOs, respectively)—and XML. We can traverse the hierarchy using the . (dot) notation. For example, the notation car.engine.power will help access an engine property of a car instance using its getEngine() method. The notation will then help get to a power property of the engine instance using its getPower() method. Instead of being an object, if we're dealing with a XML document, the notation will help us obtain a child element power of an element engine, which in turn is a child element of an element car. Instead of accessing an element, we can access a year attribute of a car, using the notation car.'@year' (or car.@year). The @ symbol indicates an attribute instead of a child element.

WorkingWithXML/UsingDOMCategory.groovy

```
document = groovy.xml.DOMBuilder.parse(new FileReader('languages.xml'))

rootElement = document.documentElement

use(groovy.xml.dom.DOMCategory) {
  println "Languages and authors"
  languages = rootElement.language

  languages.each { language ->
    println "${language.'@name'} authored by ${language.author[0].text()}"
  }

  def languagesByAuthor = { authorName ->
      languages.findAll { it.author[0].text() == authorName }.collect {
        it.'@name' }.join(', ')
  }

  println "Languages by Wirth:" + languagesByAuthor('Wirth')
}
```

Here's data extracted using the previous code:

```
Languages and authors
C++ authored by Stroustrup
Java authored by Gosling
Lisp authored by McCarthy
Modula-2 authored by Wirth
Oberon-2 authored by Wirth
Pascal authored by Wirth
Languages by Wirth:Modula-2, Oberon-2, Pascal
```

DOMCategory is useful for parsing an XML document using the DOM API with the convenience of GPath queries and Groovy's dynamic elegance.

To use the DOMCategory, we must place the code within the use() block. The other two approaches we'll see in this chapter don't have that restriction. In the previous example, we extracted the desired details from the document using the GPath syntax. We also wrote a custom method or filter to get only those languages written by Wirth.

Using XMLParser

The class groovy.util.XMLParser exploits Groovy's dynamic typing and metaprogramming capabilities. We can access the members of our document directly by name. For example, we can access an author's name using it.author[0].

Let's use the XMLParser to fetch the desired data from the language's XML document:

WorkingWithXML/UsingXMLParser.groovy
```groovy
languages = new XmlParser().parse('languages.xml')

println "Languages and authors"

languages.each {
  println "${it.@name} authored by ${it.author[0].text()}"
}

def languagesByAuthor = { authorName ->
    languages.findAll { it.author[0].text() == authorName }.collect {
      it.@name }.join(', ')
}


println "Languages by Wirth:" + languagesByAuthor('Wirth')
```

The code is much like the example we saw in *Using DOMCategory*, on page 144. The main difference is the absence of the use() block. XMLParser has added the convenience of iterators to the elements, so we can navigate easily using methods such as each(), collect(), and find().

Using XMLParser has a couple of downsides: it does not preserve the XML InfoSet, and it ignores the XML comments and processing instructions in documents. The convenience it provides makes it a great tool for most common processing needs. However, if we have other specific needs, we have to explore more-traditional parsers.

Using XMLSlurper

For large document sizes, the memory usage of XMLParser might become prohibitive. The class XMLSlurper comes to rescue in these cases. It is similar to

XMLParser in usage. The following code is almost the same as the code in *Using XMLParser*, on page 146:

```
WorkingWithXML/UsingXMLSlurper.groovy
languages = new XmlSlurper().parse('languages.xml')
println "Languages and authors"

languages.language.each {
  println "${it.@name} authored by ${it.author[0].text()}"
}

def languagesByAuthor = { authorName ->
    languages.language.findAll { it.author[0].text() == authorName }.collect {
      it.@name }.join(', ')
}
println "Languages by Wirth:" + languagesByAuthor('Wirth')
```

We can parse XML documents with namespaces in them, as well. Namespaces remind me of when I got a call from a company in Malaysia interested in training that involved extensive coding to emphasize test-driven development. I asked, in the middle of the conversation, what language I would be using. After a pause, the gentleman said reluctantly, "English, of course. Everyone on my team speaks English well." What I had actually meant was "What computer language would I be using?" This is an example of context and confusion in daily conversations. XML documents have the same issue, and namespaces can help deal with name collisions.

Remember that namespaces are not URLs, but they are required to be unique. The prefixes we use for namespaces in our XML document are *not* unique. We can make them up as we please (well, with some naming restrictions). So, to refer to a namespace in our query, we need to associate a prefix with it. We can do that using the declareNamespaces() method, which takes a map of prefixes as keys and namespaces as values. Once we define the prefixes, our GPath queries can contain prefixes for names, as well. element.name will return all child elements with name, independent of the namespace; however, element.'ns:name' will return only elements with the namespace that ns is associated with. Let's look at an example. Suppose we have an XML document with names of computer and natural languages, as shown here:

```
<languages xmlns:computer="Computer" xmlns:natural="Natural">
  <computer:language name="Java"/>
  <computer:language name="Groovy"/>
  <computer:language name="Erlang"/>
  <natural:language name="English"/>
  <natural:language name="German"/>
  <natural:language name="French"/>
</languages>
```

The element name language falls into either a "Computer" namespace or a "Natural" namespace. The following code shows how to fetch both all language names and only "Natural" languages:

WorkingWithXML/UsingXMLSlurperWithNS.groovy
```
languages = new XmlSlurper().parse(
  'computerAndNaturalLanguages.xml').declareNamespace(human: 'Natural')

print "Languages: "
println languages.language.collect { it.@name }.join(', ')

print "Natural languages: "
println languages.'human:language'.collect { it.@name }.join(', ')
```

The following data is extracted using the code:

```
Languages: Java, Groovy, Erlang, English, German, French
Natural languages: English, German, French
```

For large XML documents, we'd want to use the XMLSlurper. It performs a lazy evaluation, so it's kind on memory usage and has low overhead.

In addition to the nice parsing APIs, Groovy makes it easy to go in the opposite direction, to create XML documents—we'll glance at different ways in the next section.

8.2 Creating XML

When creating business applications, we often have a number of reasons to present data in XML format—as a way to store the state of an application, to communicate with web services, to represent some configuration data, and so on. Whatever the need, Groovy makes it quite easy to create XML documents.

We can use the full power of Java APIs to generate XML. If we have a particular favorite Java-based XML processor, such as Xerces, we can use it with Groovy as well.[1] This might be a good approach if we already have working code in Java to create XML documents in a specific format and want to use it in our Groovy projects.

If we want to create an XML document using a pure-Groovy approach, we can use GString's ability to embed expressions into a string, along with Groovy's facility for creating multiline strings. This facility is useful for creating small XML fragments that we may need in code and tests. Here's a quick example (refer to Section 5.3, *Multiline Strings*, on page 103 for more details):

---

1. http://xerces.apache.org/xerces-j

```groovy
langs = ['C++' : 'Stroustrup', 'Java' : 'Gosling', 'Lisp' : 'McCarthy']

content = ''
langs.each { language, author ->
  fragment = """
    <language name="${language}">
      <author>${author}</author>
    </language>
  """

  content += fragment
}
xml = "<languages>${content}</languages>"
println xml
```

Here is the XML document produced:

```
<languages>
  <language name="C++">
    <author>Stroustrup</author>
  </language>

  <language name="Java">
    <author>Gosling</author>
  </language>

  <language name="Lisp">
    <author>McCarthy</author>
  </language>
</languages>
```

Alternatively, we can use the MarkupBuilder or StreamingMarkupBuilder to create XML-formatted data output from an arbitrary source. This is the preferred approach in Groovy applications because the convenience the builders provide makes it easy to create XML documents. We don't have to mess with complex APIs or string manipulation; it's all plain, simple Groovy. Again, here's a quick example (refer to the discussion in Section 17.1, *Building XML*, on page 253, for details of using both the MarkupBuilder and StreamingMarkupBuilder):

```groovy
langs = ['C++' : 'Stroustrup', 'Java' : 'Gosling', 'Lisp' : 'McCarthy']

xmlDocument = new groovy.xml.StreamingMarkupBuilder().bind {
  mkp.xmlDeclaration()
  mkp.declareNamespace(computer: "Computer")
  languages {
    comment << "Created using StreamingMarkupBuilder"
    langs.each { key, value ->
      computer.language(name: key) {
```

```
        author (value)
      }
    }
  }
}
println xmlDocument
```

The XML document produced by the code is as follows:

```
<?xml version="1.0"?>
<languages xmlns:computer='Computer'>
  <!--Created using StreamingMarkupBuilder-->
    <computer:language name='C++'>
      <author>Stroustrup</author>
    </computer:language>
    <computer:language name='Java'>
      <author>Gosling</author>
    </computer:language>
    <computer:language name='Lisp'>
      <author>McCarthy</author>
    </computer:language>
</languages>
```

If our data resides in a database or a Microsoft Excel file, we can mix that with the techniques we'll look at in Chapter 9, *Working with Databases*, on page 151. Once we fetch the data from the database, we can insert it into the document using any of the approaches we have discussed.

In this chapter, we saw how Groovy helps parse XML documents. Groovy can make working with XML bearable. If our users don't like maintaining XML configuration files (who does?), they can create and maintain Groovy-based DSLs that we can transform to the XML formats our underlying frameworks or libraries expect. If we're on the receiving end of the XML documents, we can rely on Groovy to give us an object representation of the XML data.

Once we have the data on hand, we know how to use Groovy to present it in XML format. We discuss these topics in depth throughout this book, and we'll see more-detailed code examples. In the next chapter you'll learn how to fetch the data from a database right from our Groovy code.

CHAPTER 9

Working with Databases

I have a remote database that I update frequently. Accessing it through the browser was rather slow, but I had put away the task to automate the update process. I was simply not inclined to write mundane Java code for that task—nothing exciting or new to learn in that. That was before I came across Groovy SQL (GSQL). Now my updates are automated, fast, and totally effortless. With GSQL I have more data than code in my update script—that's a great signal-to-noise ratio.

Working with databases is common, but can get tedious and boring really quickly. GSQL is a wrapper around Java Database Connectivity (JDBC) that provides a number of convenience methods to easily access data. We can quickly create SQL queries and then use built-in iterators to traverse the results, all using Groovy syntax.

In this chapter we'll explore the power of GSQL. You'll learn to write SQL select queries, generate XML data from the results, perform insertions and updates of data, and see ways to access data from an Excel file.

9.1 Setting Up the Database

We'll use MySQL in the examples in this chapter; however, we can use any database that we can access using JDBC. First let's set up the database we'll use in the examples, with a table named weather. The table contains names of and temperature values for some cities.

It's easier to set up the database using an automated script than to do it manually. So, let's create a SQL script to build the database:

```
create database if not exists weatherinfo;
use weatherinfo;

drop table if exists weather;
```

```
create table weather (
  city varchar(100) not null,
  temperature integer not null
);
```

```
insert into weather (city, temperature) values ('Austin', 48);
insert into weather (city, temperature) values ('Baton Rouge', 57);
insert into weather (city, temperature) values ('Jackson', 50);
insert into weather (city, temperature) values ('Montgomery', 53);
insert into weather (city, temperature) values ('Phoenix', 67);
insert into weather (city, temperature) values ('Sacramento', 66);
insert into weather (city, temperature) values ('Santa Fe', 27);
insert into weather (city, temperature) values ('Tallahassee', 59);
```

In the script, we defined the schema for a table named "weather" and populated the table with some sample data. Let's save this script to a file named createdb.sql and run the script to create the database using the command mysql --user=root < createdb.sql.

Now the database is ready; let's look at different ways to access it from Groovy code.

9.2 Connecting to a Database

To connect to a database, simply create an instance of groovy.sql.Sql by calling the static method newInstance(). One version of this method accepts the database URL, user ID, password, and database-driver name as parameters. If we already have a java.sql.Connection instance or a java.sql.DataSource, then instead of using newInstance(), we can use one of the constructors for Sql that accepts those.

We can obtain the information about the connection by calling the Sql instance's getConnection() method (the connection property). When we're finished, we can close the connection by calling the close() method. Here is an example of connecting to the database we created for this chapter:

WorkingWithDatabases/Weather.groovy
```
def sql = groovy.sql.Sql.newInstance('jdbc:mysql://localhost:3306/weatherinfo',
            userid, password, 'com.mysql.jdbc.Driver')
```

```
println sql.connection.catalog
```

The preceding code reports the name of the database as follows:

```
weatherinfo
```

9.3 Database Select

We can use the Sql object to conveniently iterate through data in a table. Simply call the eachRow() method, provide it with a SQL query to execute, and give it a closure to process each row of data, thusly:

WorkingWithDatabases/Weather.groovy

```
println "City                    Temperature"
sql.eachRow('SELECT * from weather') {
  printf "%-20s%s\n", it.city, it[1]
}
```

The data fetched using the previous code is as follows:

```
City            Temperature
Austin          48
Baton Rouge     57
Jackson         50
Montgomery      53
Phoenix         67
Sacramento      66
Santa Fe        27
Tallahassee     59
```

We asked eachRow() to execute the SQL query on the weather table to process all its rows. We then iterated (as the name each indicates) over each row. There's more grooviness here—we can use the GroovyResultSet object that eachRow() provides to access the columns in the table either directly by name (as in it.city) or using the index (as in it[1]).

In the previous example, we hard-coded the header for the output. It would be nice to get this from the database instead. Another overloaded version of eachRow() will do that. It accepts two closures—one for metadata and the other for data. The closure for metadata is called only once (after the execution of the SQL statement) with an instance of ResultSetMetaData, and the other closure is called once for each row in the result. Let's give that a try in the following code:

WorkingWithDatabases/Weather.groovy

```
processMeta = { metaData ->
  metaData.columnCount.times { i ->
    printf "%-21s", metaData.getColumnLabel(i+1)
  }
  println ""
}

sql.eachRow('SELECT * from weather', processMeta) {
  printf "%-20s %s\n", it.city, it[1]
}
```

The output shows the header created using the metadata, followed by the rows of data:

```
city              temperature
Austin            48
Baton Rouge       57
Jackson           50
Montgomery        53
Phoenix           67
Sacramento        66
Santa Fe          27
Tallahassee       59
```

If we want to process all the rows but don't want to use an iterator, we can use the rows() method on the Sql instance. It returns an ArrayList instance of result data, as shown here:

WorkingWithDatabases/Weather.groovy
```
rows = sql.rows('SELECT * from weather')

println "Weather info available for ${rows.size()} cities"
```

The code reports this:

```
Weather info available for 8 cities
```

Call the firstRow() method instead to get only the first row of results.

We can perform stored-procedure calls using the call() methods of Sql. Use the withStatement() method to set up a closure that will be called before the execution of queries. This will help if we want to intercept and alter the SQL queries before execution.

9.4 Transforming Data to XML

We can get the data from the database and create different representations using Groovy builders. Here is an example that creates an XML representation (see Section 17.1, *Building XML*, on page 253) of the data in the weather table:

WorkingWithDatabases/Weather.groovy
```
bldr = new groovy.xml.MarkupBuilder()

bldr.weather {
  sql.eachRow('SELECT * from weather') {
    city(name: it.city, temperature: it.temperature)
  }
}
```

The code produces this XML output:

WorkingWithDatabases/Weather.output
```
<weather>
  <city name='Austin' temperature='48' />
  <city name='Baton Rouge' temperature='57' />
  <city name='Jackson' temperature='50' />
  <city name='Montgomery' temperature='53' />
  <city name='Phoenix' temperature='67' />
  <city name='Sacramento' temperature='66' />
  <city name='Santa Fe' temperature='27' />
  <city name='Tallahassee' temperature='59' />
</weather>
```

With hardly any effort, Groovy and GSQL help us create an XML representation of data from the database.

9.5 Using DataSet

In Section 9.3, *Database Select*, on page 153, we saw how to process the results set obtained from executing a SELECT query. If we want to receive only a filtered set of rows, such as only cities with temperature values below 32, we can set up the query accordingly. Alternatively, we can receive the result as a groovy.sql.DataSet to filter data. Let's examine this further.

The dataSet() method of the Sql class takes a table's name and returns a virtual proxy—it does not fetch the actual rows until we iterate. We can then iterate over the rows using the each() method of the DataSet (like the eachRow() method of Sql). In the following code, however, we'll use the findAll() method to filter the results to obtain only cities with below-freezing temperatures. When we invoke findAll(), the DataSet is further refined with a specialized query based on the select predicate we provide. The actual data is still not fetched until we call the each() method on the resulting object. As a result, DataSet is highly efficient, extracting only data that is selected.

WorkingWithDatabases/Weather.groovy
```
dataSet = sql.dataSet('weather')
citiesBelowFreezing = dataSet.findAll { it.temperature < 32 }
println "Cities below freezing:"
citiesBelowFreezing.each {
  println it.city
}
```

The output from the code using the previous DataSet is as follows:

```
Cities below freezing:
Santa Fe
```

9.6 Inserting and Updating

We can use the DataSet object to add data, not just filter data. The add() method accepts a map of data to create a row, as shown in the following code:

```
WorkingWithDatabases/Weather.groovy
println "Number of cities : " + sql.rows('SELECT * from weather').size()
dataSet.add(city: 'Denver', temperature: 19)
println "Number of cities : " + sql.rows('SELECT * from weather').size()
```

The following output shows the effect of executing that code:

```
Number of cities : 8
Number of cities : 9
```

More traditionally, however, we can insert data using the Sql class's execute() or executeInsert() method, as shown here:

```
WorkingWithDatabases/Weather.groovy
temperature = 50
sql.executeInsert("""INSERT INTO weather (city, temperature)
                    VALUES ('Oklahoma City', ${temperature})""")
println sql.firstRow(
  "SELECT temperature from weather WHERE city='Oklahoma City'")
```

The output from the previous code is as follows:

```
[temperature:50]
```

We can perform updates and deletions in a similar way by issuing the appropriate SQL commands.

9.7 Accessing Microsoft Excel

We can use the Sql class to access Microsoft Excel, as well. For information on interacting with COM or ActiveX, take a look at Groovy's Scriptom application programming interface (API).[1] In this section we'll create a really simple example using things we've seen already, except that we'll be talking to Excel instead of MySQL. Let's first create an Excel file named weather.xlsx (or weather.xls in older versions of Excel).

Create it in the c:\temp directory. The file will contain a worksheet with the name temperatures (see the bottom of the worksheet) and the content shown in Figure 8, *An Excel file that we will access using GSQL*, on page 157.

The code to access Excel is as follows:

---

1.   http://groovy.codehaus.org/COM+Scripting

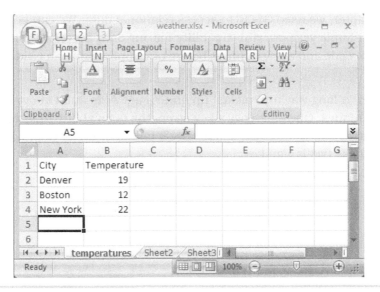

Figure 8—An Excel file that we will access using GSQL

WorkingWithDatabases/Excel/Windows/AccessExcel.groovy

```
def sql = groovy.sql.Sql.newInstance(
"""jdbc:odbc:Driver=
{Microsoft Excel Driver (*.xls, *.xlsx, *.xlsm, *.xlsb)};
DBQ=C:/temp/weather.xlsx;READONLY=false""", '', '')

println "City\t\tTemperature"
sql.eachRow('SELECT * FROM [temperatures$]') {
 println "${it.city}\t\t${it.temperature}"
}
```

Here's the data obtained from the Excel file using the previous code:

```
City           Temperature
Denver         19.0
Boston         12.0
New York       22.0
```

In the call to newInstance(), we've specified the driver for Excel and the location of the Excel file. Instead of this, we could set up a data-source name (DSN) for the Excel file and use the good old Java Database Connectivity–Open Database Connectivity (JDBC-ODBC) driver bridge if we want.

If we do that, we won't put the file location in the code. Instead, we'll configure the data source name (DSN) on Windows. The rest of the code to execute the query and process the result is familiar.

In this chapter, we used GSQL to access relational data. We can benefit from this API's simple yet powerful capability for our data access. It takes only a few lines of code and a few minutes before our application can read and write real data.

We've come a long way and picked up quite a few APIs and Groovy programming techniques. One of Groovy's key strengths is its ability to integrate and coexist with Java. In the next chapter we'll talk about how to integrate code between these two languages.

CHAPTER 10

Working with Scripts and Classes

Java is one of the most (if not the most) popular mainstream enterprise languages. Although we can use Groovy standalone, it's highly likely that we'll intermix it with Java. Groovy and Java code evolving side by side is a common usage scenario in projects that use Groovy. Learning how to intermix code written in these languages will help us to adopt Groovy quickly in our applications.

Calling Java code from within Groovy is quite trivial and straightforward. At first glance, the reverse of this does not appear simple. Groovy methods may accept closures and Groovy classes may have dynamic methods—methods that come to life at runtime. Is it even possible to access these, and if so, how hard would it be? Questions race through our minds. In this chapter we will answer these questions.

We will see how to jointly compile Java and Groovy code, use Groovy code from within Java, and create Groovy closures from within Java; we'll even explore how to call Groovy dynamic methods from within Java code—all without breaking a sweat.

10.1 The Melting Pot of Java and Groovy

In our applications, we can implement a certain functionality in a Java class, a Groovy class, or a Groovy script. Then we can call this functionality from within Java classes, Groovy classes, or Groovy scripts. Figure 9, *Ways to mix Java classes, Groovy classes, and scripts*, on page 160 shows the various options for mixing Java classes, Groovy classes, and Groovy scripts.

To use Groovy classes from Groovy code, we don't have to do anything. It just works. We simply make sure the classes we depend on are in the classpath, either as source or as bytecode. To pull a Groovy script into our Groovy code, we can use GroovyShell. To use it from within our Java classes, we can use the

ScriptEngine API provided by JSR 223. If we want to use a Groovy class from within a Java class, or vice versa, we can take advantage of the Groovy joint-compilation facility. All these are really simple, as we'll see in the rest of this chapter.

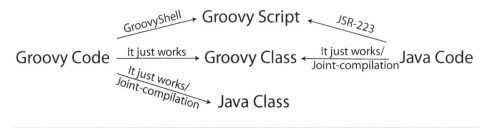

Figure 9—Ways to mix Java classes, Groovy classes, and scripts

First we'll look at the options for running Groovy. Then we'll see how to mix Groovy classes and scripts with both Java and Groovy.

10.2 Running Groovy

We have two options for running Groovy code. First, we can use the groovy command on our source code. Then Groovy automatically compiles code in memory and executes it. We don't have to take an explicit step to compile it.

Second, if we want to take a more traditional Javalike approach of explicitly compiling code to create bytecode—the .class file—we can do that using the groovyc compiler. To execute the bytecode, we'll use the java command just like we would to execute our compiled Java code. The only difference is that we need to have the groovy-all-2.1.0.jar file in the classpath. Remember to add a dot (.) to the classpath so java can find your classes in the current directory. This Java archive (JAR) is located in the embeddable directory under GROOVY_HOME. As an example, suppose we have the following Groovy code in a file named Greet.groovy:

ClassesAndScripts/Greet.groovy
```
println (['Groovy', 'Rocks!'].join(' '))
```

If we want to run it, we can simply type groovy Greet. However, if we want to explicitly compile this into Java bytecode, we type groovyc Greet.groovy to create a file named, as we'd expect, Greet.class. If our code has a package declaration, then the file will be created in the appropriate directory following the Java package-directory format. Unlike Groovy classes, Groovy scripts usually don't have package declarations. Use the -d option to specify a destination directory other than the current directory. We can run the bytecode by typing this:

```
java -classpath $GROOVY_HOME/embeddable/groovy-all-2.1.0.jar:. Greet
```

On Windows, use %GROOVY_HOME% instead of $GROOVY_HOME. Here's the output:

```
Groovy Rocks!
```

These steps show that we can compile and distribute our Groovy code as bytecode, much like we would compile and distribute our Java code. We can release it as .class files or JAR it up. java sees no difference. We can use this approach to distribute our Groovy code as bytecode along with rest of our bytecode if our deployment settings demand it.

Next we'll see some options to intermix Groovy scripts and classes.

10.3 Using Groovy Classes from Groovy

To use a Groovy class from within our Groovy code, we only have to make sure the Groovy class is in our classpath. We can use the Groovy source code as is, or we can compile it into a .class file and use it—it's our choice. When our Groovy code references a Groovy class, Groovy looks for the .groovy file with the name of the class in our classpath; if it does not find it, it looks for a .class file with the same name.

Suppose we have Groovy source code Car.groovy, shown here, in a directory named src:

ClassesAndScripts/src/Car.groovy
```
class Car
{
  int year = 2008
  int miles

  String toString() { "Car: year: $year, miles: $miles" }
}
```

Also suppose we're using this class in a file named useCar.groovy, like so:

ClassesAndScripts/useCar.groovy
```
println new Car()
```

To use this class, we type groovy -classpath src useCar. This will automatically fetch the Car class source, compile it, create an instance, and produce the output:

```
Car: year: 2008, miles: 0
```

If instead of source code we have bytecode for the Car, the steps are the same—Groovy can readily use classes from .groovy or .class files.

If we plan to intermix Groovy and Java in our projects, we'll benefit from the joint compilation facility that Groovy offers, as we'll see next.

10.4 Intermixing Groovy and Java with Joint Compilation

If the Groovy classes are precompiled, then we can use the .class files or JARs readily from Java. Java sees no difference between the bytecode from Java and Groovy; we'll have to add the Groovy JAR (discussed earlier) in our classpath, much like how we'll have JARs for Spring, Hibernate, or other frameworks/libraries we use.

What if we have Groovy source code instead of bytecode? Remember, when our Java class depends on other Java classes, javac will compile any Java classes it deems necessary if it does not find their bytecode. However, javac does not extend that kindness to Groovy. Fortunately, groovyc supports *joint compilation*. When we compile Groovy code, it determines whether any Java classes need to be compiled and takes care of compiling them. So, we can freely mix Java source code and Groovy source code in a project. We don't have to go through separate compilation steps; instead, we can simply call groovyc.

To take advantage of joint compilation, we need to use the -j compilation flag. Use the -J prefix to pass flags to the Java compiler. For example, suppose we have a Java class in a file named AJavaClass.java:

ClassesAndScripts/AJavaClass.java
```
//Java code
public class AJavaClass {
  {
        System.out.println("Created Java Class");
  }

  public void sayHello() { System.out.println("hello"); }
}
```

We also have a Groovy script in a file UseJavaClass.groovy that uses that Java class:

ClassesAndScripts/UseJavaClass.groovy
```
new AJavaClass().sayHello()
```

To compile these two files jointly, we issue the command groovyc -j AJavaClass.java UseJavaClass.groovy -Jsource 1.6. The option -Jsource 1.6 sends the optional option source = 1.6 to the Java compiler. Examine the bytecode generated using javap and notice that AJavaClass, as a regular Java class, extends java.lang.Object, whereas UseJavaClass extends groovy.lang.Script.

Execute the code to confirm all went well. Try the following command:

```
java -classpath $GROOVY_HOME/embeddable/groovy-all-2.1.0.jar:. UseJavaClass
```

We should see the following output:

```
Created Java Class
hello
```

We can intermix Groovy and Java seamlessly in our project, making Groovy a fantastic language for clean Java integration in our enterprise applications. We can focus on leveraging the advantages of each language without having to fight any integration battles.

The ease of integration goes beyond simple cases; we can invoke from Java into Groovy code that uses features with no direct support in Java, as we'll see in the next section.

10.5 Creating and Passing Groovy Closures from Java

Groovy has supported closures from day one, but Java is still toying with the idea. Surprisingly, creating closures in Java and invoking Groovy methods that take them is quite simple thanks to Groovy's dynamic nature. Whereas Java insists that we send methods instances of the proper type, Groovy is quite friendly and is happy that we use its features.

Upon close examination, we'll discover that when Groovy invokes a closure it simply uses a special method named call(). To create a closure in Java, we need only a class that has this method. If the Groovy code will pass arguments to the closure, we must make sure our call() method accepts those arguments as parameters.

It's very simple to create closures and pass them from Java, as we'll see in the next example. Let's create a Groovy class, AGroovyClass, with two methods that accept closures:

```
ClassesAndScripts/AGroovyClass.groovy
class AGroovyClass {
  def useClosure(closure) {
    println "Calling closure"
    closure()
  }

  def passToClosure(int value, closure) {
    println "Simply passing $value to the given closure"
    closure(value)
  }
}
```

The useClosure() method prints a message and calls the closure provided. The passToClosure() method passes the first parameter it receives to the closure provided.

To invoke the useClosure() method from Java, we need to provide an instance that implements the call() method, like this:

ClassesAndScripts/UseAGroovyClass.java
```java
//Java code
public class UseAGroovyClass {
  public static void main(String[] args) {
    AGroovyClass instance = new AGroovyClass();
    Object result = instance.useClosure(new Object() {
      public String call() {
        return "You called from Groovy!";
      }
    });

    System.out.println("Received: " + result);
  }
}
```

We can compile the Java and Groovy code either jointly or separately. To compile jointly, we use the command groovyc -j UseAGroovyClass.java AGroovy-Class.groovy. We can then run the Java code using the command java -classpath $GROOVY_HOME/embeddable/groovy-all-2.1.0.jar:. UseAGroovyClass. The instance of the anonymous class we created in Java is passed seamlessly to Groovy, which, in turn, calls back into the anonymous class:

```
Calling closure
Received: You called from Groovy!
```

Invoking a closure that takes parameters is not very different, as we see in the call to the passToClosure() method:

ClassesAndScripts/UseAGroovyClass2.java
```java
//Java code
System.out.println("Received: " +
  instance.passToClosure(2, new Object() {
    public String call(int value) {
      return "You called from Groovy with value " + value;
    }
  }));
```

This version of the call() method in Java takes a parameter to which the passToClosure() method assigns a value on the Groovy side, as we can see in the output:

```
Simply passing 2 to the given closure
Received: You called from Groovy with value 2
```

We must make sure the call() methods take the appropriate number and type of parameters. Groovy takes care of the rest of the details for us.

In this section we discussed calling into Groovy closures from within Java. Going the opposite direction is just as simple. At http://www.jroller.com/melix/entry/ coding_a_groovy_closure_in, Cédric Champeau shows how to treat a Java method like it's a closure on the Groovy side.

We've seen how to invoke methods with closures; next we'll see how to invoke Groovy dynamic methods from Java.

10.6 Calling Groovy Dynamic Methods from Java

In Groovy we can create methods at runtime, as we'll see in Part III, *MOPping Groovy*, on page 173. We can't directly call these methods from Java, because at compile time these methods don't exist in the bytecode. They come to life at runtime, but if we're calling them from Java we'd write the calls at compile time (or use reflection). To invoke the dynamic methods, we have to get past the Java compiler so the runtime can do the dispatching. That sounds complicated, but we can rely on Groovy!

Every Groovy object implements the GroovyObject interface, which has a special method named invokeMethod(). This method accepts the name of the method to invoke and the arguments to pass. We can use the invokeMethod() method on the Java side to invoke methods that are defined dynamically using metaprogramming in Groovy.

To see this in action, create a Groovy class that has a special method, methodMissing(), that will step in anytime a nonexistent method is called.

ClassesAndScripts/DynamicGroovyClass.groovy
```groovy
class DynamicGroovyClass {
  def methodMissing(String name, args) {
    println "You called $name with ${args.join(', ')}."
    args.size()
  }
}
```

This class is entirely dynamic; it has no real methods other than methodMissing(). Since this class accepts any method call, we can pretty much invoke any methods on it. To invoke the methods we desire from the Java side, call the invokeMethod() and pass the method name followed by an array of arguments, as in the next example.

ClassesAndScripts/CallDynamicMethod.java
```java
public class CallDynamicMethod {
  public static void main(String[] args) {
    groovy.lang.GroovyObject instance = new DynamicGroovyClass();

    Object result1 = instance.invokeMethod("squeak", new Object[] {});
```

```
    System.out.println("Received: " + result1);

    Object result2 =
      instance.invokeMethod("quack", new Object[] {"like", "a", "duck"});
    System.out.println("Received: " + result2);
  }
}
```

We created an instance of DynamicGroovyClass and assigned it to a reference of type GroovyObject, which all Groovy objects support. Using this reference, we can invoke any methods on the class, both dynamic and predefined. Once Groovy receives the methods, it takes the call through the regular Groovy method-dispatching process that we'll cover in Section 11.1, *Groovy Object*, on page 176. Groovy responds to our call from the Java side, as we see in the next output. The invokeMethod() returns any response from the invoked method is returned to the Java side.

```
You called squeak with .
Received: 0
You called quack with like, a, duck.
Received: 3
```

If Groovy could not execute the invoked method for some reason or if the method blows up, the call to invokeMethod() will fail. Be prepared to handle the exception that this method may throw our way.

There are no restrictions on using any Groovy class from Java, no matter how dynamic they are. Next we'll look at using Java classes from Groovy.

10.7 Using Java Classes from Groovy

Using Java classes from Groovy is simple and direct. If the Java classes we want to use are part of the JDK, we import the classes or their packages in Groovy just like in Java. By default Groovy imports a number of packages and classes (see Section 2.1, *From Java to Groovy*, on page 11), so if the class we want to use is imported already (such as java.util.Date), then we just use it—no import is needed.

If we want to use one of our own Java classes, or classes that are not part of the standard JDK, we can import them in Groovy just like we would in Java. Make sure to import the necessary packages or classes, or refer to the classes by their fully qualified names. When running groovy, specify the path to the .class files or JARs using the -classpath option. If the class files are in the same directory where our Groovy code is, there's no need to specify that directory using the classpath option.

Let's look at an example. Say we have a Java class named GreetJava that belongs to the package com.agiledeveloper and has a static method called sayHello(), as shown here:

```
ClassesAndScripts/GreetJava.java
// Java code
package com.agiledeveloper;

public class GreetJava {
        public static void sayHello() {
                System.out.println("Hello Java");
        }
}
```

We want to call this method from a Groovy script, so first we compile the Java class GreetJava so the class file GreetJava.class is located in the directory ./com/agiledeveloper, where . is the current directory. Then we create a Groovy script in a UseGreetJava.groovy file with the following:

```
ClassesAndScripts/UseGreetJava.groovy
com.agiledeveloper.GreetJava.sayHello()
```

To run this script, simply type groovy UseGreetJava. The script runs with no trouble and uses the sayHello() method in class GreetJava, as shown in the following output:

```
Hello Java
```

If the class file is not under the current directory, we can still use it, but we need to remember to set the classpath option. Assume that the class file GreetJava.class is located under ~/release/com/agiledeveloper, where ~ is our home directory.

To run the previously mentioned Groovy script (UseGreetJava.groovy), use the following command:

```
$groovy -classpath ~/release UseGreetJava
```

In this example, we compiled the Java code explicitly and then used the bytecode with our Groovy script. If we intend to explicitly compile our Groovy code, then we don't have to use a separate compilation step for Java and Groovy. Use the joint compilation facility instead.

Not all Groovy code needs explicit compilation. Groovy scripts are used as is via the groovy command. Next we'll cover how to intermix Groovy scripts.

10.8 Using Groovy Scripts from Groovy

Groovy scripts hold statements and expressions not necessarily confined to a particular class in the source code. We can directly exercise these using the groovy command. We can also invoke them from other Groovy scripts and classes using the GroovyShell class. Let's look at an example:

ClassesAndScripts/Script1.groovy

```
println "Hello from Script1"
```

Here we have a file named Script1.groovy, and we want to execute that script as part of executing another Groovy script, Script2.groovy, shown here:

ClassesAndScripts/Script2.groovy

```
println "In Script2"
shell = new GroovyShell()
shell.evaluate(new File('Script1.groovy'))

// or simply
evaluate(new File('Script1.groovy'))
```

The output from the previous code is as follows:

```
In Script2
Hello from Script1
Hello from Script1
```

Using the GroovyShell, we can evaluate() script in any file (or string). That was easy. But (and there is always a "but"), what if we want to pass some parameters to the scripts?

ClassesAndScripts/Script1a.groovy

```
println "Hello ${name}"
name = "Dan"
```

This script is expecting a variable name. We can use an instance of Binding to bind variables, as shown here:

ClassesAndScripts/Script2a.groovy

```
println "In Script2"

name = "Venkat"

shell = new GroovyShell(binding)
result = shell.evaluate(new File('Script1a.groovy'))

println "Script1a returned : $result"
println "Hello $name"
```

In the calling script, we created a variable name (the same variable name as in the called script). When we create the instance of GroovyShell, we pass the current Binding object to it (each script execution has one of these). The called script can now use (read and set) variables that the calling script knows about. The output from the previous code is as follows:

```
In Script2
Hello Venkat
Script1a returned : Dan
Hello Dan
```

If the script returns a value, we can receive that from the evaluate() method as the return value as well, as we saw in the previous example.

In the previous example, we passed the Binding of the calling script to GroovyShell. If we don't want our current binding to be affected and we want to keep the called script's binding separate, we simply create a new instance of Binding, call setProperty() on it to set variable names and values, and provide it as an argument when creating an instance of GroovyShell, as shown here:

ClassesAndScripts/Script3.groovy
```groovy
println "In Script3"

binding1 = new Binding()
binding1.setProperty('name', 'Venkat')
shell = new GroovyShell(binding1)
shell.evaluate(new File('Script1a.groovy'))

binding2 = new Binding()
binding2.setProperty('name', 'Dan')
shell.binding = binding2
shell.evaluate(new File('Script1a.groovy'))
```

The output from the previous code is as follows:

```
In Script3
Hello Venkat
Hello Dan
```

If we want to pass some command-line arguments to the script, we use the GroovyShell class's run() methods instead of the evaluate() methods.

We can easily load arbitrary scripts and execute them as part of our Groovy code using the GroovyShell. This feature is very useful to not only run routine tasks that may be saved in reusable scripts, but also to build and execute DSLs.

We know how to invoke Groovy scripts from Groovy code. Next we'll run through how to do that from within Java code.

10.9 Using Groovy Scripts from Java

If we want to use Groovy script as is in Java, we can use JSR 223.

Java Specification Request (JSR) 223 bridges the Java Virtual Machine (JVM) and scripting languages (see the Java Scripting Programmer's Guide in

Appendix 1, *Web Resources*, on page 309). It provides a standard way to interact between Java and several languages with implementations of the JSR 223 scripting-engine API. We can download and use JSR 223 with Java 5. It is included by default in Java 6.

JSR 223 is an option more suited to other languages on the JVM than to Groovy. Groovy's ability to jointly compile Java and Groovy lessens the need for something like JSR 223.

To call a (not-precompiled) script from Java, use the script engine. We can obtain it from ScriptEngineManager by calling the getEngineByName() method. To execute our scripts from within our Java code, call its eval() method. To use Groovy scripts, we need to make sure .../jsr223-engines/groovy/build/groovy-engine.jar is in our classpath.

Let's look at an example to execute a little Groovy script from within Java. (With Java comes the pleasure of handling exceptions we don't care about. The rest of the examples in this chapter don't show the exception-handling code, but remember to put it where needed.)

MixingJavaAndGroovy/CallingScript.java

```java
// Java code
package com.agiledeveloper;
import javax.script.*;

public class CallingScript {
  public static void main(String[] args) {
    ScriptEngineManager manager = new ScriptEngineManager();
    ScriptEngine engine = manager.getEngineByName("groovy");
    System.out.println("Calling script from Java");
    try {
      engine.eval("println 'Hello from Groovy'");
    } catch(ScriptException ex) {
      System.out.println(ex);
    }
  }
}
```

The output from the preceding code is as follows:

```
Calling script from Java
Hello from Groovy
```

In this example, our Groovy script is embedded in the string parameter to the eval() method. Unlike in this example, in reality the script may not be hard-coded. It may be in a file, an input stream, a dialog box, and so on. In that case we'll find other overloaded versions of the eval() method that make a Reader useful.

If the script returns any result to the calling Java program, we can receive it from the eval() method's Object return value.

Using this approach, we can call any arbitrary Groovy script from within our Java application. If we want to pass some parameters to the script—a Java object, created in Java but accessed from Groovy—we can use Bindings.

Bindings are an implementation of Map<String, Object> that makes objects available through a named value. ScriptContext allows the script engines to connect to the Java objects, such as Bindings, in the hosting application. We can either explicitly get access to these objects and interact with them, or simply use get() and put() on the ScriptEngine instance. If we want to execute the same script but with a different set of values for the variables, we'll create different contexts and use them in a call to eval().

Let's look at an example of passing parameters to Groovy scripts from Java:

```
MixingJavaAndGroovy/ParameterPassing.java
engine.put("name", "Venkat");
engine.eval("println \"Hello ${name} from Groovy\"; name += '!' ");
String name = (String) engine.get("name");
System.out.println("Back in Java:" + name);
```

The output from the previous code is as follows:

```
Hello Venkat from Groovy
Back in Java:Venkat!
```

We're sending a String object (with value Venkat) to the engine using the put() method. We've given the name name for the variable binding. Within the script, we use that variable (name). We can also change its value. We can obtain the variable's current value on the Java side by calling the get() method on the engine.

JSR 223 provides the capability to call instance methods, plus functions not associated with any particular class. We can use the invokeMethod() and invoke-Function() of the Invocable for that. If we plan to use a script repeatedly, we'll use the Compilable interface to avoid repeatedly recompiling the script.

Instead of using the ScriptEngineManager, we can use the GroovyScriptEngine from within Java, much like how we used the GroovyShell from within Groovy.[1] The GroovyScriptEngine's run() method takes a script filename and a binding variable that maps parameters the script expects. It can even reload and rerun the scripts if they change, making it a great candidate for embedding in Java server applications.

---

1. http://groovy.codehaus.org/Embedding+Groovy

We typically compile our Java code into .class files and JAR them up. To use other Java classes, we need only the .class files or the JARs that contain those files to be in our classpath. Groovy pretty much expects the same if we call into Java classes from Groovy. Groovy also makes our life easy by providing joint compilation. With this facility we can use Groovy and Java code side by side, plus debug and work seamlessly with the two languages on the same project.

We discussed how easily we can mix and work with Groovy scripts. Throughout this book we've seen examples of using Java classes from the JDK. In this chapter we figured out how to use our own Java classes and Groovy classes with our application. There's no impediment to creating enterprise applications mixing Java and Groovy.

Speaking of enterprise applications, in the next chapter we'll see that the dynamic, flexible Groovy language has chops for heavy lifting in the area of metaprogramming.

Part III

MOPping Groovy

CHAPTER 11

Exploring Metaobject Protocol (MOP)

In Java, we can use reflection at runtime to explore our program's structure, plus its classes, their methods, and the parameters they take. However, we're still restricted to the static structure we've created. We can't change an object's type or let it acquire behavior dynamically at runtime—at least not yet. Imagine if we could add methods and behavior dynamically based on the current state of our application or the inputs it receives. This would make our code flexible, and we could be creative and productive. Well, we don't have to imagine that anymore—metaprogramming provides this functionality in Groovy.

How extensible can we design applications to be with these features? Quite. I recently had the opportunity to consult with a company that transitioned from creating Java-based web applications to using Groovy and Grails. Their product required certain customization in the field after deployment. In their existing system, this took them weeks of effort and the time of a few programmers and testers. Working closely with their key developers, we managed to automate the customization using Groovy metaprogramming and some back-end services. Immediately, the organization realized higher throughput and productivity.

Metaprogramming means writing programs that manipulate programs, including themselves. Dynamic languages such as Groovy provide this capability through the metaobject protocol (MOP). Creating classes, writing unit tests, and introducing mock objects are all easy with Groovy's MOP.

In Groovy, we can use MOP to invoke methods dynamically and synthesize classes and methods on the fly. This can give us the feeling that our object favorably changed its class. Grails/GORM uses this facility, for example, to synthesize methods for database queries. With MOP we can create internal domain-specific languages (DSLs) in Groovy (see Chapter 19, *Creating DSLs in Groovy*, on page 295). Groovy builders (see Chapter 17, *Groovy Builders*, on page 253) rely on MOP as well. So, MOP is one of the most important concepts to learn and exploit. We'll investigate several concepts in MOP across this and the next few chapters.

In this chapter, we will explore MOP by looking at what makes a Groovy object and how Groovy resolves method calls for Java objects and Groovy objects. We'll then look at ways to query for methods and properties and, finally, see how to access objects dynamically.

Once you've absorbed the fundamentals in this chapter, you'll be ready to learn how to intercept method calls in Chapter 12, *Intercepting Methods Using MOP*, on page 185. We'll then look at how to inject and synthesize methods into classes at runtime in Chapter 13, *MOP Method Injection*, on page 193, and Chapter 14, *MOP Method Synthesis*, on page 215. Finally, we'll wrap up the discussion on MOP in Chapter 15, *MOPping Up*, on page 225.

11.1 Groovy Object

The flexibility Groovy offers can be confusing at first, so if we want to take full advantage of MOP, we need to understand Groovy objects and Groovy's method handling.

Groovy objects are Java objects with additional capabilities. Groovy objects have a greater number of dynamic behaviors than do compiled Java objects in Groovy. Also, Groovy handles method calls to Java objects differently than to Groovy objects.

In a Groovy application we'll work with three kinds of objects: POJOs, POGOs, and Groovy interceptors. Plain old Java objects (POJOs) are regular Java objects—we can create them using Java or other languages on the Java Virtual Machine (JVM). Plain old Groovy objects (POGOs) are classes written in Groovy. They extend java.lang.Object but implement the groovy.lang.GroovyObject interface. Groovy interceptors are Groovy objects that extend GroovyInterceptable and have a method-interception capability, which we'll soon discuss. Groovy defines the GroovyObject interface like this:

```
//This is an excerpt of GroovyObject.java from Groovy source code
package groovy.lang;
public interface GroovyObject {
    Object invokeMethod(String name, Object args);
    Object getProperty(String property);
    void setProperty(String property, Object newValue);
    MetaClass getMetaClass();
    void setMetaClass(MetaClass metaClass);
}
```

invokeMethod(), getProperty(), and setProperty() make Groovy objects highly dynamic. We can use them to work with methods and properties created on the fly. getMetaClass() and setMetaClass() make it very easy to create proxies to intercept method calls on POGOs, as well as to inject methods on POGOs. Once a class is loaded into the JVM, we can't change the metaobject Class for it. However, we can change its MetaClass by calling setMetaClass(). This gives us a feeling that the object changed its class at runtime.

Let's look at the GroovyInterceptable interface next. It's a marker interface that extends GroovyObject, and all method calls—both existing methods and nonexistent methods—on an object that implements this interface are intercepted by its invokeMethod().

//This is an excerpt of GroovyInterceptable.java from Groovy source code

```
package groovy.lang;

public interface GroovyInterceptable extends GroovyObject {
}
```

Groovy allows metaprogramming for POJOs and POGOs. For POJOs, Groovy maintains a MetaClassRegistry class of MetaClasses, as the following figure shows. POGOs, on the other hand, have a direct reference to their MetaClass.

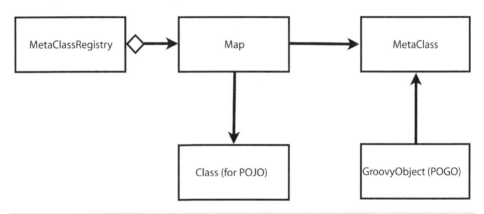

Figure 10—POJOs, POGOs, and their MetaClass

When we call a method, Groovy checks whether the target object is a POJO or a POGO. Groovy's method handling is different for each of these types.

For a POJO, Groovy fetches its MetaClass from the application-wide MetaClassRegistry and delegates method invocation to it. So, any interceptors or methods we've defined on its MetaClass take precedence over the POJO's original method.

For a POGO, Groovy takes a few extra steps, as illustrated in the following figure. If the object implements GroovyInterceptable, then *all* calls are routed to its invokeMethod(). Within this interceptor, we can route calls to the actual method, making aspect-oriented-programming–like operations possible.

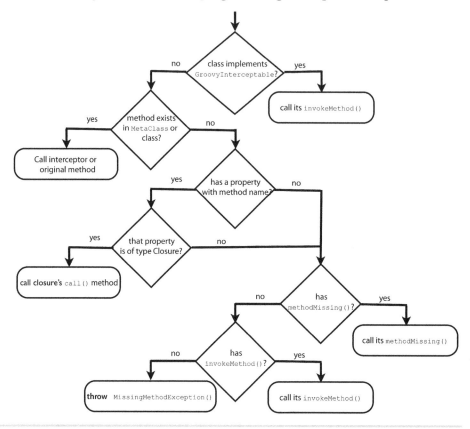

Figure 11—How Groovy handles method calls on a POGO

If the POGO does not implement GroovyInterceptable, then Groovy looks for the method first in the POGO's MetaClass and then, if it's not found, on the POGO itself. If the POGO has no such method, Groovy looks for a property or a field with the method name. If that property or field is of type Closure, Groovy invokes that in place of the method call. If Groovy finds no such property or field, it makes two last attempts. If the POGO has a method named methodMissing(), it calls it. Otherwise, it calls the POGO's invokeMethod(). If we've implemented this method on our POGO, it's used. The default implementation of invokeMethod() throws a MissingMethodException, indicating the failure of the call.

Let's see in code the mechanism discussed earlier, using classes with different options to illustrate Groovy's method handling. Study the code, and try to figure out which methods Groovy executes in each of the cases (while walking through the following code, refer to Figure 11, *How Groovy handles method calls on a POGO*, on page 178):

ExploringMOP/TestMethodInvocation.groovy

```groovy
class TestMethodInvocation extends GroovyTestCase {
  void testInterceptedMethodCallonPOJO() {
    def val = new Integer(3)
    Integer.metaClass.toString = {-> 'intercepted' }

    assertEquals "intercepted", val.toString()
  }

  void testInterceptableCalled() {
    def obj = new AnInterceptable()
    assertEquals 'intercepted', obj.existingMethod()
    assertEquals 'intercepted', obj.nonExistingMethod()
  }

  void testInterceptedExistingMethodCalled() {
    AGroovyObject.metaClass.existingMethod2 = {-> 'intercepted' }
    def obj = new AGroovyObject()
    assertEquals 'intercepted', obj.existingMethod2()
  }

  void testUnInterceptedExistingMethodCalled() {
    def obj = new AGroovyObject()
    assertEquals 'existingMethod', obj.existingMethod()
  }

  void testPropertyThatIsClosureCalled() {
    def obj = new AGroovyObject()
    assertEquals 'closure called', obj.closureProp()
  }

  void testMethodMissingCalledOnlyForNonExistent() {
    def obj = new ClassWithInvokeAndMissingMethod()
    assertEquals 'existingMethod', obj.existingMethod()
    assertEquals 'missing called', obj.nonExistingMethod()
  }

  void testInvokeMethodCalledForOnlyNonExistent() {
    def obj = new ClassWithInvokeOnly()
    assertEquals 'existingMethod', obj.existingMethod()
    assertEquals 'invoke called', obj.nonExistingMethod()
  }

  void testMethodFailsOnNonExistent() {
```

```groovy
    def obj = new TestMethodInvocation()
    shouldFail (MissingMethodException) { obj.nonExistingMethod() }
  }
}

class AnInterceptable implements GroovyInterceptable {
  def existingMethod() {}
  def invokeMethod(String name, args) { 'intercepted' }
}

class AGroovyObject {
  def existingMethod() { 'existingMethod' }
  def existingMethod2() { 'existingMethod2' }
  def closureProp = { 'closure called' }
}

class ClassWithInvokeAndMissingMethod {
  def existingMethod() { 'existingMethod' }
  def invokeMethod(String name, args) { 'invoke called' }
  def methodMissing(String name, args) { 'missing called' }
}

class ClassWithInvokeOnly {
  def existingMethod() { 'existingMethod' }
  def invokeMethod(String name, args) { 'invoke called' }
}
```

The following output confirms that all the tests pass and Groovy handles the method as discussed:

```
.........
Time: 0.047

OK (9 tests)
```

11.2 Querying Methods and Properties

At runtime, we can query an object's methods and properties to find out if the object supports a certain behavior. This is especially useful for behavior we add dynamically at runtime. We can add behavior not only to classes, but also to select instances of a class.

We can use MetaObjectProtocol's getMetaMethod() (MetaClass extends MetaObjectProtocol) to get a metamethod. We can use getStaticMetaMethod() if we're looking for a static method. To get a list of overloaded methods, we use the plural forms of these methods—getMetaMethods() and getStaticMetaMethods(). Similarly, we can use getMetaProperty() and getStaticMetaProperty() for a metaproperty. If we want simply to check for existence and not get the metamethod or metaproperty, we use respondsTo() to check for methods and hasProperty() to check for properties.

MetaMethod "represents a Method on a Java object a little like Method except without using reflection to invoke the method," according to the Groovy documentation. If we have a method name as a string, we can call getMetaMethod() and use the resulting MetaMethod to invoke our method, like so:

ExploringMOP/UsingMetaMethod.groovy
```
str = "hello"
methodName = 'toUpperCase'
// Name may come from an input instead of being hard coded

methodOfInterest = str.metaClass.getMetaMethod(methodName)

println methodOfInterest.invoke(str)
```

The dynamically invoked method produces this output:

```
HELLO
```

We don't have to know a method name at coding time. We can get it as input and invoke the method dynamically.

To find out whether an object would respond to a method call, we can use the respondsTo() method. It takes as parameters the instance we're querying, the name of the method we're querying for, and an optional comma-separated list of arguments intended for that method. It returns a list of MetaMethods for the matching methods. Let's use that in an example:

ExploringMOP/UsingMetaMethod.groovy
```
print "Does String respond to toUpperCase()? "
println String.metaClass.respondsTo(str, 'toUpperCase')? 'yes' : 'no'

print "Does String respond to compareTo(String)? "
println String.metaClass.respondsTo(str, 'compareTo', "test")? 'yes' : 'no'

print "Does String respond to toUpperCase(int)? "
println String.metaClass.respondsTo(str, 'toUpperCase', 5)? 'yes' : 'no'
```

Here's the output from the code:

```
Does String respond to toUpperCase()? yes
Does String respond to compareTo(String)? yes
Does String respond to toUpperCase(int)? no
```

getMetaMethod() and respondsTo() offer a nice convenience. We can simply send these methods the arguments for a method we're looking for. getMetaMethod() and respondsTo() don't insist on an array of the arguments' Class like the getMethod() method in Java reflection. Even better, if the method we're interested in does not take any parameters, don't send any arguments, not even a null. This is because the last parameter to these methods is an array of parameters and Groovy treats it as optional.

There was one more magical thing taking place in the previous code: we used Groovy's special treatment of boolean (for more information, see Section 2.7, *Groovy Boolean Evaluation*, on page 30). The respondsTo() method returns a list of MetaMethods, and since we used the result in a conditional statement (the ?: operator), Groovy returned true if there were any methods, and false otherwise. So, we don't have to explicitly check whether the size of the returned list is greater than zero—Groovy does that for us.

11.3 Dynamically Accessing Objects

We've looked at ways to query for methods and properties, and at ways to invoke them dynamically. There are other convenient ways to access properties and call methods in Groovy. We will look at them now using an instance of String as an example. Suppose we get the names of properties and methods as input at runtime and want to access these dynamically. Here are some ways to do that:

```
ExploringMOP/AccessingObject.groovy
def printInfo(obj) {
  // Assume user entered these values from standard input
  usrRequestedProperty = 'bytes'
  usrRequestedMethod = 'toUpperCase'

  println obj[usrRequestedProperty]
  //or
  println obj."$usrRequestedProperty"

  println obj."$usrRequestedMethod"()
  //or
  println obj.invokeMethod(usrRequestedMethod, null)
}

printInfo('hello')
```

Here's the output from the previous code:

```
[104, 101, 108, 108, 111]
[104, 101, 108, 108, 111]
HELLO
HELLO
```

To invoke a property dynamically, we can use the index operator [] or use the dot notation followed by a GString evaluating the property name, as shown in the previous code. To invoke a method, use the dot notation or call the invokeMethod on the object, giving it the method name and list of arguments (null in this case).

To iterate over all of an object's properties, we can use the properties property (or the getProperties() method), as shown here:

ExploringMOP/AccessingObject.groovy
```
println "Properties of 'hello' are: "
'hello'.properties.each { println it }
```

The output is as follows:

```
Properties of 'hello' are:
class=class java.lang.String
bytes=[B@74f2ff9b
empty=false
```

In this chapter, we looked at the fundamentals for metaprogramming in Groovy. With this foundation, we're well equipped to explore MOP further, understand how Groovy works, and take advantage of the MOP concepts we'll see in the next few chapters.

CHAPTER 12

Intercepting Methods Using MOP

In Groovy we can implement aspect-oriented programming (AOP)—such as method interception or method advice—fairly easily.[1] There are three types of advice. And, no, they're not the good advice, the bad advice, and the unsolicited advice we receive every day. We'll focus on the *before*, *after*, and *around* advice. The before advice is code for a concern we'd want to execute before a certain operation. The after advice is executed after an operation's execution. The around advice is executed *instead of* the intended operation. We can use MOP to implement these advice types or interceptors. We don't need any complex tools or frameworks to do that in Groovy.

Here we'll discuss two approaches in Groovy to intercept method calls: either let the object do it or let its MetaClass do it. If we want the object to handle it, we need to implement the GroovyInterceptable interface. This is not desirable if we're not the author of the class, if the class is a Java class, or if we want to introduce interception dynamically. The second approach is better in these cases. We'll look at both of these approaches in this chapter. There's one more way to intercept methods, using categories, but we'll defer discussing that until Section 13.1, *Injecting Methods Using Categories*, on page 193.

12.1 Intercepting Methods Using GroovyInterceptable

If a Groovy object implements GroovyInterceptable, then its invokeMethod() is called when *any* of its methods are called—both existing methods and nonexistent methods. That is, GroovyInterceptable's invokeMethod() hijacks all calls to the object.

If we want to perform an *around advice*, we simply implement our logic in this method, and we're done. However, if we want to implement the *before* or *after advice* (or both), we first implement our before/after logic, then route

---

1. For a thorough discussion of AOP, see *AspectJ in Action [Lad03]*, by Ramnivas Laddad.

the call to the actual method at the appropriate time. To route the call, we'll use the MetaMethod for the method we can obtain from the MetaClass (see Section 11.2, *Querying Methods and Properties*, on page 180).

---

invokeMethod, GroovyInterceptable, and GroovyObject

If a Groovy object implements the GroovyInterceptable interface, then its invokeMethod() is called for *all* its method calls. For other Groovy objects, it is called only for methods that are nonexistent at call time. The exception to this is if we implement invokeMethod() on an object's MetaClass. In that case, it is called always for both types of methods.

Suppose we want to run filters—such as validation, login verification, logging, and so on—before we run some methods of a class. We don't want to manually edit each method to call the filters, because such effort is redundant, tedious, and error-prone. We don't want to ask callers of our methods to invoke the filters, either, because there's no guarantee they'll call. Intercepting method calls to apply the filters is a good option. It'll be seamless and automatic.

We use System.out.println() instead of println() in the examples in this chapter to avoid the interception of informational print messages. Whereas println() is a Groovy-injected method in Object, calls to which the code we write will intercept, System.out.println() is a static method on the PrintStream class that's not affected by our interceptions.

Let's look at an example in which we want to run a filter method check() on a Car before any other method is executed. Here's the code that uses GroovyInterceptable to achieve this:

InterceptingMethodsUsingMOP/InterceptingCalls.groovy

```
class Car implements GroovyInterceptable {
  def check() { System.out.println "check called..." }

  def start() { System.out.println "start called..." }

  def drive() { System.out.println "drive called..." }

  def invokeMethod(String name, args) {
    System.out.print("Call to $name intercepted... ")

    if (name != 'check') {
      System.out.print("running filter... ")
      Car.metaClass.getMetaMethod('check').invoke(this, null)
    }

    def validMethod = Car.metaClass.getMetaMethod(name, args)
```

```
        if (validMethod != null) {
          validMethod.invoke(this, args)
        } else {
20        Car.metaClass.invokeMethod(this, name, args)
        }
      }
    }

25  car = new Car()

    car.start()
    car.drive()
    car.check()
30  try {
      car.speed()
    } catch(Exception ex) {
      println ex
    }
```

The output shows the proper interception of methods:

```
Call to start intercepted... running filter... check called...
start called...
Call to drive intercepted... running filter... check called...
drive called...
Call to check intercepted... check called...
Call to speed intercepted... running filter... check called...
groovy.lang.MissingMethodException:
  No signature of method: Car.speed()
  is applicable for argument types: () values: []
```

Since Car implements GroovyInterceptable, all method calls on an instance of Car are intercepted by its invokeMethod(). In that method, if the method name is not check, we invoke the before filter, which is the check() method. With the help of the MetaClass's getMetaMethod(), we determine whether the method called is a valid existing method. If it is, we call that method using the MetaMethod's invoke() method, as on line number 18.

If the method is not found, we simply route the request to the MetaClass, as on line number 20. This creates an opportunity for the method to be synthesized dynamically, as we'll see in Section 14.1, *Method Synthesis Using methodMissing*, on page 216. If the method does not exist, MetaClass's invokeMethod() will throw a MissingMethodException.

In this example, we created a *before advice*. We can easily create an *after advice* by placing the desired code after line number 18. If we want to implement *around advice*, then we can eliminate, or replace with an alternate code, the code on line number 18.

12.2 Intercepting Methods Using MetaClass

We used GroovyInterceptable to intercept method calls in Section 12.1, *Intercepting Methods Using GroovyInterceptable*, on page 185. That approach is good if we're the author of the class whose methods we want to intercept. However, that approach won't work if we don't have the privileges to modify the class source code or if it is a Java class. Furthermore, we may decide at runtime to start intercepting calls based on some condition or application state. In these cases, we can intercept methods by implementing the invokeMethod() method on the MetaClass.

Let's rewrite the example from Section 12.1, *Intercepting Methods Using GroovyInterceptable*, on page 185, this time using the MetaClass. In this version, the Car does not implement GroovyInterceptable and does not have the invokeMethod(). Even if it has invokeMethod(), the invokeMethod() we add to MetaClass takes precedence if Car does not implement GroovyInterceptable. Here's the code:

InterceptingMethodsUsingMOP/InterceptingCallsUsingMetaClass.groovy

```
Line 1  class Car {
          def check() { System.out.println "check called..." }

          def start() { System.out.println "start called..." }

 5
          def drive() { System.out.println "drive called..." }
        }

        Car.metaClass.invokeMethod = { String name, args ->
10        System.out.print("Call to $name intercepted... ")

          if (name != 'check') {
            System.out.print("running filter... ")
            Car.metaClass.getMetaMethod('check').invoke(delegate, null)
15        }

          def validMethod = Car.metaClass.getMetaMethod(name, args)
          if (validMethod != null) {
            validMethod.invoke(delegate, args)
20        } else {
            Car.metaClass.invokeMissingMethod(delegate, name, args)
          }
        }

25
        car = new Car()

        car.start()
        car.drive()
30      car.check()
```

```
   try {
     car.speed()
   } catch(Exception ex) {
     println ex
35 }
```

Let's observe the method interceptions in the output:

```
Call to start intercepted... running filter... check called...
start called...
Call to drive intercepted... running filter... check called...
drive called...
Call to check intercepted... check called...
Call to speed intercepted... running filter... check called...
groovy.lang.MissingMethodException:
  No signature of method: Car.speed()
  is applicable for argument types: () values: []
```

On line number 9, we implemented, in the form of a closure, the invokeMethod()
and set it on Car's MetaClass. This method will now intercept all calls on an
instance of Car. There are two differences between this version of invokeMethod()
and the version we implemented on Car in Section 12.1, *Intercepting Methods
Using GroovyInterceptable*, on page 185. The first difference is the use of delegate
instead of this (see line number 14, for example). The delegate within the intercepting closure refers to the target object whose methods are being intercepted.
The second difference is on line number 21, where we call invokeMissingMethod()
on the MetaClass instead of calling invokeMethod. We're already in invokeMethod(),
so we should not call it recursively here.

As we saw earlier, one nice aspect of using the MetaClass to intercept calls is
that we can intercept calls on POJOs as well. To see this in action, let's
intercept calls to methods on an Integer and perform AOP-like advice:

InterceptingMethodsUsingMOP/InterceptInteger.groovy
```
Integer.metaClass.invokeMethod = { String name, args ->
  System.out.println("Call to $name intercepted on $delegate... ")

  def validMethod = Integer.metaClass.getMetaMethod(name, args)
  if (validMethod == null) {
    Integer.metaClass.invokeMissingMethod(delegate, name, args)
  } else {
    System.out.println("running pre-filter... ")
    result = validMethod.invoke(delegate, args) // Remove this for around-advice

    System.out.println("running post-filter... ")
    result
  }
}
```

```
println 5.floatValue()
println 5.intValue()
try {
  println 5.empty()
} catch(Exception ex) {
  println ex
}
```

The output shows the interception of methods on an Integer:

```
Call to floatValue intercepted on 5...
running pre-filter...
running post-filter...
5.0
Call to intValue intercepted on 5...
running pre-filter...
running post-filter...
5
Call to empty intercepted on 5...
groovy.lang.MissingMethodException:
  No signature of method: java.lang.Integer.empty()
  is applicable for argument types: () values: []
```

The invokeMethod() we added on Integer's MetaClass intercepts method calls on 5, an instance of Integer. To intercept calls on any Object and not only Integers, we should add the interceptor to Object's MetaClass.

If we're interested in intercepting calls only to nonexistent methods, then we should use methodMissing() instead of invokeMethod(). You'll learn about this in Chapter 14, *MOP Method Synthesis*, on page 215.

We can provide both invokeMethod() and methodMissing() on MetaClass. invokeMethod() takes precedence over methodMissing(). However, by calling invokeMissingMethod(), we're letting methodMissing() handle nonexistent methods.

The ability to intercept method calls using MetaClass was influenced by Grails. It was originally introduced in Grails and was later moved into Groovy.[2] Take a minute to examine the MetaClass that's giving us so much power:

InterceptingMethodsUsingMOP/ExamineMetaClass.groovy
```
Integer.metaClass.invokeMethod = { String name, args -> /* */ }
println Integer.metaClass.getClass().name
```

Here is the class the output reports:

```
groovy.lang.ExpandoMetaClass
```

---

2.   http://graemerocher.blogspot.com/2007/06/dynamic-groovy-groovys-equivalent-to.html

ExpandoMetaClass is an implementation of the MetaClass interface and is one of the key classes responsible for implementing dynamic behavior in Groovy. We can add methods to this class to inject behavior into our class, and we can even specialize individual objects using this class.

There is a gotcha here, depending on ExpandoMetaClass. It is one among many different implementations of MetaClass. By default, Groovy currently does not use ExpandoMetaClass. When we add a method to the metaClass, the default metaClass is replaced with an instance of ExpandoMetaClass.

Here's an example that shows this behavior. We'll examine an instance's metaclass before and after dynamically adding a method.

InterceptingMethodsUsingMOP/MetaClassUsed.groovy
```groovy
def printMetaClassInfo(instance) {
  print "MetaClass of ${instance} is ${instance.metaClass.class.simpleName}"
  println " with delegate ${instance.metaClass.delegate.class.simpleName}"
}

printMetaClassInfo(2)
println "MetaClass of Integer is ${Integer.metaClass.class.simpleName}"
println "Adding a method to Integer metaClass"
Integer.metaClass.someNewMethod = { -> /* */ }
printMetaClassInfo(2)
println "MetaClass of Integer is ${Integer.metaClass.class.simpleName}"

@groovy.transform.Immutable
class MyClass {
  String name
}

obj1 = new MyClass("obj1")

printMetaClassInfo(obj1)
println "Adding a method to MyClass metaClass"
MyClass.metaClass.someNewMethod = { -> /* */}
printMetaClassInfo(obj1)

println "obj2 created later"
obj2 = new MyClass("obj2")
printMetaClassInfo(obj2)
```

From the output we can see that Groovy switched the default metaClass it started with.

```
MetaClass of 2 is HandleMetaClass with delegate MetaClassImpl
MetaClass of Integer is HandleMetaClass
Adding a method to Integer metaClass
MetaClass of 2 is HandleMetaClass with delegate ExpandoMetaClass
MetaClass of Integer is ExpandoMetaClass
```

```
MetaClass of MyClass(obj1) is HandleMetaClass with delegate MetaClassImpl
Adding a method to MyClass metaClass
MetaClass of MyClass(obj1) is HandleMetaClass with delegate MetaClassImpl
obj2 created later
MetaClass of MyClass(obj2) is HandleMetaClass with delegate ExpandoMetaClass
```

To begin with, the metaclass that an instance of Integer used was an instance of HandleMetaClass with an underlying instance of MetaClassImpl it *delegated* the calls to. When we added a method to the Integer's metaClass, an instance of ExpandoMetaClass replaced it. When we queried after this addition, we saw that the instance's metaClass delegated to an ExpandoMetaClass instead of the original MetaClassImpl. For our own Groovy classes, the MetaClass used for instances created before the query for metaClass on our class is different from the instances created after we added a method. This behavior has caused some surprises when working with metaprogramming. We can find examples in Section 13.2, *Injecting Methods Using ExpandoMetaClass*, on page 198, and in Section 14.1, *Method Synthesis Using methodMissing*, on page 216. It would be nice if Groovy consistently used ExpandoMetaClass as the default implementation. There are discussions about this change in the Groovy community.

In this chapter, we saw how to intercept methods calls to realize AOP-like method advice capabilities. We'll find this feature useful to mock up methods for the sake of testing, to temporarily replace problem methods, to study alternate implementations for algorithms without having to modify existing code, and more. We can go further with MOP by adding methods dynamically. We'll explore that in the next chapter.

CHAPTER 13

MOP Method Injection

We've heard groans like, "It would be so convenient if the String class supported an encrypt() method." Object-oriented programming is about extensibility, but languages often limit how far we can extend. What if we could open any class and add methods we desire, based on the needs of the application on hand? This would give us unbounded extensibility—make it easy to write expressive code. In Groovy we can do just that, with little effort.

In Groovy we can open a class at any time. That is, we can add methods to classes dynamically, allowing them to change behavior at runtime. Rather than working with a static structure and a predefined set of methods, objects can be agile and flexible, and assimilate behavior based on what's going on in our application. We can add a method based on a certain input we receive, for example. The ability to modify the behavior of our classes is central to metaprogramming and Groovy's metaobject protocol (MOP).

Using Groovy's MOP, we can inject behavior using any of the following:

- Categories
- ExpandoMetaClass
- Mixins

In this chapter we'll discuss MOP facilities for method injection using these techniques.

13.1 Injecting Methods Using Categories

Groovy categories provide a controlled way to inject methods—the effect of method injection is contained within a block of code. A *category* is an object that has the ability to alter a class's MetaClass. It does so within the scope of the block and the executing thread. It reverses the change when we exit the block. Categories can be nested, and we can also apply multiple categories in a single block. We will explore the behavior and use of categories using examples in this section.

Suppose we have a Social Security number in a String or StringBuilder. We want to inject a method toSSN() that will return the string in the format xxx-xx-xxxx. Let's discuss some ways to achieve this.

Say the first plan of attack is to create a class, SSNStringBuilder, that extends StringBuilder and write the method toSSN() in it. Unfortunately, users of StringBuilder won't have this method. It's available only on SSNStringBuilder. Also, we can't extend the *final* class String, so we don't have this method in it.

Instead, we can take advantage of Groovy's categories by creating a class StringUtil and adding a static method toSSN() in it. This method takes one parameter, the target object on which the method is to be injected. The method checks the size of the string and returns a string in the intended format. To use the new method, call a special method, use(), that takes two parameters: a category and a closure code block within which the injected methods are in effect.

The code is as follows:

InjectionAndSynthesisWithMOP/UsingCategories.groovy
```
class StringUtil {
  def static toSSN(self) { //write toSSN(String self) to restrict to String
    if (self.size() == 9) {
      "${self[0..2]}-${self[3..4]}-${self[5..8]}"
    }
  }
}
use(StringUtil) {
  println "123456789".toSSN()
  println new StringBuilder("987654321").toSSN()
}

try {
  println "123456789".toSSN()
} catch(MissingMethodException ex) {
  println ex.message
}
```

Let's exercise the injected methods and view the output:

```
123-45-6789
987-65-4321
No signature of method: java.lang.String.toSSN()
  is applicable for argument types: () values: []
Possible solutions: toSet(), toSet(), toURI(),
  toURL(), toURL(), toURI()
```

The methods we injected are available only within the *use* block. When we called toSSN() outside the block, we got a MissingMethodException.

The calls to toSSN() on instances of String and StringBuilder within the block are routed to the static method in the category StringUtil. toSSN()'s self parameter is assigned to the target instance. Since we did not define the self parameter's type, its type defaults to Object, and toSSN() is available on any object. If we want to restrict the method to only Strings and StringBuilders, we will have to create two versions of toSSN() with explicit parameter types, one with String self and the other with StringBuilder self.

If we use the syntax in the previous example, Groovy categories will require the injection method to be static and take at least one parameter. The first parameter (called self in this example) refers to the method call's target. Any parameters that our injected method takes will trail. The parameters can be any legal Groovy parameters—objects and closures.

Groovy also provides an alternative syntax for categories. Rather than writing static methods, we can ask the Groovy compiler to convert instance methods of a class to static methods with the format discussed previously. We can do this using a special @Category annotation. We can implement the StringUtil using this annotation, like this:

```
InjectionAndSynthesisWithMOP/UsingCategories.groovy
@Category(String)
class StringUtilAnnotated {
  def toSSN() {
    if (size() == 9) {
      "${this[0..2]}-${this[3..4]}-${this[5..8]}"
    }
  }
}
use(StringUtilAnnotated) {
  println "123456789".toSSN()
}
```

The @Category annotation converts the toSSN() method of the newly defined StringUtilAnnotated class to public static toSSN(String self) {...} based on the parameter String we passed to the annotation. The way to use the category is still the same, and the output from the previous code is shown here:

```
123-45-6789
```

The annotated syntax reduces ceremony. We don't have to declare the methods of the category class static, and we don't have to pass the additional first parameter. However, if we use the annotation syntax, we're restricting the method to only the type specified in the parameter (String in this example), and it is not reusable for other types, such as StringUtil, unless we make the parameter more general, like Object.

Let's take a moment to understand the magic that happened when we called use() in the previous examples. Groovy routes the use() method call in our script to the public static Object use(Class categoryClass, Closure closure) method of the GroovyCategorySupport class. This method defines a new scope—a fresh property/method list on the stack for the target objects' MetaClass. It then examines each of the static methods in the given category class and adds its static methods with at least one parameter to the property/method list. Finally, it calls the closure attached. Any method calls from within the closure are intercepted and sent to the implementation provided by the category, if present. This is true for new methods we add and for existing methods that we're intercepting. Finally, upon return from the closure, use() ends the scope created earlier, discarding the injected methods in the category.

Injected methods can take objects and closures as parameters. Here is an example to show that. Let's write another category, FindUtil. Here we are providing a method called extractOnly() that will extract part of a string specified by a closure parameter:

```
InjectionAndSynthesisWithMOP/UsingCategories.groovy
class FindUtil {
  def static extractOnly(String self, closure) {
    def result = ''
    self.each {
      if (closure(it)) { result += it }
    }
    result
  }
}
use(FindUtil) {
  println "121254123".extractOnly { it == '4' || it == '5' }
}
```

The result of the previous call is as follows:

54

Built-in Categories

Groovy comes with a couple of categories to make our lives easier. DOMCategory (see *Using DOMCategory*, on page 144) helps treat DOM objects like JavaBeans and use Groovy path expressions (GPath) (see *Using XMLParser*, on page 146). ServletCategory provides Servlet API objects' attributes using the JavaBeans convention.

We can apply more than one category at the same time—to bring in multiple sets of methods. use() takes either one category or a list of categories. Here's an example to use both the categories we created earlier:

```
InjectionAndSynthesisWithMOP/UsingCategories.groovy
use(StringUtil, FindUtil) {
  str = "123487651"
  println str.toSSN()
  println str.extractOnly { it == '8' || it == '1' }
}
```

The output from the previous code is as follows:

```
123-48-7651
181
```

Even though use() takes a List of Class instances, Groovy is quite happy to accept a comma-separated list of class names. This is because Groovy turns the name of a class, once defined, into a reference to the Class metaobject. String, for example, is equivalent to String.class; in other words, String == String.class.

When we mix multiple categories, the obvious question is about the order in which method calls get resolved when there is a method-name collision. The last category in the list takes the highest precedence.

We can nest calls to use. That is, we can call use() from within a closure of another call to use(). An inner category takes precedence over an outer one.

So far, we've seen how to inject new methods into an existing class. In Chapter 12, *Intercepting Methods Using MOP*, on page 185, we saw ways to intercept existing methods. We can use categories for that, as well. Suppose we want to intercept calls to toString() and pad the response with two exclamation points on each side. Here's how to do that using categories:

```
InjectionAndSynthesisWithMOP/UsingCategories.groovy
class Helper {
  def static toString(String self) {
    def method = self.metaClass.methods.find { it.name == 'toString' }
    '!!' + method.invoke(self, null) + '!!'
  }
}

use(Helper) {
  println 'hello'.toString()
}
```

The output from the previous code is as follows:

```
!!hello!!
```

The Helper's toString() is used to intercept calls to that method on String "hello." However, within this interceptor, we want to call the original toString(). We get access to it using the MetaClass of String.

Using categories for method interception is not as elegant as the other approaches we saw in Chapter 12, *Intercepting Methods Using MOP*, on page 185. We can't use it for filtering all method calls to an instance. We would have to write separate methods for each method we wanted to intercept. Also, when we have nested categories, we can't reach into the interception of the top-level categories. Use categories for method injection, but not for method interception.

Categories provide a nice method-injection protocol. Their effect is contained within the flow of control in the use block. We leave the block, and the injected methods disappear. When we receive a parameter on our methods, we can apply our own categories to that parameter. It feels like we augmented the type of the object we received. When we leave our method, we're returning the object with its class unaffected. We can implement different versions of intercepted/injected methods by using different categories.

Categories have some limitations, however. Their effect is contained within the use() block, and therefore limited to the executing thread. So, injected methods are restricted. Existing methods can be called from anywhere, but injected methods have to be called within the block. If we enter and exit the block multiple times, there is overhead. Each time we enter, Groovy has to examine static methods and add them to a method list in the new scope. At the end of the block, it has to clean up the scope.

If the calls are not too frequent and we want the isolation that controlled method-injection categories provide, we can use them. If those features turn into limitations, we can use ExpandoMetaClass for injecting methods. We'll discuss that next.

13.2 Injecting Methods Using ExpandoMetaClass

To create domain-specific languages (DSLs), we need to be able to add arbitrary methods to different classes and even hierarchies of classes. We need to inject instance methods and static methods, manipulate constructors, and convert a method to a property for the sake of fluency. We'll want these capabilities for creating mock objects to stand in for collaborators. In this section, we'll discuss the techniques to alter and enhance a class's structure.

We can inject methods into a class by adding methods to its MetaClass. The methods we inject are available globally. We're not restricted to a block like in categories. We discussed ExpandoMetaClass in Section 12.2, *Intercepting Methods Using MetaClass*, on page 188. Using ExpandoMetaClass, we can add methods, properties, constructors, and static methods; borrow methods from other classes; and even inject methods into POGOs and POJOs.

Let's look at an example of using ExpandoMetaClass to inject a method called daysFromNow() into Integer. We want the statement 5.daysFromNow() to return the date five days from today. Here's the code:

InjectionAndSynthesisWithMOP/UsingExpandoMetaClass.groovy
```
Integer.metaClass.daysFromNow = { ->
  Calendar today = Calendar.instance
  today.add(Calendar.DAY_OF_MONTH, delegate)
  today.time
}
println 5.daysFromNow()
```

The previous code reports the following:

```
Thu Sep 20 13:16:03 MST 2012
```

In this code, we implemented daysFromNow() using a closure and introduced that into Integer's MetaClass. (To inject the method on any object, add it to MetaClass of Object.) Within the closure, we need to get access to Integer's target object. The delegate refers to the target. See Section 4.9, *Closure Delegation*, on page 86, and Section 7.1, *Using Object Extensions*, on page 128, for discussions on delegates and closures.

We could drop the parentheses at the end of the method call to make it fluent (see Section 19.2, *Fluency*, on page 297) so we can call 5.daysFromNow. However, this requires a little trick (see Section 19.9, *The Parentheses Limitation and a Workaround*, on page 303). We need to set up a property instead of a method because without the parentheses Groovy thinks the method is a property. To define a property named daysFromNow, we have to create a method named getDaysFromNow(), so let's do that:

InjectionAndSynthesisWithMOP/UsingExpandoMetaClass.groovy
```
Integer.metaClass.getDaysFromNow = { ->
  Calendar today = Calendar.instance
  today.add(Calendar.DAY_OF_MONTH, delegate)
  today.time
}
println 5.daysFromNow
```

The output from the previous code is shown next. The call to the property daysFromNow is now routed to the method getDaysFromNow().

```
Thu Sep 20 13:16:03 MST 2012
```

We injected a method on Integer, but what about its cousins Short and Long? The previous method is not available on these classes. We certainly don't want to redundantly add the method to those classes. One idea is to store the closure in a variable and then assign it to these classes, as shown here:

InjectionAndSynthesisWithMOP/MethodOnHierarchy.groovy
```
daysFromNow = { ->
  Calendar today = Calendar.instance
  today.add(Calendar.DAY_OF_MONTH, (int)delegate)
  today.time
}

Integer.metaClass.daysFromNow = daysFromNow
Long.metaClass.daysFromNow = daysFromNow

println 5.daysFromNow()
println 5L.daysFromNow()
```

The output is as follows:

```
Thu Sep 20 13:26:43 MST 2012
Thu Sep 20 13:26:43 MST 2012
```

Alternatively, we can provide the method in the base class Number of Integer. Let's add a method named someMethod() on Number and see whether it's available on Integer and Long:

InjectionAndSynthesisWithMOP/MethodOnHierarchy.groovy
```
Number.metaClass.someMethod = { ->
  println "someMethod called"
}

2.someMethod()
2L.someMethod()
```

The output from the previous code, shown here, confirms that the methods are available on the derived classes:

```
someMethod called
someMethod called
```

We saw how to inject a method into a class hierarchy. We might also want to introduce methods into an interface hierarchy so the methods are available on all classes implementing that interface. We'll take a look at adding a method to an interface in Section 19.11, *ExpandoMetaClass and DSLs*, on page 307.

We can inject static methods into a class, as well, by adding them to the Meta-Class's static property.

Let's add a static method isEven() to Integer:

```
InjectionAndSynthesisWithMOP/UsingExpandoMetaClass.groovy
Integer.metaClass.'static'.isEven = { val -> val % 2 == 0 }

println "Is 2 even? " + Integer.isEven(2)
println "Is 3 even? " + Integer.isEven(3)
```

Exercising the code will produce the following output:

```
Is 2 even? true
Is 3 even? false
```

We figured out how to inject instance methods and static methods. The third type of method a class can have is the constructor. We can add constructors by defining a special property with the name constructor. Since we're adding a constructor and not replacing an existing one, we use the << operator. Use caution; if we use << to override existing constructors or methods, we'll get an error. Let's introduce a constructor for Integer that accepts a Calendar so the instance will hold the number of days in the year as of that date:

```
InjectionAndSynthesisWithMOP/UsingExpandoMetaClass.groovy
Integer.metaClass.constructor << { Calendar calendar ->
    new Integer(calendar.get(Calendar.DAY_OF_YEAR))
}

println new Integer(Calendar.instance)
```

The output from the previous code is as follows:

```
349
```

In the injected constructor we are using the existing constructor of Integer that accepts an int. We could have returned the result of the call to Calendar's get() instead of creating a new instance of Integer. In that case, autoboxing will take care of creating an Integer instance. Make sure that the implementation doesn't recursively call itself, leading to a StackOverflowError.

Instead of adding a new constructor, if we want to replace (or override, though strictly speaking constructors are not overrideable) a constructor, we can do that by using the = operator instead of the << operator.

```
InjectionAndSynthesisWithMOP/UsingExpandoMetaClass.groovy
Integer.metaClass.constructor = { int val ->
  println "Intercepting constructor call"
  constructor = Integer.class.getConstructor(Integer.TYPE)
  constructor.newInstance(val)
}

println new Integer(4)
println new Integer(Calendar.instance)
```

The output from the previous code is as follows:

```
Intercepting constructor call
4
Intercepting constructor call
349
```

From within the constructor override, we can still call the original implementation using reflection. As we can see, other constructors—predefined and injected—are still intact. So, when we create an Integer using a Calendar instance, it uses the constructor injected earlier, which in turn now uses the constructor override we provided previously.

Adding methods to the metaClass using the syntax ClassName.metaClass.method = {...} is simple and convenient if we want to add one or two methods. If we want to add a bunch of methods, the declaration and setup will soon feel like a burden. Groovy provides a way to group these methods into a convenient syntax called an ExpandoMetaClass (EMC) DSL. In the previous example we added a few methods to the Integer metaClass individually. Instead we can group them, as we see next.

InjectionAndSynthesisWithMOP/UsingEMCDSL.groovy

```groovy
Integer.metaClass {
    daysFromNow = { ->
      Calendar today = Calendar.instance
      today.add(Calendar.DAY_OF_MONTH, delegate)
      today.time
    }

    getDaysFromNow = { ->
      Calendar today = Calendar.instance
      today.add(Calendar.DAY_OF_MONTH, delegate)
      today.time
    }

    'static' {
      isEven = { val -> val % 2 == 0 }
    }

    constructor = { Calendar calendar ->
      new Integer(calendar.get(Calendar.DAY_OF_YEAR))
    }

    constructor = { int val ->
      println "Intercepting constructor call"
      constructor = Integer.class.getConstructor(Integer.TYPE)
      constructor.newInstance(val)
    }
}
```

We group methods we'd like to inject into a class's metaClass in a closure we pass to ClassName.metaClass. Wrap the code for each instance method in a closure and assign it to the method name we'd like to inject. To inject static methods, define a closure with the word 'static' prefixed and place our definition for static methods within that closure, as in the example. To define a constructor, we use the word "constructor," as before.

The EMC DSL reduces code noise and makes it easier to see in one place the bunch of methods we're adding to a class.

ExpandoMetaClass is very flexible for injecting methods. We can use the injected methods from anywhere in our application. We invoke injected methods just like we invoke regular methods. With ExpandoMetaClass, we can inject methods into plain old Java objects and plain old Groovy objects (POJOs and POGOs). So, we can enjoy the dynamic capabilities for all classes.

ExpandoMetaClass has some limitations, however. The injected methods are available only for calls within Groovy code. We can't use these methods from within compiled Java code. They can't be used with reflection from Java code, either. For a workaround to invoke them from Java, see Section 10.6, *Calling Groovy Dynamic Methods from Java*, on page 165.

13.3 Injecting Methods into Specific Instances

We saw ways to inject methods into a class dynamically. We can add behavior to specific instances of a class much like how we added behavior to the class. Suppose we receive a Person and, based on a certain condition or state, we want to perform some operations on it. We figure it would be easier to inject a set of reusable methods or utility functions on it; however, we don't want to apply those globally on all Persons. Groovy makes it fairly simple to inject instances with methods.

The MetaClass is per-instance. If we want an instance to have a different behavior than the other objects instantiated from the same class, we inject the methods into the metaClass obtained from the specific instance. Alternatively, we can create an instance of ExpandoMetaClass, add the desired methods to it (including the methods we'd like to preserve from the instance's current metaClass), initialize it (required to indicate the completion of method/property additions), and attach it to the instance we desire to enhance. Here is an example of adding a method to an instance of Person:

```
InjectionAndSynthesisWithMOP/InjectInstance.groovy
class Person {
  def play() { println 'playing...' }
}
```

```
def emc = new ExpandoMetaClass(Person)
emc.sing = { ->
  'oh baby baby...'
}
emc.initialize()

def jack = new Person()
def paul = new Person()

jack.metaClass = emc

println jack.sing()

try {
  paul.sing()
} catch(ex) {
  println ex
}
```

The previous code reports the following:

```
oh baby baby...
groovy.lang.MissingMethodException:
  No signature of method: Person.sing()
  is applicable for argument types: () values: []
Possible solutions: find(), find(groovy.lang.Closure),
  is(java.lang.Object), any(), print(java.lang.Object),
  print(java.io.PrintWriter)
```

We injected sing() on our courageous friend jack by setting the instance of MetaClass on it. We can now invoke sing() on jack. However, if we try to call it on any other instance of Person, it will fail.

We added the method sing() to jack, but if his vocal abilities are like mine, we'd want him to sing only in the bathroom. Groovy provides a convenient way to strip these injected methods off the instances—simply set the metaClass property to null.

InjectionAndSynthesisWithMOP/InjectInstance.groovy
```
jack.metaClass = null
try {
  jack.play()
  jack.sing()
} catch(ex) {
  println ex
}
```

Now that we've removed the method we added, any call to it will fail, as we can see in the following output. Only injected methods are affected—any predefined methods, such as play(), are still available.

```
playing...
groovy.lang.MissingMethodException:
  No signature of method: Person.sing() is applicable ...
```

We took a few steps to create the ExpandoMetaClass, add methods to it, and then initialize it. We don't have to go through that much trouble. We can simply set the methods on the instance's metaClass property, as we see here:

```groovy
class Person {
  def play() { println 'playing...' }
}
def jack = new Person()
def paul = new Person()

jack.metaClass.sing = { ->
  'oh baby baby...'
}
println jack.sing()

try {
  paul.sing()
} catch(ex) {
  println ex
}

jack.metaClass = null
try {
  jack.play()
  jack.sing()
} catch(ex) {
  println ex
}
```

We eliminated quite a bit of noise in this version of code to inject a method. The output from this code is the same as from the previous version.

We can inject multiple methods into an instance individually, like we injected the sing() method, or we can group them using the EMC DSL as we did in Section 13.2, *Injecting Methods Using ExpandoMetaClass*, on page 198. The syntax to group methods is as follows:

```groovy
jack.metaClass {
  sing = { ->
    'oh baby baby...'
  }
  dance = { ->
    'start the music...'
  }
}
```

Using the `ExpandoMetaClass` we can inject methods into both Groovy and Java classes. We can also inject methods into specific instances as we saw in this section. If we want to inject a group of methods into multiple classes, the `ExpandoMetaClass` offers yet another convenience through mixins, as we'll see next.

13.4 Injecting Methods Using Mixins

In Java we can inherit from multiple interfaces, but we're allowed to extend from only one class. Groovy carries the Java semantics, but in addition offers the flexibility to pull in implementations from multiple classes.

The issues surrounding multiple interfaces in languages like C++ prompted the restrictions in Java. When multiple implementations are pulled together, the implementations can collide and cause a great deal of confusion. Groovy avoids those issues by allowing methods to compose and collaborate rather than collide, as we'll see in this section.

Groovy mixins are a runtime capability that we can use to bring in or *mix in* implementations from multiple classes. If we mix a class into another, Groovy will chain the instances of these classes in memory. When we invoke a method, Groovy will first route the call to the mixed-in class, if present. If the method does not exist in that class, the main class will handle it. We can also mix multiple classes into a class, and the last-added mixin takes precedence.

We can mix a class into multiple classes and mix multiple classes into a single class. We'll create a `Friend` class and inject its methods into a few classes as a way to learn about mixins.

InjectionAndSynthesisWithMOP/mixin.groovy
```groovy
class Friend {
  def listen() {
    "$name is listening as a friend"
  }
}
```

The class `Friend` looks like a regular class. It has a `listen()` method to represent the behavior of a friend—a good friend is someone who listens. In this method we simply print the value of the `name` property along with a small message. The property itself is not defined anywhere in this class; the class this is mixed into will provide it.

Here we'll examine the options Groovy provides for mixing in classes.

First, inject the mixin into a `Person` class using the `@Mixin` annotation syntax illustrated in the following code. Alternatively, we could introduce the mixin into the class using a static initializer, like so: class Person { static { mixin Friend} ...}.

```
InjectionAndSynthesisWithMOP/mixin.groovy
@Mixin(Friend)
class Person {
  String firstName
  String lastName
  String getName() { "$firstName $lastName"}
}

john = new Person(firstName: "John", lastName: "Smith")
println john.listen()
```

The @Mixin annotation adds the methods of the class provided as an argument to the annotated class. In this example, the methods of Friend are added to the Person class. We can mix in more than one class by providing a list of class names to the annotation, like so: @Mixin([Friend, Teacher]).

We can invoke the methods injected using the mixin on any instance of the Person class, as in the previous example. The next output shows the person responding to the mixed-in listen method.

```
John Smith is listening as a friend
```

The syntax for a mixin is quite elegant and concise, but the use of an annotation limits it to only the authors of the class. We can't use this approach if we don't have the source code for the class or if we don't want to modify it.

We can mix behavior into existing classes to inject methods into both Groovy and Java classes. We don't need the source code for the class to mix in classes. Let's look at the syntax to dynamically mix in at runtime, create a Dog class—man's best friend—and then mix the Friend class into it.

```
InjectionAndSynthesisWithMOP/mixin.groovy
class Dog {
  String name
}

Dog.mixin Friend

buddy = new Dog(name: "Buddy")
println buddy.listen()
```

Instead of using the annotation, we called the mixin() method on the class and passed it the name of the class we'd like to mix in. The methods of this mixed-in class are now available to all instances of Dog. The next output shows the result of calling the listen() method.

```
Buddy is listening as a friend
```

We saw how to mix in classes using annotation and then using the special mixin() method. We can also selectively mix into specific instances of a class. Write a Cat class to see how this works:

```
InjectionAndSynthesisWithMOP/mixin.groovy
class Cat {
  String name
}

try {
  rude = new Cat(name: "Rude")
  rude.listen()
} catch(ex) {
  println ex.message
}
```

The instance of Cat named rude does not support any of the methods of Friend, as cats in general aren't friendly, at least not the way we expect. So, our attempt to call the listen() method on it ended up...well, *cata*strophic. Check out the output:

```
No signature of method: Cat.listen() is applicable
  for argument types: () values: []
Possible solutions: ...
```

Not all cats are the same, and we can genetically alter specific instances to our liking. In the next example we create another instance of the Cat class, but socks is special; using the mixin() method on its metaClass, we mixed in the Friend behavior.

```
InjectionAndSynthesisWithMOP/mixin.groovy
socks = new Cat(name: "Socks")
socks.metaClass.mixin Friend
println socks.listen()
```

Our newfound friend socks purrs on call to listen().

```
Socks is listening as a friend
```

We've seen how to mix behavior into classes and specific instances. We can mix in multiple behaviors as well, as we'll see next.

13.5 Decorating Classes with Multiple Mixins

When we mix in multiple classes, all of those classes' methods are available in the target class. By default, methods hide on collision. That is, if two or more classes being mixed in have methods with the same name and parameters' signature, the method in the latest-added mixin hides the method that has already been injected.

We can program these methods to instead collaborate in a way that the call can result in a chain of methods calls. Let's create a chain of filters to transform the parameters they receive; we'll see how mixins can provide such a design option.

An application needs different types of writers; the target may be a file, a socket, a web service, a simple string, and so on. We've generalized these into an abstract base class named Writer.

```
InjectionAndSynthesisWithMOP/Filters.groovy
abstract class Writer {
  abstract void write(String message)
}
```

One specific implementation of this class is a StringWriter that writes the given message in the write() method to a StringBuilder.

```
InjectionAndSynthesisWithMOP/Filters.groovy
class StringWriter extends Writer {
  def target = new StringBuilder()

  void write(String message) {
    target.append(message)
  }

  String toString() { target.toString() }
}
```

We can write other implementations of the Writer as we please. Let's use the StringWriter we created to write some stuff into, using the methods shown next.

```
InjectionAndSynthesisWithMOP/Filters.groovy
def writeStuff(writer) {
  writer.write("This is stupid")
  println writer
}

def create(theWriter, Object[] filters = []) {
  def instance = theWriter.newInstance()
  filters.each { filter -> instance.metaClass.mixin filter }
  instance
}
writeStuff(create(StringWriter))
```

In the writeStuff() method we receive an instance of the Writer, write an intelligent message using the write() method, and, right after that, print the content the Writer holds. We use the create() method to create an instance of a specific Writer-derived class provided as the first parameter. We then mix an *optional* list of classes into this instance and return the mixed-in instance.

Here's result of calling the writeStuff() method with an instance of StringWriter without any behavior mixed in:

```
This is stupid
```

We now have the code to merely write the given message to the targets, such as StringWriter or one of the other Writer specializations we could implement. In the meantime, our requirements have evolved and we're asked to write the value of the given parameter in uppercase.

We don't want to change any of the concrete writers, such as StringWriter or the base Writer class. The request to print in uppercase may be a harbinger of more such transformations or filtering to follow, and any change to these classes would render them nonextensible when such requests emerge.

To see how mixins can help achieve a flexible design here, create a separate UpperCaseFilter class:

```
InjectionAndSynthesisWithMOP/Filters.groovy
class UppercaseFilter {

  void write(String message) {
    def allUpper = message.toUpperCase()

    invokeOnPreviousMixin(metaClass, "write", allUpper)
  }
}
```

In UpperCaseFilter's write() method, we transform the given parameter message to all uppercase and invoke a yet-to-be-written method invokeOnPreviousMixin(). This write() method is focused on its piece of responsibility, to filter and transform the message. It then promptly passes the modified message to the next object or filter to its left in the chain of mixins it's part of.

Now we need the invokeOnPreviousMixin() method. We could write this as a standalone method or inject this into the Object base class so it's available as an instance method on any class. In this method we need to fetch the previous mixin in the list of mixins for the instance we're working with.

We use the mixin() method to add one or more mixins to a class or an instance. Groovy provides a property named mixedIn that holds an ordered list of mixins for an instance.

Remember that the mixins we add form a chain leading to the target we mixed into. We can walk the list of mixins to find the mixin or the final target instance ahead in the list, as we'll see next.

InjectionAndSynthesisWithMOP/Filters.groovy

```
Object.metaClass.invokeOnPreviousMixin = {
  MetaClass currentMixinMetaClass, String method, Object[] args ->
  def previousMixin = delegate.getClass()
  for(mixin in mixedIn.mixinClasses) {
    if(mixin.mixinClass.theClass ==
      currentMixinMetaClass.delegate.theClass) break
    previousMixin = mixin.mixinClass.theClass
  }
  mixedIn[previousMixin]."$method"(*args)
}
```

The type of the leftmost instance in the chain is the target instance, which we obtain using delegate.getClass(). We then walk through the list of classes held in the mixedIn LinkedHashSet until we reach the mixin prior to the current mixin. Finally, from the context of a mixin we invoke the given method on the mixin or target ahead in the list.

To see the fruit of these efforts, invoke the writeStuff() method with an instance of StringWriter that's mixed in with an UpperCaseFilter.

InjectionAndSynthesisWithMOP/Filters.groovy

```
writeStuff(create (StringWriter, UppercaseFilter))
```

To the writeStuff() method in the previous call we send an instance of StringWriter chained with an instance of UpperCaseFilter, as in the following figure.

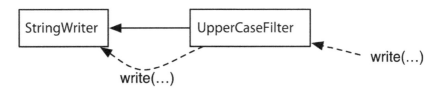

Figure 12—Chaining of the UpperCaseFilter mixin to a StringWriter instance

The call to the write() method on this instance of StringWriter is first routed to the chained instance of UpperCaseFilter. This transforms the given parameter and forwards the call to the target instance, as we can see here:

```
THIS IS STUPID
```

Our efforts to devise this extensible design are quickly rewarded—we've been asked to filter out profanity in the messages being written. Removing profane words can be one hell of a task, so in this first version we will simply remove the word "stupid," which responsible parents often advise their children to avoid.

InjectionAndSynthesisWithMOP/Filters.groovy
```
class ProfanityFilter {
  void write(String message) {
    def filtered = message.replaceAll('stupid', 's*****')
    invokeOnPreviousMixin(metaClass, "write", filtered)
  }
}
```

```
writeStuff(create (StringWriter, ProfanityFilter))
```

The ProfanityFilter's write() method replaces all lowercase occurrences of the offending word and forwards it to the method on the instance to its left in the chain. The target receives the appropriate filtered message, as the next output shows.

```
This is s*****
```

The flexibility and extensibility of our design with mixins shines in the next example, where we chain both the filters in sequence.

InjectionAndSynthesisWithMOP/Filters.groovy
```
writeStuff(create(StringWriter, UppercaseFilter, ProfanityFilter))
writeStuff(create(StringWriter, ProfanityFilter, UppercaseFilter))
```

In the first call we created a chain of UpperCaseFilter followed by the ProfanityFilter. In the second call we reversed the order of these two filters, as in the following figure.

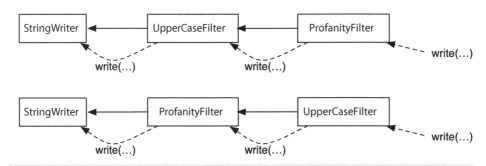

Figure 13—Chaining the **UpperCaseFilter** mixin to a **StringWriter** instance

The order we use to mix in the behavior matters. Method calls propagate right to left in the chain, as we see in the output:

```
THIS IS S*****
THIS IS STUPID
```

Since our kiddie version of the ProfanityFilter looked for only a lowercase word, when the first filter in line was UpperCaseFilter the word escaped in bold. We can use this idiosyncrasy to observe the order of execution.

In this section we saw the power of mixins, how to create them at the class and instance level, and how to design for extensibility by chaining them. If we're design-pattern aficionados, we'll recognize this as an implementation of the Decorator pattern. Dynamically injecting methods into classes is quite powerful, but we're ready to take the Groovy metaprogramming flexibility up a notch with method synthesis. We'll cover that next.

In this chapter, we saw how to intercept and inject methods. Groovy MOP makes it easy to perform AOP-like activities. We can create code that is highly dynamic, and we can create highly reusable code that takes only a few lines. In the next chapter we'll up the dynamic behavior one more notch—we'll see how to synthesize or generate methods dynamically.

CHAPTER 14

MOP Method Synthesis

We can separate ways of adding behavior into two types: injection and synthesis.

We'll use the term *method injection* to refer to the case in which, at code-writing time, we know the names of methods we want to add to one or more classes. With method injection we can add behavior dynamically into classes. We can add to any number of classes a set of reusable methods—like utility functions—that represent a certain functionality. We can inject methods by using categories, by using ExpandoMetaClass, or through the Groovy Mixin facility. We saw these techniques in Chapter 13, *MOP Method Injection*, on page 193.

On the other hand, *method synthesis* will refer to the case in which we want to dynamically figure out the behavior for methods upon invocation. Groovy's invokeMethod(), methodMissing(), and GroovyInterceptable are useful for method synthesis. For example, Grails/GORM synthesizes finder methods like findByFirstName() and findByFirstNameAndLastName() for domain objects upon invocation.

A synthesized method may not exist as a separate method until we call it. When we call a nonexistent method, Groovy can intercept the call, allow our application to implement it on the fly, let us cache that implementation for future invocation, and then invoke it—Graeme Rocher, the creator of Grails, calls it the "Intercept, Cache, Invoke" pattern.

In this chapter, we'll add dynamic methods to both classes and specific instances. Rather than having a prescribed set of methods (and behavior) defined at compile time, we can make classes assimilate behavior based on the execution path through the application or their current state. Our objects will appear to be active and intelligent, acquiring new behavior as they evolve. The techniques we learn in this chapter will help us quickly relate to how dynamic methods are used in Groovy related tools. For example, these techniques will help us see how the persistent objects (GORM) are implemented in Grails and how build tools like Gradle provide such flexible, dynamic behaviors with so little code.

14.1 Method Synthesis Using methodMissing

So far we've been able to inject specific methods into a class or an instance. In this section, we'll synthesize methods with flexible and dynamic names. We don't decide the names ahead of time. In fact, we can let the users of our class decide the names as long as they follow conventions we set. When they call a nonexistent method, we can intercept it and create an implementation on the fly. The implementation is made to measure. In other words, it is created only when the users ask for it.

Method synthesis is implemented in Grails/GORM for domain classes. Suppose we have a domain class (a class that represents information persistent in a database table) Person with a number of fields (columns in the table), such as firstName, lastName, cityOfResidence, and so on. Assume other fields can be added at any time. GORM allows users of our Person class to call methods such as findByFirstName(), findByLastName(), findByFirstNameAndLastName(), or even findByFirstNameAndAge() if age is a field on Person. Our Person class will not have any of these methods precreated. Each method is synthesized at runtime on the first call. In the rest of this chapter, we'll discuss how to synthesize methods in Groovy.

We can intercept calls to nonexistent methods in Groovy by implementing methodMissing(). Likewise, we can intercept access to nonexistent properties by implementing propertyMissing(). Within these methods we can implement the logic for the method or property dynamically. We infer the semantics based on certain conventions we define. For instance, method names that start with *find* might imply a query, method names that start with *update* may imply a save, and so on.

Let's look at an example of synthesizing methods. We are going to turn jack, a boring, all-work-no-play Person, into a multiathlete. He'll play all kinds of sports.

InjectionAndSynthesisWithMOP/MethodSynthesisUsingMethodMissing.groovy
```
class Person {
  def work() { "working..." }

  def plays = ['Tennis', 'VolleyBall', 'BasketBall']

  def methodMissing(String name, args) {
    System.out.println "methodMissing called for $name"
```

```
    def methodInList = plays.find { it == name.split('play')[1]}
    if (methodInList) {
      "playing ${name.split('play')[1]}..."
    } else {
      throw new MissingMethodException(name, Person.class, args)
    }
  }
}

jack = new Person()

println jack.work()
println jack.playTennis()
println jack.playBasketBall()
println jack.playVolleyBall()
println jack.playTennis()

try {
  jack.playPolitics()
} catch(Exception ex) {
  println "Error: " + ex
}
```

The output from the previous code is as follows:

```
working...
methodMissing called for playTennis
playing Tennis...
methodMissing called for playBasketBall
playing BasketBall...
methodMissing called for playVolleyBall
playing VolleyBall...
methodMissing called for playTennis
playing Tennis...
methodMissing called for playPolitics
Error: groovy.lang.MissingMethodException:
  No signature of method: Person.playPolitics()
  is applicable for argument types: () values: []
```

work() is the only predefined domain method on Person. The call to work() went
to that method directly. However, calls to nonexistent methods are routed to
the methodMissing() method. In methodMissing(), we accept a call if it starts with
play and ends with one of the names in the plays array, and we can dynamically modify this list to add other sports we want, giving the impression that
jack is assimilating new skills. If the method is not one we support (such as
playPolitics()), we throw a MissingMethodException.

From the caller's point of view, there is no difference between calling a regular
method and a synthesized method.

The previous implementation is quite dynamic, but there's a catch. Repeated calls to a nonexistent method, such as playTennis(), involve identical performance hits to evaluate. We can make this efficient by injecting the method on first invocation. Again, Graeme Rocher calls this technique the "Intercept, Cache, Invoke" pattern. We're going to synthesize the method on first call, inject it into the MetaClass (cache it), and then invoke this injected method. Here is the code for that:

InjectionAndSynthesisWithMOP/MethodSynthesisUsingMethodMissing2.groovy
```groovy
class Person {
  def work() { "working..." }

  def plays = ['Tennis', 'VolleyBall', 'BasketBall']

  def methodMissing(String name, args) {
    System.out.println "methodMissing called for $name"
    def methodInList = plays.find { it == name.split('play')[1]}

    if (methodInList) {
      def impl = { Object[] vargs ->
          "playing ${name.split('play')[1]}..."
      }

      Person instance = this
      instance.metaClass."$name" = impl //future calls will use this

      impl(args)
    } else {
      throw new MissingMethodException(name, Person.class, args)
    }
  }
}

jack = new Person()
println jack.playTennis()
println jack.playTennis()
```

The output from the previous code shows that the synthesized method is cached on first call:

```
methodMissing called for playTennis
playing Tennis...
playing Tennis...
```

The methodMissing() method is called only on the first call to a supported nonexistent method. The second call (and subsequent ones) to the same supported method goes directly to the implementation (closure) we injected into the instance's MetaClass.

methodMissing and GroovyInterceptable

Unlike invokeMethod(), which is called for all methods on objects that implement GroovyInterceptable, methodMissing() is called only for methods that are nonexistent at the time of call. If an object implements GroovyInterceptable, its invokeMethod() is called (if present). Only if the object forwards control to its MetaClass's invokeMethod() does method-Missing() get called.

In Section 12.2, *Intercepting Methods Using MetaClass*, on page 188, we intercepted calls using GroovyInterceptable. We can mix that with methodMissing() to intercept calls to both existing methods and synthesized methods, as shown here:

InjectionAndSynthesisWithMOP/InterceptingMissingMethods.groovy

```groovy
class Person implements GroovyInterceptable {
  def work() { "working..." }
  def plays = ['Tennis', 'VolleyBall', 'BasketBall']
  def invokeMethod(String name, args) {
    System.out.println "intercepting call for $name"

    def method = metaClass.getMetaMethod(name, args)

    if (method) {
      method.invoke(this, args)
    } else {
      metaClass.invokeMethod(this, name, args)
    }
  }

  def methodMissing(String name, args) {
    System.out.println "methodMissing called for $name"
    def methodInList = plays.find { it == name.split('play')[1]}

    if (methodInList) {
      def impl = { Object[] vargs ->
          "playing ${name.split('play')[1]}..."
        }

      Person instance = this
      instance.metaClass."$name" = impl //future calls will use this

      impl(args)
    } else {
      throw new MissingMethodException(name, Person.class, args)
    }
  }
}
```

```
jack = new Person()
println jack.work()
println jack.playTennis()
println jack.playTennis()
```

The output from the previous code is as follows:

```
intercepting call for work
working...
intercepting call for playTennis
methodMissing called for playTennis
playing Tennis...
intercepting call for playTennis
playing Tennis...
```

Method synthesis is one of the most powerful features of Groovy. This feature is widely used in libraries and frameworks written on top of Groovy, like easyb and GORM. I've used this feature quite a bit to write extensible code for complex business-logic processing with only a few lines of code.

14.2 Method Synthesis Using ExpandoMetaClass

In Section 14.1, *Method Synthesis Using methodMissing*, on page 216, we saw how to synthesize methods. However, if we don't have the privilege of editing the class source file or if the class is not a POGO, that approach will not work. We can synthesize methods using the ExpandoMetaClass in these cases.

We already saw how to interact with MetaClass in Section 12.2, *Intercepting Methods Using MetaClass*, on page 188. Instead of providing an interceptor for a domain method, we implement the methodMissing() method on it. Let's take the Person class (and the boring jack) from Section 14.1, *Method Synthesis Using methodMissing*, on page 216, but instead ExpandoMetaClass, as shown here:

InjectionAndSynthesisWithMOP/MethodSynthesisUsingEMC.groovy
```
class Person {
  def work() { "working..." }
}

Person.metaClass.methodMissing = { String name, args ->
  def plays = ['Tennis', 'VolleyBall', 'BasketBall']

  System.out.println "methodMissing called for $name"
  def methodInList = plays.find { it == name.split('play')[1]}

  if (methodInList) {
    def impl = { Object[] vargs ->
        "playing ${name.split('play')[1]}..."
    }
```

```
    Person.metaClass."$name" = impl //future calls will use this
    impl(args)
  } else {
    throw new MissingMethodException(name, Person.class, args)
  }
}
jack = new Person()
println jack.work()
println jack.playTennis()
println jack.playTennis()

try {
  jack.playPolitics()
} catch(ex) {
  println ex
}
```

The output from the previous code is as follows:

```
working...
methodMissing called for playTennis
playing Tennis...
playing Tennis...
methodMissing called for playPolitics
groovy.lang.MissingMethodException:
  No signature of method: Person.playPolitics()
  is applicable for argument types: () values: []
```

The MetaClass's methodMissing() will take precedence over methodMissing() if present in our class. Methods of our class's MetaClass override the methods in our class.

When we called work() on jack, Person's work() was executed directly. If we call a nonexistent method, however, it is routed to the Person's MetaClass's methodMissing(). In this method we implement logic similar to the solution in Section 14.1, *Method Synthesis Using methodMissing*, on page 216. Repeated calls to supported nonexistent methods do not incur overhead, as we can see in the preceding output for the second call to playTennis(). We cached the implementation on the first call.

In Section 12.2, *Intercepting Methods Using MetaClass*, on page 188, we intercepted calls using ExpandoMetaClass's invokeMethod(). We can mix that with methodMissing() to intercept calls to both existing methods and synthesized methods, as shown here:

InjectionAndSynthesisWithMOP/MethodSynthesisAndInterceptionUsingEMC.groovy
```
class Person {
  def work() { "working..." }
}
```

```
Person.metaClass.invokeMethod = { String name, args ->
  System.out.println "intercepting call for ${name}"

  def method = Person.metaClass.getMetaMethod(name, args)

  if (method) {
    method.invoke(delegate, args)
  } else {
    Person.metaClass.invokeMissingMethod(delegate, name, args)
  }
}

Person.metaClass.methodMissing = { String name, args ->
  def plays = ['Tennis', 'VolleyBall', 'BasketBall']

  System.out.println "methodMissing called for ${name}"
  def methodInList = plays.find { it == name.split('play')[1]}

  if (methodInList) {
    def impl = { Object[] vargs ->
        "playing ${name.split('play')[1]}..."
    }

    Person.metaClass."$name" = impl //future calls will use this

    impl(args)
  } else {
    throw new MissingMethodException(name, Person.class, args)
  }
}

jack = new Person()
println jack.work()
println jack.playTennis()
println jack.playTennis()
```

The output from the previous code is as follows:

```
intercepting call for work
working...
intercepting call for playTennis
methodMissing called for playTennis
playing Tennis...
intercepting call for playTennis
playing Tennis...
```

14.3 Synthesizing Methods for Specific Instances

We saw how to inject methods into specific instances of a class in Section 13.3, *Injecting Methods into Specific Instances*, on page 203. We can dynamically

invokeMethod vs. methodMissing

invokeMethod() is a method of GroovyObject. methodMissing() was introduced later in Groovy and is part of the MetaClass-based method handling. If our objective is to handle calls to nonexistent methods, we implement methodMissing() because this involves low overhead. If our objective is to intercept calls to both existing and nonexistent methods, we use invokeMethod().

synthesize methods into specific instances, as well, by providing the instance(s) with a specialized MetaClass. Here is an example:

InjectionAndSynthesisWithMOP/SynthesizeInstance.groovy
```groovy
class Person {}

def emc = new ExpandoMetaClass(Person)
emc.methodMissing = { String name, args ->
  "I'm Jack of all trades... I can $name"
}
emc.initialize()

def jack = new Person()
def paul = new Person()

jack.metaClass = emc

println jack.sing()
println jack.dance()
println jack.juggle()

try {
  paul.sing()
} catch(ex) {
  println ex
}
```

That code reports the following:

```
I'm Jack of all trades... I can sing
I'm Jack of all trades... I can dance
I'm Jack of all trades... I can juggle
groovy.lang.MissingMethodException:
  No signature of method: Person.sing()
  is applicable for argument types: () values: []
```

This ability to synthesize methods at the instance level is quite useful. We can alter the behavior of a select instance, in tests or particular web requests in a web application, without affecting the related class within the Java Virtual Machine.

The ability to create dynamic methods or behavior on objects based on the current state of the instances and input received is quite powerful and paves the way to creating and implementing highly dynamic DSLs, as we'll see later.

In this chapter, we covered how to synthesize methods. In the next chapter we'll talk about how to create classes dynamically and get a feel for which of the metaprogramming techniques to use.

CHAPTER 15

MOPping Up

We've seen how to synthesize methods, and in this chapter we'll see how to synthesize an entire class. Rather than creating explicit classes ahead of time, we can create classes on the fly, which gives us more flexibility. Delegation is better than inheritance, yet it has been hard to implement in Java. We'll see how Groovy's metaobject protocol (MOP) allows method delegation with only one line of code. We'll wrap up this chapter by reviewing the MOP techniques we've seen in the preceding chapters.

15.1 Creating Dynamic Classes with Expando

In Groovy we can create a class entirely at runtime. Suppose we're building an application that will configure devices. We don't have a clue what these devices are—we know only that devices have properties and configuration scripts. We don't have the luxury of creating an explicit class for each device at coding time. So, we'll want to synthesize classes at runtime to interact with and configure these devices. In Groovy, classes can come to life at runtime based on our command.

The Groovy Expando class gives us the ability to synthesize classes dynamically. It got its name because it is dynamically expandable. We can assign properties and methods to it either at construction time using a Map or at any time dynamically. Let's start with an example to synthesize a class Car. We'll see two ways to create it using Expando.

```
MOPpingUp/UsingExpando.groovy
carA = new Expando()
carB = new Expando(year: 2012, miles: 0)
carA.year = 2012
carA.miles = 10

println "carA: " + carA
println "carB: " + carB
```

The output from the previous code is as follows:

```
carA: {year=2012, miles=10}
carB: {year=2012, miles=0}
```

We created carA, the first instance of Expando, without any properties or methods. We injected the year and miles later. On the other hand, we created carB, the second instance of Expando, with the year and miles initialized at construction time.

We're not restricted to properties. We can define methods as well, and invoke them like we would invoke any method. Let's give that a try. Once again, we can define a method at construction time or inject it later at will:

MOPpingUp/UsingExpando.groovy

```
car = new Expando(year: 2012, miles: 0, turn: { println 'turning...' })
car.drive = {
  miles += 10
  println "$miles miles driven"
}

car.drive()
car.turn()
```

The output from the previous code is as follows:

```
10 miles driven
turning...
```

Suppose we have an input file with some data for Cars, as shown here:

MOPpingUp/car.dat

```
miles, year, make
42451, 2003, Acura
24031, 2003, Chevy
14233, 2006, Honda
```

We can easily work with Car objects without explicitly creating a Car class, as in the following code. We parse the file's content, first extracting the property names. Then we create instances of Expando, one for each line of data in the input file, and populate those instances with values for the properties. We even add a method, in the form of a closure, to compute the average miles driven per year until 2008. Once the objects are created, we can access the properties and call methods on them dynamically. We can also address the methods/properties by name, as shown in the end of the following code.

MOPpingUp/DynamicObjectsUsingExpando.groovy

```
data = new File('car.dat').readLines()

props = data[0].split(", ")
```

```
data -= data[0]

def averageMilesDrivenPerYear = { miles.toLong() / (2008 - year.toLong()) }

cars = data.collect {
  car = new Expando()
  it.split(", ").eachWithIndex { value, index ->
    car[props[index]] = value
  }

  car.ampy = averageMilesDrivenPerYear

  car
}

props.each { name -> print "$name " }
println " Avg. MPY"

ampyMethod = 'ampy'
cars.each { car ->
  for(String property : props) { print "${car[property]} " }
  println car."$ampyMethod"()
}

// You may also access the properties/methods by name
car = cars[0]
println "$car.miles $car.year $car.make ${car.ampy()}"
```

The output from that code is as follows:

```
miles year make  Avg. MPY
42451 2003 Acura 8490.2
24031 2003 Chevy 4806.2
14233 2006 Honda 7116.5
42451 2003 Acura 8490.2
```

We can use Expando whenever we want to synthesize classes on the fly. It's lightweight and flexible. For example, this feature shines when we create mock objects for unit testing, as we'll see in Section 18.8, *Mocking Using Expando*, on page 285.

15.2 Method Delegation: Putting It All Together

We use inheritance to extend a class's behavior. On the other hand, we use delegation to rely upon contained or aggregated objects to provide a class's behavior. We should choose inheritance if we intend to use an object in place of another object, and delegation if we intend to simply use an object. Reserve inheritance for *is-a* or *kind-of* relationships; we should prefer delegation over inheritance most of the time (see *Effective Java [Blo08]*). However, it's easy to program inheritance—it takes only one keyword, extends. But it's hard to pro-gram delegation, because we have to write all those methods that route the call to the contained objects. Groovy helps us do the right thing. By using MOP, we can easily implement delegation with a single line of code, as we'll see in this section.

In the following example, a Manager wants to delegate work to either a Worker or an Expert. We're using methodMissing() and ExpandoMetaClass to realize this. If a method called on the instance of Manager does not exist, its methodMissing() routes it to either the Worker or the Expert, whichever successfully evaluates the respondsTo() method (see Section 11.2, *Querying Methods and Properties*, on page 180). If there are no takers for a method among the delegates and the Manager does not handle the method.

MOPpingUp/Delegation.groovy

```groovy
class Worker {
  def simpleWork1(spec) { println "worker does work1 with spec $spec" }
  def simpleWork2() { println "worker does work2" }
}

class Expert {
  def advancedWork1(spec) { println "Expert does work1 with spec $spec" }
  def advancedWork2(scope, spec) {
    println "Expert does work2 with scope $scope spec $spec"
  }
}

class Manager {
  def worker = new Worker()
  def expert = new Expert()
  def schedule() { println "Scheduling ..." }
  def methodMissing(String name, args) {
    println "intercepting call to $name..."
    def delegateTo = null

    if(name.startsWith('simple')) { delegateTo = worker }
    if(name.startsWith('advanced')) { delegateTo = expert }
    if (delegateTo?.metaClass.respondsTo(delegateTo, name, args)) {
      Manager instance = this
      instance.metaClass."${name}" = { Object[] varArgs ->
          delegateTo.invokeMethod(name, varArgs)
      }
      delegateTo.invokeMethod(name, args)
    } else {
      throw new MissingMethodException(name, Manager.class, args)
    }
  }
}
```

```
peter = new Manager()
peter.schedule()
peter.simpleWork1('fast')
peter.simpleWork1('quality')
peter.simpleWork2()
peter.simpleWork2()
peter.advancedWork1('fast')
peter.advancedWork1('quality')
peter.advancedWork2('prototype', 'fast')
peter.advancedWork2('product', 'quality')
try {
  peter.simpleWork3()
} catch(Exception ex) {
  println ex
}
```

The output from the previous code is as follows:

```
Scheduling ...
intercepting call to simpleWork1...
worker does work1 with spec fast
worker does work1 with spec quality
intercepting call to simpleWork2...
worker does work2
worker does work2
intercepting call to advancedWork1...
Expert does work1 with spec fast
Expert does work1 with spec quality
intercepting call to advancedWork2...
Expert does work2 with scope prototype spec fast
Expert does work2 with scope product spec quality
intercepting call to simpleWork3...
groovy.lang.MissingMethodException:
  No signature of method: Manager.simpleWork3()
  is applicable for argument types: () values: []
```

We figured out a way to delegate calls, but that's a lot of work. We don't want to put in so much effort each time we want to delegate. We can refactor this code for reuse. Let's look at how the refactored code will look when used in the Manager class:

```
MOPpingUp/DelegationRefactored.groovy
class Manager {
  { delegateCallsTo Worker, Expert, GregorianCalendar }

  def schedule() { println "Scheduling ..." }
}
```

That is short and sweet. In the initializer block we call a yet-to-be-implemented method named delegateCallsTo() and send the names of classes to which we want to delegate unimplemented methods. If we want to use delegation in another class, all it takes now is that code in the initialization block. Let's look at the fancy delegateCallsTo() method:

MOPpingUp/DelegationRefactored.groovy
```groovy
Object.metaClass.delegateCallsTo = {Class... klassOfDelegates ->
  def objectOfDelegates = klassOfDelegates.collect { it.newInstance() }
  delegate.metaClass.methodMissing = { String name, args ->
      println "intercepting call to $name..."
      def delegateTo = objectOfDelegates.find {
                    it.metaClass.respondsTo(it, name, args) }
      if (delegateTo) {
        delegate.metaClass."${name}" = { Object[] varArgs ->
            delegateTo.invokeMethod(name, varArgs)
        }
        delegateTo.invokeMethod(name, args)
      } else {
        throw new MissingMethodException(name, delegate.getClass(), args)
      }
    }
}
```

When we call delegateCallsTo() from within our class's instance initializer, it adds a methodMissing() to the class, which is known within this closure as delegate. It takes the Class list provided as an argument to delegateCallsTo() and creates a list of delegates, which are the candidates to implement delegated methods. In methodMissing(), the call is routed to an object among the delegates that will respond to the method. If there are no takers, the call fails. The list of classes given to delegateCallsTo() also represents the order of precedence; the first one has the highest precedence. Of course, we have to see all this in action, so here is the code to exercise the previous example:

MOPpingUp/DelegationRefactored.groovy
```groovy
peter = new Manager()
peter.schedule()
peter.simpleWork1('fast')
peter.simpleWork1('quality')
peter.simpleWork2()
peter.simpleWork2()
peter.advancedWork1('fast')
peter.advancedWork1('quality')
peter.advancedWork2('prototype', 'fast')
peter.advancedWork2('product', 'quality')
println "Is 2008 a leap year? " + peter.isLeapYear(2008)
try {
  peter.simpleWork3()
} catch(Exception ex) {
  println ex
}
```

That code produces the following output:

```
Scheduling ...
intercepting call to simpleWork1...
worker does work1 with spec fast
worker does work1 with spec quality
intercepting call to simpleWork2...
worker does work2
worker does work2
intercepting call to advancedWork1...
Expert does work1 with spec fast
Expert does work1 with spec quality
intercepting call to advancedWork2...
Expert does work2 with scope prototype spec fast
Expert does work2 with scope product spec quality
intercepting call to isLeapYear...
Is 2008 a leap year? true
intercepting call to simpleWork3...
groovy.lang.MissingMethodException:
  No signature of method: Manager.simpleWork3()
  is applicable for argument types: () values: []
```

We can build on this idea to meet our needs. For instance, if we want to mix in some precreated objects, we can send them as an array to the first parameter of delegateCallsTo() and have those objects used along with the ones created from the delegate classes. The previous example shows how we can use Groovy's MOP to implement dynamic behavior such as method delegation.

We can learn from the example in this section how to dynamically change an instance's behavior at runtime. If we like, we can modify the delegation based on the current state of the object. If the delegation is static, that is decided ahead of time and no runtime change is necessary. Then we can simply use the @Delegate annotation (a compile-time metaprogramming technique), as we saw in *Using @Delegate*, on page 41.

15.3 Review of MOP Techniques

We've seen a number of options to intercept, inject, and synthesize methods. In this section, we'll figure out which option is right for us.

Options for Method Interception

We discussed method interception in Chapter 12, *Intercepting Methods Using MOP*, on page 185, and Section 13.1, *Injecting Methods Using Categories*, on page 193. We can use GroovyInterceptable, ExpandoMetaClass, or categories.

If we have the privileges to modify the class source, we can implement GroovyInterceptable on the class we want to intercept method calls. The effort is as simple as implementing invokeMethod().

If we can't modify the class or if the class is a Java class, then we can use ExpandoMetaClass or categories. ExpandoMetaClass clearly stands out in this case because a single invokeMethod() can take care of intercepting any methods of our class. Categories, on the other hand, would require separate methods, one per intercepted method. Also, if we use categories we're restricted by the use() block.

Options for Method Injection

We discussed method injection in Section 13.1, *Injecting Methods Using Categories*, on page 193. We can use categories or ExpandoMetaClass.

Categories compete well with ExpandoMetaClasses for method injection. If we use categories, we can control the location where methods are injected. We can easily implement different versions of method injection by using different categories. We can easily nest and mix multiple categories, as well. The control that categories offer—that method injection takes effect only within the use() blocks and is limited to the executing thread—may also be considered a restriction. If we want to use the injected methods at any location and also want to inject static methods and constructors, ExpandoMetaClass is a better choice. Beware, though, that ExpandoMetaClass is not the default MetaClass in Groovy.

Using the ExpandoMetaClass, we can inject methods into specific instances of a class instead of affecting the entire class.

Options for Method Synthesis

We discussed method injection in Section 14.1, *Method Synthesis Using methodMissing*, on page 216. We can use methodMissing() on a Groovy object or ExpandoMetaClass.

If we have the privileges to modify the class source, we can implement the methodMissing() method on the class for which we want to synthesize methods. We can improve performance by injecting the method on the first call. If we need to intercept our methods at the same time, we can implement GroovyInterceptable.

If we can't modify the class or if the class is a Java class, then we can add the method methodMissing() to the class's ExpandoMetaClass. If we want to intercept method calls at the same time, we can implement invokeMethod() on the ExpandoMetaClass.

Using the ExpandoMetaClass, we can synthesize methods into specific instances of a class instead of affecting the entire class.

Metaprogramming is a key feature that makes Groovy really shine. It gives us the ability to extend programs at runtime and reap the language's dynamic capabilities. The metaprogramming techniques we've picked up so far provide us the ability to alter the behavior of programs at runtime. Groovy also allows us to alter the behavior of a program, just in time, during compilation. We'll talk about compile-time metaprogramming in the next chapter.

CHAPTER 16

Applying Compile-Time Metaprogramming

Unlike some dynamically typed languages with only runtime capabilities, Groovy offers both runtime and compile-time metaprogramming.

With runtime metaprogramming, explored in the previous chapters, we can postpone to runtime the decisions to intercept, inject, and even synthesize methods of classes and instances. For the most part, that's all we need for metaprogramming. Compile-time metaprogramming is an advanced feature that's useful in some special situations and is mostly used by framework/tool writers.

With Groovy we can analyze and modify a program's structure at compile time. This can help make applications highly extensible, allowing us to add new cross-cutting features. For example, we can inspect classes for thread safety, log messages, or perform pre- and postcheck operations in different parts of the code without explicitly modifying the source code.

Compile-time metaprogramming is the magic behind some powerful features and Groovy-based tools. For example, the type checker in Groovy 2 is implemented as an abstract syntax tree (AST) transformation. The elegant unit-testing tool Spock uses this approach to facilitate fluent test cases.[1] It's also used extensively in the code-analysis tool CodeNarc to detect potential errors and code smells.[2] This feature powers Groovy annotations, such as @Delegate and @Immutable that we saw in Section 2.10, *Using Groovy Code-Generation Transformations*, on page 40.

In this chapter we'll cover how to use of compile-time metaprogramming to analyze code structure, to intercept methods, and to inject behavior.

---

1. http://spockframework.org
2. http://codenarc.sourceforge.net

16.1 Analyzing Code at Compile Time

Senior developers and software architects often champion coding standards, and they try to ensure consistent practices are followed in their teams. We can use Groovy's power to automate code review for smells and poor practices. We'll see here how to use compile-time metaprogramming to detect smells.

Naming variables is difficult and takes effort, but using single-letter variables is morally wrong. Rather than manually policing the code, we'll leverage compile-time metaprogramming to inspect poor variable and method names.

AST/CodeAnalysis/smelly.groovy
```
def canVote(a) {
  a > 17 ? "You can vote" : "You can't vote"
}

def p(instance) {
  //code to print the instance...
}
```

The canVote() method takes a parameter a that represents an age, and decides if a person of that age can vote. We'd like to automatically detect the smelly parameter a and the odd name p() for a method in the code. The earliest opportunity to do this is during the compilation of code. Since the code is syntactically correct, the compiler will not detect these smells, but we can. We'll instruct the compiler to fail when compiling this smelly code, even though it's syntactically correct.

Understanding the Code Structure

To detect code smells, we need to traverse the code structure and analyze class names, method names, field names, parameter names, and so on. We could write a parser, but the compiler already parses and analyzes the code, so we might as well ride on that to minimize our efforts.

The Groovy compiler allows us to step into its compilation phases and peek at the AST it's working with. The AST tree structure, which depicts the expressions and statements in a program, is represented using nodes. As the code is compiled, the program's AST is transformed—nodes are inserted, removed, or rearranged. We can review the AST as it evolves during compilation, make changes to it, and instruct the compiler to flag warnings or errors.

canVote() is a short method that just returns the result of the ternary operator, but its AST is quite rich, with fine-grained details (see the following figure).

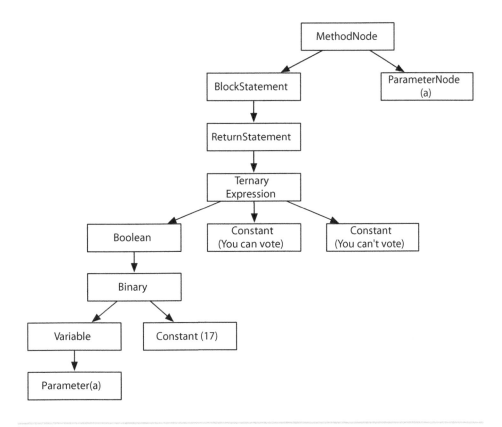

Figure 14—AST for the canVote() method

To use compile-time metaprogramming, we have to understand and work with the AST. This is a complex task, but fortunately we have help. The groovyConsole tool has a nice feature to display the AST of our code. Open the Groovy source code in this tool and select the Script | "Inspect AST" menu item. See the AST structure that the groovyConsole tool displays for the smelly code in Figure 15, *groovyConsole's AST Browser view for the canVote method*, on page 238.

Navigating the Code Structure

Now that we have a grasp of the AST for the smelly code, it's time to navigate through this structure to inspect the code. The AST-transformation application programming interface (API) provided in Groovy makes this task approachable. To navigate the code, let's create a class called CodeCheck and implement the ASTTransformation interface.

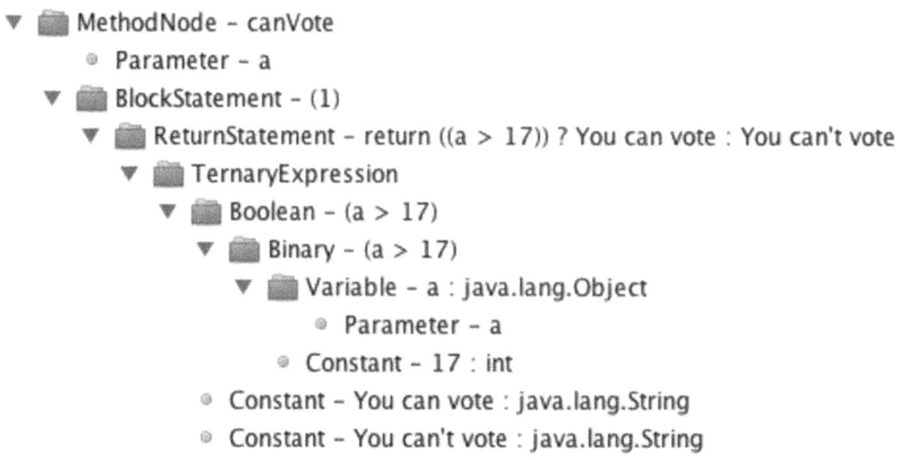

▼ 📁 MethodNode – canVote
    ◦ Parameter – a
  ▼ 📁 BlockStatement – (1)
    ▼ 📁 ReturnStatement – return ((a > 17)) ? You can vote : You can't vote
      ▼ 📁 TernaryExpression
        ▼ 📁 Boolean – (a > 17)
          ▼ 📁 Binary – (a > 17)
            ▼ 📁 Variable – a : java.lang.Object
              ◦ Parameter – a
            ◦ Constant – 17 : int
        ◦ Constant – You can vote : java.lang.String
        ◦ Constant – You can't vote : java.lang.String

Figure 15—groovyConsole's AST Browser view for the canVote() method

AST/CodeAnalysis/com/agiledeveloper/CodeCheck.groovy

```
@GroovyASTTransformation(phase = CompilePhase.SEMANTIC_ANALYSIS)
class CodeCheck implements ASTTransformation {
    void visit(ASTNode[] astNodes, SourceUnit sourceUnit) {
        sourceUnit.ast.classes.each { classNode ->
            classNode.visitContents(new OurClassVisitor(sourceUnit))
        }
    }
}
```

We first tell the compiler, using the annotation GroovyASTTransformation, when we'd like to inspect the AST. The Groovy compiler is multiphased and allows us to intervene between any of the phases: initialization, parsing, conversion, semantic analysis, canonicalization, instruction selection, class generation, output, and finalization. The first logical opportunity to intervene is after the semantic-analysis phase, when the AST is formed. We can intervene in later stages if we want to work with a denser AST. In our example we indicated that the AST transformation must be applied right after the semantic-analysis phase.

As the compiler reaches the indicated phase, it will invoke our class's visit() method, providing it a list of ASTNode instances and a reference to the SourceUnit that represents the code being compiled. Within the visit() method we can iterate over the nodes to inspect various elements, or even alter the nodes if we desire.

In this example, we want to visit the entire structure and look for code smells. The AST-transformation API makes our life simple by providing a visitor named GroovyClassVisitor. For each class node, method node, field node, and so on, the visitor's methods will be invoked with the appropriate node information. Rather than having to step through the hierarchy of classes and methods, we can sit back and take the appropriate actions in these methods, allowing the API to do the tough job of navigation.

Within the visit() method we register an implementation of the GroovyClassVisitor with each of the class nodes we find in the given source unit.

Let's implement the GroovyClassVisitor interface.

AST/CodeAnalysis/com/agiledeveloper/CodeCheck.groovy
```
class OurClassVisitor implements GroovyClassVisitor {
 SourceUnit sourceUnit
 OurClassVisitor(theSourceUnit) { sourceUnit = theSourceUnit }
 private void reportError(message, lineNumber, columnNumber) {
   sourceUnit.addError(new SyntaxException(message, lineNumber, columnNumber))
 }

 void visitMethod(MethodNode node) {
   if(node.name.size() == 1)
     reportError "Make method name descriptive, avoid single letter names",
         node.lineNumber, node.columnNumber

   node.parameters.each { parameter ->
     if(parameter.name.size() == 1)
       reportError "Single letter parameters are morally wrong!",
           parameter.lineNumber, parameter.columnNumber
   }
 }

 void visitClass(ClassNode node) {}
 void visitConstructor(ConstructorNode node) {}
 void visitField(FieldNode node) {}
 void visitProperty(PropertyNode node) {}
}
```

The AST-transformation API will invoke the visitor's methods as it navigates down the class elements of a class—the constructor, fields, methods, and so on. Since we're working to detect smells, in the visitMethod() method we check for a single-letter method name and add an error message if found. The compiler, in turn, reports this error and fails the compilation. Instead of reporting an error, we could report it as a warning.

In addition to detecting a smell in the method name, we examine the method's parameter names. We can expand this to detecting smells in field names, property names, and so on by implementing code in the other methods (such as visitField() and visitProperty()).

We're almost finished with the implementation of our little smell-checker, but we have to help the compiler find and apply this AST transformation during compilation. Here we'll use an approach called *global transformation* in which the transformation can be applied to any piece of code without the need for any special markers on the code. The Groovy compiler will look for such global transformations in each of the JAR files in the classpath. To make this search efficient, it expects us to declare the transformation class name in a special manifest file in the respective JAR files. Here's the content of this special file, manifest/META-INF/services/org.codehaus.groovy.transform.ASTTransformation, for the code-checker example:

```
com.agiledeveloper.CodeCheck
```

Let's summarize what we have seen so far. The manifest file tells the compiler the name of the transformation class. The transformation class is annotated to indicate the compilation phase during which it should be invoked. The transformation class's visit() method takes care of the appropriate actions, using the help of a visitor in this example.

We need to compile the CodeCheck class and create a JAR file with the class files and the manifest file. The Groovy compiler will then apply the smell-checker whenever that JAR file is in the classpath. Let's look at the steps for accomplishing this:

```
$ groovyc -d classes com/agiledeveloper/CodeCheck.groovy
$ jar -cf checkcode.jar -C classes com -C manifest .
$ groovyc -classpath checkcode.jar smelly.groovy
```

Let's run the commands to check for smells in the example we created. The compiler will output a few error messages and fail the compilation due to the detected code smells.

```
org.codehaus.groovy.control.MultipleCompilationErrorsException:
  startup failed:
smelly.groovy: 1: Single letter parameters are morally wrong! @
  line 1, column 13.
   def canVote(a) {
               ^

smelly.groovy: 5: Make method name descriptive, avoid single letter names @
  line 5, column 1.
   def p(instance) {
   ^

2 errors
```

The code inspection happens during the compilation phase, not during the runtime. This takes a bit of getting used to. Play with the example, place some output messages as we navigate the AST, and take time to learn how and when the transformation gets applied.

We saw how to use the AST transformations to inspect code. If we're simply looking for some common code smells, we don't have to go to such lengths. Instead we can use CodeNarc, a Groovy code-quality tool. We can readily use the standard code-quality checks that come with CodeNarc and even extend the rules to check for code smells we desire to keep an eye on. The example we looked at helps us see the power of AST transformations, and can come in handy if we want to perform domain-specific constraint checks in the code.

The power of AST transformation goes well beyond the ability to analyze code. We can intercept method calls and even inject code into programs at compile time, as we will see next.

16.2 Intercepting Method Calls Using AST Transformations

Imagine we're in the middle of developing some banking software and the businesspeople throw a curveball at us. They want every $10K-plus deposit, withdrawal, or transfer involving a checking account to be audited. We want to respond to this request quickly, so let's consider some options.

Our least favorable option would have us hunt for all places we perform a transaction on any checking account. Even with our favorite high-octane integrated development environment, finding and modifying the calls would not be fun. Furthermore, each time we call one of the methods, we would have to remember to perform the audit operation.

Another option is to modify the methods of the checking-account class to perform the additional operation. This is more reliable and requires less effort than the first option. However, it would lead to code duplication and we would have to keep an eye out for the new functions we add.

Chapter 12, *Intercepting Methods Using MOP*, on page 185 covered how to use runtime metaprogramming to intercept method calls. That technique prevails over the preceding two options by a great margin. There will be no code duplication, and the solution extends nicely for addition of new methods in the class. The method interception itself happens only at runtime and incurs a slight penalty during execution. In this section we will learn how to avoid that by intercepting the methods at compile time.

Let's look at the CheckingAccount class with the newly added audit() method. We want this method to be invoked at the appropriate time when one of the other methods of the class is called.

AST/InterceptingCalls/UsingCheckingAccount.groovy
```groovy
class CheckingAccount {
  def audit(amount) { if(amount > 10000) print "auditing..." }
  def deposit(amount) { println "depositing ${amount}..." }
  def withdraw(amount) { println "withdrawing ${amount}..." }
}

def account = new CheckingAccount()
account.deposit(1000)
account.deposit(12000)
account.withdraw(11000)
```

We'll use AST transformations to add a call to the audit() method in each of the CheckingAccount class's methods (except the audit() method itself). Let's write a transformation class for this:

AST/InterceptingCalls/com/agiledeveloper/InjectAudit.groovy
```groovy
@GroovyASTTransformation(phase = CompilePhase.SEMANTIC_ANALYSIS)
class InjectAudit implements ASTTransformation {
    void visit(ASTNode[] astNodes, SourceUnit sourceUnit) {
      def checkingAccountClassNode =
        astNodes[0].classes.find { it.name == 'CheckingAccount' }
      injectAuditMethod(checkingAccountClassNode)
    }
```

The InjectAudit class implements the ASTTransformation interface and provides the necessary visit() method. Using the annotation, we've indicated to the compiler to apply this transformation at the end of the semantic-analysis phase.

Since this is a global transformation, the compiler will trigger it for all nodes it finds in the code being compiled. Within the visit() method we extract, using the find() method, only the node that represents the CheckingAccount class. We then use a helper method, injectAuditMethod(), to take the appropriate action:

AST/InterceptingCalls/com/agiledeveloper/InjectAudit.groovy
```groovy
static void injectAuditMethod(checkingAccountClassNode) {
  def nonAuditMethods =
    checkingAccountClassNode?.methods.findAll { it.name != 'audit' }
  nonAuditMethods?.each { injectMethodWithAudit(it) }
}
```

Using the findAll() method, we extract all methods except audit(). We then add, using the helper method injectMethodWithAudit(), a call to the audit() method at the top of each selected method.

injectMethodWithAudit() is where the real action is. We want to place a call to the audit() method at the beginning. Unfortunately, the steps are not a simple call to the method. We have to create the AST for the method call and insert it into the list of expressions in the method's AST. Let's do that next.

```
AST/InterceptingCalls/com/agiledeveloper/InjectAudit.groovy
    static void injectMethodWithAudit(methodNode) {
      def callToAudit = new ExpressionStatement(
        new MethodCallExpression(
          new VariableExpression('this'),
          'audit',
          new ArgumentListExpression(methodNode.parameters)
        )
      )

      methodNode.code.statements.add(0, callToAudit)
    }
}
```

To understand the AST we created for the method call, use the groovyConsole to view the internal AST structure for the call. This will help you relate to and figure out what needs to be created. A simple call like audit(amount) can take quite a few lines of code and a number of expression objects, as we see in this example.

The MethodCallExpression represents the call at the AST level. Its first argument, the VariableExpression, indicates that the method call is on the current object in the execution context (this). The second argument indicates the name of the method to be called, and the third argument represents the parameter to be passed to the method—in this example, an ArgumentListExpression with the parameters of the containing method node.

Finally, we add the created expression node into the list of statements for the method.

One last step before we can put this transformation to use—we must make it known to the compiler. Create the manifest file META-INF/services/org.code-haus.groovy.transform.ASTTransformation to list the transformation class name.

```
com.agiledeveloper.InjectAudit
```

Let's compile the transformation and JAR it first.

```
$ groovyc -d classes com/agiledeveloper/InjectAudit.groovy
$ jar -cf injectAudit.jar -C classes com -C manifest .
```

The transformation is ready to add the method calls into the CheckingAccount class. To study the effect of this transformation, let's run UsingCheckingAccount.groovy without the transformation:

```
$ groovy UsingCheckingAccount.groovy
```

The calls to the three methods simply result in direct calls:

```
depositing 1000...
depositing 12000...
withdrawing 11000...
```

Let's use the transformation to modify this behavior—include injectAudit.jar in the classpath.

```
$ groovy -classpath injectAudit.jar UsingCheckingAccount.groovy
```

The compiler will recognize the transformation in injectAudit.jar and add calls to the audit() method:

```
depositing 1000...
auditing...depositing 12000...
auditing...withdrawing 11000...
```

Each call to a method on the CheckingAccount class is preceded by a call to audit(), but the transformation will not affect any direct call to the audit() method.

We ran the code as a script, so each time we run it we'll have to include injectAudit.jar in the classpath for this behavior to take effect. We can avoid this by precompiling the code. Simply compile the script using groovyc and include the injectAudit.jar in the classpath. The bytecode created will include the appropriate calls to audit(). We can then run the bytecode using either the groovy or the java command.

We used AST transformation to add method calls at compile time. This can give better performance than runtime metaprogramming. However, it took a lot more effort. Next we will see ways to alleviate that.

Easing the Pain of Creating AST Nodes

A simple call like this.audit() took multiple objects and a few lines of code to create during transformation. For more-complex calls, this is daunting and can quickly dissuade even the most enthusiastic coders. Thankfully, there's an ASTBuilder class to ease the burden.

The ASTBuilder provides three different ways to create an AST subtree: buildFromSpec(), buildFromString(), and buildFromCode(). Let's use these to implement the injectMethodWithAudit() method.

The buildFromSpec() method helps reduce the noisy new operations to instantiate instances of expressions and such. We can simply use a methodCall block to create an instance of MethodCallExpression and a variable to define a variable, as in the next version of injectMethodWithAudit():

AST/EasingThePain/com/agiledeveloper/InjectAudit.groovy

```groovy
    static void injectMethodWithAudit(methodNode) {
      List<Statement> statements = new AstBuilder().buildFromSpec {
        expression {
          methodCall {
            variable 'this'
            constant 'audit'
            argumentList {
              methodNode.parameters.each { variable it.name }
            }
          }
        }
      }
      def callToCheck = statements[0]
      methodNode.code.statements.add(0, callToCheck)
    }
}
```

The creation of the AST is fluent with the buildFromSpec() method, but this approach introduces some complexities. We have to get familiar with the DSL syntax this API expects. We must know the structure of the AST we're creating; this API only makes the syntax fluent.

Rather than going through so much effort, we can simply use the buildFromString() method to get an AST transformation from a piece of code embedded in a string. Let's rewrite the injectMethodWithAudit() method using this builder method.

AST/EasingThePain2/com/agiledeveloper/InjectAudit.groovy

```groovy
    static void injectMethodWithAudit(methodNode) {
      def codeAsString = 'audit(amount)'
      List<Statement> statements = new AstBuilder().buildFromString(codeAsString)

      def callToAudit = statements[0].statements[0].expression
      methodNode.code.statements.add(0, new ExpressionStatement(callToAudit))
    }
}
```

We simply dropped into a string the code we want inserted, and let the builder take care of the rest. The buildFromString() saved us quite a bit of effort in creating the AST, but the result it delivered, unfortunately, is wrapped in a return statement. We have to put forth some effort to extract what we need, and then place that into an ExpressionStatement before inserting it into the target method's statements.

The buildFromString() method has one more problem—it requires us to place the code in a string. Dealing with escape characters and multiple lines of code can get messy. Even with the help of heredocs syntax (see Section 5.3, *Multiline Strings*, on page 103), this can get difficult.

The buildFromCode() prevails over the other approaches. We can write code like we naturally do and place it in to a code block. The buildFromCode() takes this block, like a good samaritan, and produces the AST transformation. Let's use that facility to rewrite the injectMethodWithAudit() method:

AST/EasingThePain3/com/agiledeveloper/InjectAudit.groovy
```
  static void injectMethodWithAudit(methodNode) {
    List<Statement> statements = new AstBuilder().buildFromCode { audit(amount) }
    def callToAudit = statements[0].statements[0].expression
    methodNode.code.statements.add(0, new ExpressionStatement(callToAudit))
  }
}
```

This approach helped us quite a bit:

• We didn't struggle with the AST structure for the code we created.

• We don't have to worry if the AST structure changes in future versions of Groovy; the AstBuilder will evolve with that, sparing us the effort of modifying the AST structure.

• We can clearly see the code we're generating without being lost in the details of the AST structure.

The buildFromCode() method is quite appealing, but there are a few caveats to its use. It does not totally absolve us of the need to know the AST structure. We still have to extract the appropriate parts from the produced AST and know where to place them. There are limits to code we can generate with this facility. The code we generate is carried as is in the transformation's compiled bytecode, and not hidden from prying eyes. Finally, the ASTBuilder's build methods themselves go through a compile-time AST transformation. This restricts us to using Groovy to write the transformation code. Transformations not using the ASTBuilder can be written in any JVM language.

We saw how to intercept methods and add behavior into them at compile time. We can also use this technique to add new methods and fields to classes, as we'll see next.

16.3 Injecting Methods Using AST Transformations

We saw how to inject code into existing methods. We can also inject new methods and fields into classes by using AST transformations. This gives us the full power of aspect-oriented programming (AOP) at compile time without the need for any third-party libraries.

In the Execute Around Method pattern from Section 4.5, *Using Closures for Resource Cleanup*, on page 78, a static method helped create and clean up instances. This method yielded the instance for arbitrary use in between these two operations. Let's implement that pattern using AST transformations. Rather than asking the programmer to implement the use() method by hand, we can create it; the programmer just has to ask—nicely.

The AST transformations we've seen so far in this chapter are all global transformations. They were applied on all pieces of code being compiled. Within the transformations we decided whether to perform some transformation action or simply skip performing any transformation. That approach is nonintrusive; the code being transformed is oblivious to the transformation and doesn't need anything special.

That approach, though, is too sweeping for the problem at hand. We need to know which class to inject the use() method into. This is where the asking *nicely* part comes in. We'll write a local transformation, one that is applied only in select places the programmer marks with special annotations we provide. Local transformations provide an advantage; we don't have to create the extra manifest file.

Let's create that transformation-triggering annotation.

```
AST/EAM/com/agiledeveloper/EAM.groovy
@Retention(RetentionPolicy.SOURCE)
@Target([ElementType.TYPE])
@GroovyASTTransformationClass("com.agiledeveloper.EAMTransformation")

public @interface EAM {
}
```

Using the Target, we specified that this annotation can be placed only on classes. Using the GroovyASTTransformationClass, we indicated to the compiler that the mentioned transformation com.agiledeveloper.EAMTransformation should be applied on any class with this EAM annotation.

We will insert the static use() method into the annotated class. That could sound a bit scary, but writing a local transformation is not much different from writing a global transformation, and we know how to do that. This transformation is invoked only on the targeted class, so we can start working with it directly in the visit() method:

```
AST/EAM/com/agiledeveloper/EAMTransformation.groovy
Line 1  @GroovyASTTransformation(phase = CompilePhase.SEMANTIC_ANALYSIS)
      -  class EAMTransformation implements ASTTransformation {
      -    void visit(ASTNode[] astNodes, SourceUnit sourceUnit) {
      -
      5      astNodes.findAll { node -> node instanceof ClassNode }.each { classNode ->
      -
      -        def useMethodBody = new AstBuilder().buildFromCode {
      -          def instance = newInstance()
      -          try {
     10            instance.open()
      -            instance.with block
      -          } finally {
      -            instance.close()
      -          }
     15        }
      -
      -        def useMethod = new MethodNode(
      -          'use', ACC_PUBLIC | ACC_STATIC, ClassHelper.OBJECT_TYPE,
      -          [new Parameter(ClassHelper.OBJECT_TYPE, 'block')] as Parameter[],
     20          [] as ClassNode[], useMethodBody[0])
      -
      -        classNode.addMethod(useMethod)
      -      }
      -    }
     25  }
```

At the center of the EAM pattern is the special use() method we want to inject into the class. In this method we need to pass the instance to a closure that will use it. The invocation of the closure itself needs to be wrapped in a try-finally block. We'll invoke the cleanup code in the finally block.

Within the visit() method we'll use ASTBuilder's buildFromCode() method to create the use() method and inject it into the class. We'll assume the targeted class has an open() and a close() method. If these methods are absent, a runtime error will result. We can also raise a compile-time error if we desire. For this we'll have to walk the AST node for the class, and if we don't find the methods, report into the errors object as we did in Section 16.1, *Analyzing Code at Compile Time*, on page 236.

In the visit() method, using buildFromCode() we created only the body of the use() method on line number 7. We have to attach that body to a method node that represents the use() method. On line number 17 we create an instance of MethodNode and attach the body to it.

Let's take a closer look at the MethodNode's creation. We indicate the name of the method (use) in the first parameter. We use the second parameter to indicate that the method should have both the public and the static modifiers.

We indicate the return type (Object) using the third parameter. Methods generally take parameters, but our use() method expects a closure. We indicate that, using the fourth parameter, with a list of parameter types and names. The fifth parameter helps indicate the exceptions that a method will throw—none in this example. Finally, the last parameter refers to the body of the created method.

As the last step, let's add this created method to the class using the addMethod() method.

Quite a bit went on in that concise code, and we've devised a way to inject a use() method into any class annotated with our EAM annotation. Let's try this on a class—but first we need to compile the transformation code and bundle it up into a JAR.

```
$ groovyc -d classes \
  com/agiledeveloper/EAM.groovy \
  com/agiledeveloper/EAMTransformation.groovy
$ jar -cf eam.jar -C classes com
```

We'll create a Resource class that can benefit from the method injection.

AST/EAM/resource.groovy
```
@com.agiledeveloper.EAM
class Resource {
  private def open() { print "opened..." }
  private def close() { print "closed" }
  def read() { print "read..." }
  def write() { print "write..." }
}
println "Using Resource"
Resource.use  {
  read()
  write()
}
```

The Resource class has the expected open() and close() methods. We're calling the anticipated use() method. Don't worry that the method doesn't exist; our transformation will inject it because we've marked the Resource class with the EAM annotation. As a final step, lets make sure eam.jar is in the classpath when we compile the Resource class:

```
$ groovy -classpath eam.jar resource.groovy
```

The output from the command should show the EAM pattern in action, implemented through compile-time metaprogramming.

```
Using Resource
opened...read...write...closed
```

In Section 4.5, *Using Closures for Resource Cleanup*, on page 78, we manually created the use() method. In this section we injected that method into the Resource class, or any class annotated with @EAM, using an AST transformation. Once we get a handle on AST transformations, we can do quite powerful transformations with them.

There's a caveat to using such a powerful tool—we need to ensure that the transformations actually behave as we intend. Thankfully, there's some help in this area. Groovy ships with an AST transformation, invoked using the @ASTTest annotation, to help test other AST transformation and assert expectations on various AST nodes.[3]

Metaprogramming is one of the most powerful concepts. When used properly, it can help create highly extensible software. Frameworks like Grails make extensive use of it. Groovy is special because it provides both runtime and compile-time metaprogramming capabilities. In this chapter we discussed how this capability enables us to not just use the language, but also to flex it to inject behavior into existing code.

In Part III of this book we've covered how to create classes, methods, and properties on the fly. We can intercept calls to existing methods and even method that don't exist. The extent to which we use metaprogramming depends on our application-specific needs. We know, however, that when our application demands metaprogramming, we can implement it quickly. In Part IV we'll see several scenarios in which metaprogramming plays a vital role—when unit-testing with mock objects, creating builders, and creating DSLs.

---

3. See http://groovy.codehaus.org/gapi/groovy/transform/ASTTest.html.

Part IV

Using Metaprogramming

CHAPTER 17

Groovy Builders

Builders are internal DSLs that provide ease in working with certain types of problems. For instance, if we need to work with nested, hierarchical structures, such as tree structures, XML, HTML, or JavaScript Object Notation (JSON) representations, we'll find builders to be very useful. They provide syntax that does not tie us tightly to the underlying structure or implementation. They don't replace the underlying implementation; instead, they provide an elegant way to work with it.

We can use Groovy builders for a number of everyday tasks, including working with XML, JSON, HTML, DOM, SAX, Swing, and even Ant. In this chapter we'll look at a few tasks to get a feel for builders. We'll then explore two techniques to create our own builders.

17.1 Building XML

Most of us love to hate XML. Working with XML gets harder as the document size increases, and the tools and API support are not pleasant. My theory is that XML is like a human: it starts out cute when it's small and gets annoying when it becomes bigger.

XML may be a fine format for machines to handle, but it's rather unwieldy to work with directly. No one really wants to do it, but we're forced to. Groovy alleviates this a great deal by making working with XML almost fun.

Let's look at an example of creating XML documents in Groov using a builder:

```
UsingBuilders/UsingXMLBuilder.groovy
bldr = new groovy.xml.MarkupBuilder()
bldr.languages {
  language(name: 'C++') { author('Stroustrup')}
  language(name: 'Java') { author('Gosling')}
  language(name: 'Lisp') { author('McCarthy')}
}
```

This code uses the groovy.xml.MarkupBuilder to create an XML document. When we call arbitrary methods or properties on the builder, it kindly assumes that we're referring to either an element name or an attribute name in the resulting XML document, depending on the context of the call. Here's the output from the previous code:

```
<languages>
  <language name='C++'>
    <author>Stroustrup</author>
  </language>
  <language name='Java'>
    <author>Gosling</author>
  </language>
  <language name='Lisp'>
    <author>McCarthy</author>
  </language>
</languages>
```

We called a method named languages() that does not exist on the instance of the MarkupBuilder class. Instead of rejecting it, the builder smartly assumed our call meant to define a root element of our XML document, which is a rather nice assumption.

The closure attached to that method call now provides an internal context. Domain-specific languages are context-sensitive. Any nonexistent method called within that closure is assumed to be a child element name. If we pass Map parameters to the method calls (such as language(name: value)), they're treated as attributes of the elements. Any single parameter value (such as author(value)) indicates element content instead of attributes. We can study the previous code and the related output to see how the MarkupBuilder inferred the code.

In the previous example, the data that went into the XML document was hard-coded, and the builder wrote to the standard output. In a real project, neither of those conditions may be usual. We'd want data to come from a collection that can be populated from a data source or input stream. Also, we'd want to write the XML content out to a Writer instead of to the standard output.

The builder can readily attach to a Writer that it can take as a constructor argument. So, attach a StringWriter to the builder. The data may come from arbitrary source—for example, from a database. See Section 9.3, *Database Select*, on page 153. The following example takes data from a map, creates an XML document, and writes the document into a StringWriter:

UsingBuilders/BuildXML.groovy
```groovy
langs = ['C++' : 'Stroustrup', 'Java' : 'Gosling', 'Lisp' : 'McCarthy']

writer = new StringWriter()
bldr = new groovy.xml.MarkupBuilder(writer)
bldr.languages {
  langs.each { key, value ->
      language(name: key) {
        author (value)
    }
  }
}
println writer
```

The output from the previous code is as follows:

```
<languages>
  <language name='C++'>
    <author>Stroustrup</author>
  </language>
  <language name='Java'>
    <author>Gosling</author>
  </language>
  <language name='Lisp'>
    <author>McCarthy</author>
  </language>
</languages>
```

The MarkupBuilder is quite adequate for small to medium-sized documents. However, if our document is large (a few megabytes), we can use StreamingMarkup-Builder, which is kinder in terms of memory usage. Let's rewrite the previous example using the StreamingMarkupBuilder, but to add some flavor let's also include namespaces and XML comments:

UsingBuilders/BuildUsingStreamingBuilder.groovy
```groovy
langs = ['C++' : 'Stroustrup', 'Java' : 'Gosling', 'Lisp' : 'McCarthy']

xmlDocument = new groovy.xml.StreamingMarkupBuilder().bind {
  mkp.xmlDeclaration()
  mkp.declareNamespace(computer: "Computer")
  languages {
    comment << "Created using StreamingMarkupBuilder"
    langs.each { key, value ->
      computer.language(name: key) {
        author (value)
      }
    }
  }
}
println xmlDocument
```

Here's the output this new version produces:

```
<?xml version="1.0"?>
<languages xmlns:computer='Computer'>
  <!--Created using StreamingMarkupBuilder-->
    <computer:language name='C++'>
      <author>Stroustrup</author>
    </computer:language>
    <computer:language name='Java'>
      <author>Gosling</author>
    </computer:language>
    <computer:language name='Lisp'>
      <author>McCarthy</author>
    </computer:language>
</languages>
```

Using StreamingMarkupBuilder, we can declare namespaces, XML comments, and so on, using the builder-support property mkp. Once we define a namespace, to associate an element with a namespace we can use the dot notation on the prefix, such as computer.language, where computer is a prefix.

The builders for XML make the syntax easy and elegant. We don't have to deal with the XML's pointy syntax to create XML documents. Creating XML output is easy. If we need to create JSON output instead, Groovy still has us covered, as we'll see next.

17.2 Building JSON

Groovy provides convenient solutions for when we're creating web services and need to generate a JSON-formatted object.[1] Its as simple as sending our instances to groovy.json.JsonBuilder's constructor, and the builder takes care of the rest. We can write the generated JSON format to a Writer by calling the writeTo() method, as in the next example.

UsingBuilders/BuildJSON.groovy
```groovy
class Person {
  String first
  String last
  def sigs
  def tools
}
john = new Person(first: "John", last: "Smith",
  sigs: ['Java', 'Groovy'], tools: ['script': 'Groovy', 'test': 'Spock'])
bldr = new groovy.json.JsonBuilder(john)
writer = new StringWriter()
bldr.writeTo(writer)
println writer
```

---

1.   http://www.json.org/

The builder uses the field names and their values as keys and values in the JSON format, as we can see here:

```
{"first":"John","last":"Smith","tools":{"script":"Groovy","test":"Spock"},
  "sigs":["Java","Groovy"]}
```

It took little effort to produce that output. Customizing the output takes only a few more steps. We can use the builder's fluency to create the desired output, as in the next example.

```
UsingBuilders/BuildJSON.groovy
bldr = new groovy.json.JsonBuilder()
bldr {
  firstName john.first
  lastName john.last
  "special interest groups" john.sigs
  "preferred tools" {
    numberOfTools john.tools.size()
    tools john.tools
  }
}
writer = new StringWriter()
bldr.writeTo(writer)
println writer
```

Rather than using the instance's property names directly, we chose different names for each property. We can also add new properties, such as numberOfTools in this example. The builder uses the DSL syntax we provided to create the next output:

```
{"firstName":"John","lastName":"Smith",
  "special interest groups":["Java","Groovy"],
  "preferred tools":{"numberOfTools":2,
    "tools":{"script":"Groovy","test":"Spock"}}}
```

The JsonBuilder can produce JSON-formatted output from JavaBeans, hashmaps, and lists. The JSON output is stored in memory, and we can later write it to a stream or use it for further processing. Instead of storing it in memory, if we want to directly stream the data as it's created, we can use StreamingJsonBuilder instead of the JsonBuilder.

Groovy also makes it easy to go the opposite direction; it provides a JsonSlurper to create a HashMap from JSON data. We can use the parseText() method to read the JSON data contained in a String. We can also read JSON data from a Reader, or a file, using the parse() method.

Let's parse the JSON output we created in the earlier example, now stored in the file person.json.

UsingBuilders/person.json
{"first":"John","last":"Smith","tools":{"script":"Groovy","test":"Spock"},
  "sigs":["Java","Groovy"]}

The JSON data, rather than coming from a file, may come from a web service. Once we get access to the data stream, as an instance of Reader, we can pass it to the parse() method like in the next example. Here's the code to process the JSON data in the file person.json:

UsingBuilders/ParseJSON.groovy
```groovy
def sluper = new JsonSlurper()
def person = sluper.parse(new FileReader('person.json'))

println "$person.first $person.last is interested in ${person.sigs.join(', ')}"
```

We create a FileReader to fetch the data in the file. We then pass that to the parse() method, which returns an instance of HashMap with the data. We can either use the key-values in the HashMap as is, or create a Groovy object from the data—remember, we can create Groovy objects using the HashMap as constructor parameter (see Section 2.2, *JavaBeans*, on page 19).

Here's the output from the code to parse the JSON data:

```
John Smith is interested in Java, Groovy
```

It took little effort to parse the JSON data; the convenience is embarrassingly simple.

Groovy builders go beyond merely producing data; they can even make our Swing programming experience pretty hip, as we'll see next.

17.3 Building Swing

The elegance of builders is not restricted to XML structure. Groovy provides a builder for creating Swing applications, as well. When working with Swing, we need to perform some mundane tasks such as creating components (like buttons), registering event handlers, and so on. Typically, to implement an event handler we write an anonymous inner class and, in the implementation handler methods, we receive parameters (such as ActionEvent) even if we don't care for them. SwingBuilder, along with Groovy closures, eliminates the drudgery.

We can use the builder-provided nested or hierarchical structure to create a container (such as JFrame) and its components (such as buttons, text boxes, and so on). Initialize components by using Groovy's flexible key-value pair initialization facility. Defining an event handler is trivial. Simply provide it a closure. We're building the familiar Swing application, but we will find the code is smaller than when writing this in Java. This helps us quickly make changes, experiment, and get feedback. We're still using the underlying Swing API, but the syntax is a lot different. We're using the Groovy idioms to talk to Swing.[2] Now let's create a Swing application using the SwingBuilder class:

```
UsingBuilders/BuildSwing.groovy
bldr = new groovy.swing.SwingBuilder()

frame = bldr.frame(
  title: 'Swing',
  size: [50, 100],
  layout: new java.awt.FlowLayout(),
  defaultCloseOperation:javax.swing.WindowConstants.EXIT_ON_CLOSE
) {
  lbl = label(text: 'test')
  btn = button(text: 'Click me', actionPerformed: {
    btn.text = 'Clicked'
    lbl.text = "Groovy!"
    } )
}

frame.show()
```

The following figure shows the output from the previous code.

Figure 16—A little Swing application created using SwingBuilder

We initialized an instance of JFrame, assigned its title, size, and layout, and set the default close operation, all in one simple statement. This is equivalent to five separate statements in Java. Also, registering the event handler was as simple as providing a closure to the actionPerformed property of button (for JButton). This eliminated the effort in Java to create an anonymous inner class and implement the actionPerformed() method with the ActionEvent parameter. Sure, there was a lot of syntax sugar, but the elegance and reduced code size make it easier to work with the Swing API.

The SwingBuilder builder shows us Groovy's expressive power. It's charming, but to create any nontrivial Swing application, check out the Griffon project.[3]

---

2. http://blog.agiledeveloper.com/2007/05/its-not-languages-but-their-idioms-that.html
3. http://griffon.codehaus.org

Griffon is a framework built on Groovy to create Swing applications using the convention-over-configuration principle. It not only eases the pain of creating the GUI, but also can take care of handling events properly across multiple threads.

17.4 Custom Builder Using Metaprogramming

As we saw earlier, builders provide a way to create an internal DSL for specialized complex tasks that use a nested or hierarchical structure or format. When working with a specialized task in our application, we can check for a builder that can solve the problem. If we don't find any builders, we can create our own.

We have two ways to create a custom builder: take the entire effort on our shoulders by using Groovy's metaprogramming capabilities, as we'll see in this section, or use the BuilderSupport (Section 17.5, *Using BuilderSupport*, on page 262) or FactoryBuilderSupport (Section 17.6, *Using FactoryBuilderSupport*, on page 266) Groovy provides.

To help understand the BuilderSupport's benefits, let's build a to-do list. Here's the code that's using the builder we'll create:

UsingBuilders/UsingTodoBuilder.groovy
```
bldr = new TodoBuilder()

bldr.build {
  Prepare_Vacation (start: '02/15', end: '02/22') {
    Reserve_Flight (on: '01/01', status: 'done')
    Reserve_Hotel(on: '01/02')
    Reserve_Car(on: '01/02')
  }
  Buy_New_Mac {
    Install_QuickSilver
    Install_TextMate
    Install_Groovy {
      Run_all_tests
    }
  }
}
```

The output of that code (once we create the ToDoBuilder) is as follows:

```
To-Do:
 - Prepare Vacation [start: 02/15 end: 02/22]
  x Reserve Flight [on: 01/01]
  - Reserve Hotel [on: 01/02]
  - Reserve Car [on: 01/02]
 - Buy New Mac
  - Install QuickSilver
```

```
    - Install TextMate
    - Install Groovy
      - Run all tests
```

Completed tasks are marked with an x. Indentation shows nesting of tasks, and task parameters such as start date appear next to the tasks' names.

In the preceding DSL for the to-do list, we created item names such as "Reserve Car" using an underscore instead of a space so we can use them as method names in Groovy. The only known method is build(). The rest of the methods and properties are handled using methodMissing() and propertyMissing(), as shown next.

UsingBuilders/TodoBuilder.groovy
```groovy
class TodoBuilder {
  def level = 0
  def result = new StringWriter()
  def build(closure) {
    result << "To-Do:\n"
    closure.delegate = this
    closure()
    println result
  }

  def methodMissing(String name, args) {
    handle(name, args)
  }

  def propertyMissing(String name) {
    Object[] emptyArray = []
    handle(name, emptyArray)
  }

  def handle(String name, args) {
    level++
    level.times { result << " "}
    result << placeXifStatusDone(args)
    result << name.replaceAll("_", " ")
    result << printParameters(args)
    result << "\n"

    if (args.length > 0 && args[-1] instanceof Closure) {
      def theClosure = args[-1]
      theClosure.delegate = this
      theClosure()
    }

    level--
  }
```

```
def placeXifStatusDone(args) {
  args.length > 0 && args[0] instanceof Map &&
    args[0]['status'] == 'done' ? "x " : "- "
}

def printParameters(args) {
  def values = ""
  if (args.length > 0 && args[0] instanceof Map) {
    values += " ["
    def count = 0
    args[0].each { key, value ->
      if (key == 'status') return
      count++
      values += (count > 1 ? " " : "")
      values += "${key}: ${value}"
    }
    values += "]"
  }

  values
}
}
```

The result is mostly standard straightforward Groovy code with a good use of metaprogramming. When a nonexistent method or property is called, we assume it's an item. To check whether a closure is attached, we test the last parameter in args, obtained using the index -1. We then set the delegate of the presented closure to the builder and invoke the closure to traverse down the nested tasks.

Creating our own custom builder is not difficult. Do not hesitate to do it. For very complex cases with deeper nesting and extensive use of Map and regular parameters, BuilderSupport, which we'll see next, will help.

17.5 Using BuilderSupport

We saw how to create a custom builder using methodMissing() and propertyMissing(). If we're creating more than one builder, chances are we'll refactor some of the method-recognition code into a common base class. That has been done for us; the class BuilderSupport provides convenience methods that recognize the node structure. Instead of writing the logic to deal with the structure, we simply listen to calls as Groovy traverses the structure and takes appropriate action. Extending the abstract class BuilderSupport feels like working with Simple API for XML (SAX)—a popular event-driven parser for XML. It triggers events on a handler we provide as it parses and recognizes elements and attributes in a document.

Let's look at what the builder does before we explore how to implement it:

```groovy
UsingBuilders/UsingTodoBuilderWithSupport.groovy
bldr = new TodoBuilderWithSupport()

bldr.build {
  Prepare_Vacation (start: '02/15', end: '02/22') {
    Reserve_Flight (on: '01/01', status: 'done')
    Reserve_Hotel(on: '01/02')
    Reserve_Car(on: '01/02')
  }
  Buy_New_Mac {
    Install_QuickSilver
    Install_TextMate
    Install_Groovy {
      Run_all_tests
    }
  }
}
```

The output of running the previous code (once we create the ToDo-BuilderWithSupport) is as follows:

```
To-Do:
 - Prepare Vacation [start: 02/15 end: 02/22]
 x Reserve Flight [on: 01/01]
 - Reserve Hotel [on: 01/02]
 - Reserve Car [on: 01/02]
 - Buy New Mac
  - Install QuickSilver
  - Install TextMate
  - Install Groovy
   - Run all tests
```

BuilderSupport expects us to implement two specific sets of methods: setParent() and overloaded versions of createNode(). Optionally, we can implement other methods, such as nodeCompleted(). Remember the options we have in calling a method; we can call a method with no parameters (foo()), call it with some value (foo(6)), call it with a map (foo(name:'Brad', age: 12)), or call it with a map and a value (foo(name:'Brad', age:12, 6)). BuilderSupport provides four versions of createNode(), one for each of the previous options. The appropriate method is called when we invoke methods on an instance of the builder. The setParent() is called to let the builder's author know the parent of the current node being processed. Whatever we return from createNode() is considered to be a node, and the builder support sends that as a parameter to nodeCompleted().

The BuilderSupport does not handle missing properties like it handles missing methods. However, we can still use the propertyMissing() method to handle those cases.

Next we'll look at the code for the TodoBuilderWithSupport that extends the Builder-Support. The format for the to-do list chosen supports only method calls with no parameters (and properties) and method calls that accept a Map. So in the versions of createNode() that accept an Object parameter, we throw an exception to indicate an invalid format. In the other two versions of that method, and in the propertyMissing() method, we keep track of the level of nesting by incre-menting the level variable. We decrement level in the nodeCompleted() method since that's called when we leave a nesting level. In the createNode() methods, we return the name of the node created so we can compare that to nodeComplet-ed() to find when we exit the topmost node build. If our need is more complex, we can return an instance of our own custom class that represents different nodes. If we need to perform some other operations when a node is creat-ed—such as attaching the child nodes to their parent—we can use setParent() to do so. This method receives the instances of Node for the parent and the child—the node object that createNode() returns when those nodes are created. The rest of the code for the TodoBuilderWithSupport is processing the nodes found and creating the desired output.

Play around to see which methods get called in which order. We can insert a few println statements in these methods to understand the sequence.

UsingBuilders/TodoBuilderWithSupport.groovy
```groovy
class TodoBuilderWithSupport extends BuilderSupport {
  int level = 0
  def result = new StringWriter()
  void setParent(parent, child) {}

  def createNode(name) {
    if (name == 'build') {
      result << "To-Do:\n"
      'buildnode'
    } else {
      handle(name, [:])
    }
  }
  def createNode(name, Object value) {
    throw new Exception("Invalid format")
  }

  def createNode(name, Map attribute) {
    handle(name, attribute)
  }
```

```
def createNode(name, Map attribute, Object value) {
  throw new Exception("Invalid format")
}

def propertyMissing(String name) {
  handle(name, [:])
  level--
}

void nodeCompleted(parent, node) {
  level--
  if (node == 'buildnode') {
    println result
  }
}

def handle(String name, attributes) {
  level++
  level.times { result << " "}
  result << placeXifStatusDone(attributes)
  result << name.replaceAll("_", " ")
  result << printParameters(attributes)
  result << "\n"
  name
}

def placeXifStatusDone(attributes) {
   attributes['status'] == 'done' ? "x " : "- "
}

def printParameters(attributes) {
  def values = ""
  if(attributes.size() > 0) {
    values += " ["
    def count = 0
    attributes.each { key, value ->
      if (key == 'status') return
      count++
      values += (count > 1 ? " " : "")
      values += "${key}: ${value}"
    }
    values += "]"
  }
  values
}
}
```

We saw the advantage of refactoring common code into the BuilderSupport, but we can take advantage of another level of refactoring, as we'll see next.

17.6 Using FactoryBuilderSupport

We'll use FactoryBuilderSupport if we're working with well-defined node names such as button, checkbox, label, and so on, in the SwingBuilder. The BuilderSupport we saw in Section 17.5, *Using BuilderSupport*, on page 262, is good for working with hierarchical structures. However, it's not convenient for dealing with different types of nodes. Suppose we have to work with twenty different node types. Our implementation of createNode() will get complicated. Based on the node name, we'll create different nodes, which leads to a messy switch statement. Chances are we'll quickly lean toward an abstract factory (see *Design Patterns: Elements of Reusable Object-Oriented Software [GHJV95]*) approach to create these nodes. That's what FactoryBuilderSupport does. Based on the node name, it delegates the node creation to different factories. We only have to map the names to the factories.

FactoryBuilderSupport was inspired by the SwingBuilder, and later SwingBuilder was modified to extend FactoryBuilderSupport instead of BuilderSupport. Let's see an example of implementing and using a builder that extends FactoryBuilderSupport.

Let's create a builder named RobotBuilder that we can use to create and program a robot. As a first step, think about how we will use it:

UsingBuilders/UsingFactoryBuilderSupport.groovy
```
def bldr = new RobotBuilder()

def robot = bldr.robot('iRobot') {
    forward(dist: 20)
    left(rotation: 90)
    forward(speed: 10, duration: 5)
}

robot.go()
```

We'd like RobotBuilder produce this output from the code:

```
Robot iRobot operating...
move distance... 20
turn left... 90 degrees
move distance... 50
```

Now let's look at the builder. RobotBuilder extends FactoryBuilderSupport. In its instance initializer, we map the node names robot, forward, and left to the corresponding factories using FactoryBuilderSupport's registerFactory() method. That's all we have in RobotBuilder. FactoryBuilderSupport does all the hard work of traversing the hierarchy of nodes and calling the appropriate factory. The factories and nodes, which we'll see soon, take care of the rest of the details:

UsingBuilders/UsingFactoryBuilderSupport.groovy
```groovy
class RobotBuilder extends FactoryBuilderSupport {
  {
    registerFactory('robot', new RobotFactory())

    registerFactory('forward', new ForwardMoveFactory())

    registerFactory('left', new LeftTurnFactory())
  };
}
```

The classes Robot, ForwardMove, and LeftTurn, shown next, represent the nodes robot, forward, and left, respectively.

UsingBuilders/UsingFactoryBuilderSupport.groovy
```groovy
class Robot {
  String name
  def movements = []

  void go() {
    println "Robot $name operating..."
    movements.each { movement -> println movement }
  }
}

class ForwardMove {
  def dist
  String toString() { "move distance... $dist"}
}

class LeftTurn {
  def rotation
  String toString() { "turn left... $rotation degrees"}
}
```

The Robot has a name property and an ArrayList of movements. Its go() method traverses each movement and prints the details. The other two classes, ForwardMove and LeftTurn, have one property each. Even though the class ForwardMove has only one property named dist, in the code shown at the beginning of this section we've assigned the properties speed and duration for the left node. The factory will take care of working with these properties, as we'll see soon.

Take a look at the factories. FactoryBuilderSupport relies upon the Factory interface. This interface provides methods to control the creation of a node, handles setting the node's properties, sets the parent and child relationships between nodes, and determines whether the node is a leaf node. A default implementation of Factory called AbstractFactory is already provided in Groovy, as shown here:

```
// Excerpt of AbstractFactory.java - part of Groovy
public abstract class AbstractFactory implements Factory
{
    public boolean isLeaf() { return false; }

    public boolean onHandleNodeAttributes(FactoryBuilderSupport builder,
            Object node, Map attributes ) { return true; }

    public void onNodeCompleted(FactoryBuilderSupport builder,
            Object parent, Object node ) { }

    public void setParent(FactoryBuilderSupport builder,
            Object parent, Object child ) { }

    public void setChild(FactoryBuilderSupport builder,
            Object parent, Object child ) { }
}
```

The default implementation of isLeaf() returns false to indicate that the node can have a closure with subnodes. onHandleNodeAttributes() is a good place for any special handling of properties, like the duration and speed of the left node. Within this method, we'll remove from attributes any property that we have processed. If we return true, as in the default implementation, FactoryBuilderSupport will populate into the node instance any remaining properties found in attributes. The method onNodeCompleted() is called when the node-processing is completed, and we can perform any final operations at the end of node creation. setParent() is called on the child node's factory, so we can set up any parent-child relationship. Similarly, setChild() is called on the parent node's factory. The only method from Factory that's missing in AbstractFactory is the newInstance() method responsible for instantiating the actual node.

In this example, we need a factory for Robot, ForwardMove, and LeftTurn. The classes RobotFactory, ForwardMoveFactory, and LeftTurnFactory are as follows:

UsingBuilders/UsingFactoryBuilderSupport.groovy
```
class RobotFactory extends AbstractFactory {
  def newInstance(FactoryBuilderSupport builder, name, value, Map attributes ) {
      new Robot(name: value)
  }

  void setChild(FactoryBuilderSupport builder, Object parent, Object child) {
    parent.movements << child
  }
}

class ForwardMoveFactory extends AbstractFactory {
  boolean isLeaf() { true }
```

```
    def newInstance(FactoryBuilderSupport builder, name, value, Map attributes ) {
      new ForwardMove()
    }

    boolean onHandleNodeAttributes(FactoryBuilderSupport builder,
                Object node, Map attributes) {
      if (attributes.speed && attributes.duration) {
          node.dist = attributes.speed * attributes.duration
          attributes.remove('speed')
          attributes.remove('duration')
      }

      true
    }
}

class LeftTurnFactory extends AbstractFactory {
  boolean isLeaf() { true }

    def newInstance(FactoryBuilderSupport builder, name, value, Map attributes) {
      new LeftTurn()
    }
}
```

In each factory's newInstance() method, we instantiate the appropriate node. In the RobotFactory's setChild(), we add the movement node to Robot's list of movements. Since forward and left are leaf nodes, in their factory's isLeaf() method we return true. We support the forward node's special properties in the ForwardMoveFactory's onHandle-NodeAttributes().

Let's take a minute to see the benefit of the isLeaf() methods. In the following example, we provide a closure to the forward node:

UsingBuilders/UsingFactoryBuilderSupport.groovy
```
def robotBldr = new RobotBuilder()
robotBldr.robot('bRobot') {
  forward(dist: 20) { }
}
```

The FactoryBuilderSupport class realizes that the forward node can't have nested levels and so rejects it, as shown here:

```
java.lang.RuntimeException: 'forward' doesn't support nesting.
```

The implementation of a builder to deal with multiple well-defined nodes is a lot cleaner with FactoryBuilderSupport than with BuilderSupport. FactoryBuilderSupport provides other convenience methods to intercept the life cycle of node creation, so we can take more control of the node traversal if we want. For example, we can use the preInstantiate() method to perform actions before the factory creates a node, or we can override postNodeCompletion() to perform actions after a node is completed. If we need to perform other tasks while building, we can use convenience methods such as FactoryBuilderSupport's getCurrentNode() and getParentNode() to easily work with the hierarchical structure we're creating. Refer to http://groovy.codehaus.org/FactoryBuilderSupport as well as http://groovy.codehaus.org/api/groovy/util/FactoryBuilderSupport.html for more details on the builder and its API.

In this chapter we saw how to use Groovy's builders. Builders provide us with DSL syntax to perform mundane tasks such as creating an XML or HTML document. We can use one of the builders provided or create a custom builder. And if we create a useful builder, we should consider contributing it to the community!

We've come to realize and appreciate Groovy's power. The dynamic nature of Groovy does require discipline on our part—automated testing of our code is important. In the next chapter we'll explore how to write unit tests.

CHAPTER 18

Unit Testing and Mocking

Unit testing is essential for metaprogramming. However weak the checks performed by a compiler might be in a statically typed language, we don't have even that level of support in a dynamic language. That's why unit testing is necessary in dynamic languages. (See *Test Driven Development: By Example [Bec02], Pragmatic Unit Testing in Java with JUnit [TH03]*, and *JUnit Recipes: Practical Methods for Programmer Testing [Rai04]*.) Although we can easily take advantage of dynamic capabilities and metaprogramming in these languages, we have to take the time to make sure our program is doing what we expect and not just what we typed.

There has been greater awareness of unit testing among developers in the past few years; unfortunately, though, the adoption is not sufficient. Unit testing is the software equivalent of exercise: most developers would agree that it improves the health of their code, yet they offer various excuses for not doing it.

Unit testing is not only critical for programming Groovy; it is also easy and fun in Groovy. JUnit is built into Groovy. Metaprogramming capabilities make it easy to create mock objects. Groovy also has a built-in mock library. Let's take a look at how we can use Groovy to unit-test our Java and Groovy applications.

18.1 Code in This Book and Automated Unit Tests

Unit testing is not something I provide as abstract advice. I have used automated unit tests for all the code in this book because I'm working with an evolving language. Groovy features change, its implementations change, bugs are being fixed, new features are added, and so on. I updated my installation of Groovy on my machines quite a few times as I was writing these chapters and code examples. If an update broke an example because of a feature or implementation change, I needed to know that quickly without expending too much effort. Furthermore, I refactored several examples in this book as the writing process progressed. The automated unit tests helped me sleep better at night because I knew the examples were still working as expected after a language update or my own refactoring.

Soon after writing the first few examples, I decided to take a break and figure out a way to automate the testing of all examples while keeping them independent and in isolated files. Some of the examples are functions and some are stand-alone programs or scripts. Groovy's metaprogramming capabilities, along with the ExpandoMetaClass and the ability to load and execute scripts, made it a breeze to create and execute automated unit tests.

It took me a couple of hours to figure out how to get going. Whenever I write a new example, I spend about two minutes at most to get the test written for that example. That effort and time paid off within the first few days, and several times since. A handful of examples failed as I upgraded Groovy. More important, these tests gave me assurance that the other examples are working and are valid.

These tests benefitted me in at least five ways:

- Furthered my understanding of Groovy features

- Raised questions in the Groovy users mailing list that helped fix a few Groovy bugs

- Helped find and fix an inconsistency in Groovy documentation

- Assisted me in ensuring that all my examples are valid and working well with the most recent version of Groovy

- Gave me the courage to refactor any example at will, at any time, with full confidence that my refactoring improved the code structure but did not affect its intended behavior

18.2 Unit Testing Java and Groovy Code

Thanks to excellent Java-Groovy integration, we can use any Java-based testing framework and mock-objects framework (such as EasyMock, JMock, and Mockito), with Groovy. We're not limited to those, however. When we install Groovy, we automatically get a unit-testing framework built on JUnit. We can use it to test any code on the Java Virtual Machine—our Java code, our Groovy code, and so on. We simply extend our test class from GroovyTestCase and implement our test methods, and we're all set to run our tests.

Unit Tests Must be FAIR

When we write unit tests, keep in mind that the tests must be FAIR—that is, *fast, automated, isolated, and repeatable.*

Tests must be fast. As we evolve our code and refactor, we want to quickly get feedback that the code continues to meet our expectations. If the tests are slow, our developers won't bother to run them. We want a very quick edit-and-run cycle.

Tests must be automated. Manual testing is tiring, is error-prone, and will take our time away from important tasks. Automated tests are like angels on our shoulder—they watch quietly as we write code, and whisper in our ears if our code violates set expectations. They give us early feedback if our code begins to fall apart. We'd probably agree that we'd much rather hear from our computer that our code sucks than from our coworker. Automated unit tests make us look good and dependable. When we say we're done, we know our code works as intended.

Tests must be isolated. If we get 1,031 compilation errors, the usual problem is a missed semicolon, right? That's not helpful; there's no point in one small error cascading into several reported errors. We want a direct correlation between a creeping bug or error and a failed test case. That will help us identify and fix problems quickly rather than being overwhelmed by large failed tests. Isolation ensures that one test does not leave behind a residual state that may affect another test. It also lets us run the tests in any order and to run all tests, one test, or a select few.

Tests must be repeatable. We must be able to run the tests any number of times and get deterministic predictable results. The worst kind of test is the one that fails on one run and passes on a following run without there having been any change to the code. Threading issues may bring about some of these problems. As another example, if a test inserts into a database data with unique column constraints, then a subsequent run of the same test without our having cleaned up the database will fail. If the test rolls back the transaction, though, this will not happen and the test will be repeatable. The repeatability of tests is key to staying sane while we rapidly evolve our application code.

Let's start by writing a simple test:

UnitTestingWithGroovy/ListTest.groovy
```groovy
class ListTest extends GroovyTestCase {
  void testListSize() {
    def lst = [1, 2]
    assertEquals "ArrayList size must be 2", 2, lst.size()
  }
}
```

Even though Groovy is dynamically typed, JUnit expects the return type of test methods to be void. That means we had to explicitly use void instead of def when defining the test method. Groovy's optional typing helped here. To run the preceding code, we simply execute it like we would execute any Groovy program. Type the following command:

```
groovy ListTest
```

The output is as follows:

```
.
Time: 0.006

OK (1 test)
```

If we're familiar with JUnit, we already understand this output—one test was executed successfully.

If we're fans of the red-green bar, we can run our unit tests from within our integrated development environment (IDE) if it supports running tests.

We can also call junit.swingui.TestRunner's run() method and provide it our Groovy test's class name to run our tests within the Swing GUI to see those red-green bars.

We may use any of the assert methods we're already familiar with in JUnit. Groovy adds more assert methods for our convenience: assertArrayEquals(), assertLength(), assertContains(), assertToString(), assertInspect(), assertScript(), and shouldFail(), to mention a few.

When writing unit tests, consider writing three types of tests: positive, negative, and exception. Positive tests help ensure that code is behaving as expected. We can call this the test of the happy path. For instance, we deposit $100 in an account and check whether the balance went up by $100. Negative tests check whether the code handles, as we expect, the failure of preconditions, invalid input, and so on. We make the deposit amount negative and see what the code does. What if the account is closed? Exception tests help determine whether the code is throwing the correct exceptions and behaving as expected when exceptional situations arise. What if an automated withdrawal kicks in after an account is closed? Trust me on this one—I had a creative bank that provided just that scenario. Situations like this can benefit from exception tests.

Thinking about tests in these terms helps us think through the logic we're implementing. We not only handle code that implements logic, but also consider boundary conditions and edge cases that often get us into trouble.

We can easily implement positive tests by using the asserts provided in Groovy and JUnit. Implementing negative tests and exception tests requires a bit more work, but Groovy has a mechanism to help, as we'll see in Section 18.3, *Testing for Exceptions*, on page 277.

Even if our main project code is in Java, we should consider writing our test code in Groovy. Since Groovy is lightweight, we'll find it is easier, faster, and more fun to write our tests in Groovy while our main code is in Java. This is also a nice way to practice Groovy on our Java-intense projects.

Suppose we have a Java class Car, as shown in the following code, in the src directory. Also suppose that we've compiled it into the classes directory using javac.

Car.class resides in the classes/com/agiledeveloper directory.

UnitTestingWithGroovy/src/Car.java
```java
// Java code
package com.agiledeveloper;

public class Car
{
  private int miles;
  public int getMiles() { return miles; }
  public void drive(int dist)
  {
    miles += dist;
  }
}
```

We can write a unit test for this class in Groovy, and we don't have to compile the test code to run it. Here are a few positive tests for the Car. These tests are in a file named CarTest.groovy in the test directory.

UnitTestingWithGroovy/test/CarTest.groovy
```groovy
class CarTest extends GroovyTestCase
{
  def car
  void setUp()
  {
    car = new com.agiledeveloper.Car()
  }
  void testInitialize()
  {
    assertEquals 0, car.miles
  }
  void testDrive()
  {
    car.drive(10)
    assertEquals 10, car.miles
  }
}
```

The setUp() method and the corresponding tearDown() method (not shown in the previous example) sandwich each test call. We can initialize objects in setUp() and optionally clean up or reset in tearDown(). These two methods help avoid duplicating code and, at the same time, help isolate the tests from each other.

To run this test, type the command groovy -classpath classes test/CarTest. We should see the following output:

```
..
Time: 0.003

OK (2 tests)
```

This output shows that two tests were executed, and both, not surprisingly, passed. The first test confirmed that the Car has zero miles on the odometer to begin with, and driving a certain distance increases the miles by that distance. Now write a negative test:

```
void testDriveNegativeInput()
{
  car.drive(-10)
  assertEquals 0, car.miles
}
```

We set the parameter for drive() to the negative value -10. We decide that the Car must ignore our drive request in this case, so we expect the miles value to be unchanged. The Java code, however, does not handle this condition. It modifies the miles without checking the input parameter. When we run the previous test, we will get an error:

```
...F
Time: 0.004
There was 1 failure:
1) testDriveNegativeInput(CarTest)
   junit.framework.AssertionFailedError:
   expected:<0> but was:<-10>

...

FAILURES!!!
Tests run: 3,  Failures: 1,  Errors: 0
```

This output shows that the two positive tests passed, but the negative test failed. We can now fix the Java code to handle this case property and rerun our test. We can see that using Groovy to test our Java code is pretty straightforward and simple.

18.3 Testing for Exceptions

Let's now look at writing exception tests. We could wrap the method in try-catch. If the method throws the expected exception—that is, if we land in the catch block—all is well.

If the code does not throw any exceptions, we'll invoke fail() to indicate the failure of the test, as shown here:

```
UnitTestingWithGroovy/ExpectException.groovy
try {
  divide(2, 0)
  fail "Expected ArithmeticException ..."
} catch(ArithmeticException ex) {
  assertTrue true // Success
}
```

The previous code is Java-style JUnit testing and works with Groovy, as well. However, Groovy makes it easier to write exception tests by providing a method shouldFail() that elegantly wraps up the boilerplate code. Let's use that to write an exception test:

```
UnitTestingWithGroovy/ExpectException.groovy
shouldFail { divide(2, 0) }
```

The method shouldFail() accepts a closure. It invokes the closure in a guarded try-catch block. If no exception is thrown, it raises an exception by calling the fail() method. If we're interested in catching a specific exception, we can specify that information to the shouldFail() method:

```
UnitTestingWithGroovy/ExpectException.groovy
shouldFail(ArithmeticException) { divide(2, 0) }
```

In this case, shouldFail() expects the closure to throw ArithmeticException. If the code throws ArithmeticException or something that extends it, it is happy. If some other exception is thrown or if no exception is thrown, then shouldFail() fails. We can take advantage of Groovy's flexibility with parentheses (see Section 19.9, *The Parentheses Limitation and a Workaround*, on page 303) and write the previous call as follows:

```
UnitTestingWithGroovy/ExpectException.groovy
shouldFail ArithmeticException, { divide(2, 0) }
```

18.4 Mocking

It's very hard, if not impossible, to unit-test a large piece of code that has dependencies. (What's large? Any code we can't see entirely without scrolling down in an editor—no, don't make the font size smaller now.) One advantage of unit testing is that it forces us to make the unit of code smaller. Smaller code is cohesive code. It also forces us to decouple the code from its surroundings. This means less coupling. Higher cohesion and lower coupling are qualities of good design. In this section we'll discuss ways to deal with dependencies; ways to unit-test code with dependencies are covered in the rest of this chapter.

Coupling comes in two forms: code that depends on our code, and code that our code depends on. We need to address both types before we can unit-test our code.

The code being tested has to be separated or decoupled from where it is used within an application. Suppose we have some logic in a button handler within the GUI. It's hard to unit-test that logic. Therefore, we have to separate this code into a method for unit testing.

Suppose we have logic that depends heavily on some resource. That resource may be slow to respond, expensive to use, unpredictable, or currently under development. Thus, we have to separate that dependency from our code before we can effectively unit-test our code. Stubs and mocks help.

Stubs vs. Mocks

A *stub* stands in for a real object. It simply reciprocates the coached expected response when the code being tested calls it. The response is set up to satisfy the needs for the test to pass. A *mock* object does a lot more than a stub. It helps us ensure our code is interacting with its dependencies, the collaborators, as expected. It can keep track of the sequence and number of calls our code makes on the collaborator it stands in for. It ensures proper parameters are passed in to method calls. Whereas stubs verify state, mocks verify behavior. When we use a mock in our test, it verifies not only the state, but also the behavior of our code's interaction with its dependencies.[a]

Groovy provides support for creating both stubs and mocks, as we will see in Section 18.10, *Mocking Using the Groovy Mock Library*, on page 289.

---

a.   In the article "Mocks Aren't Stubs," Martin Fowler discusses the difference between stubs and mocks. See http://martinfowler.com/articles/mocksArentStubs.html.

The code that our code depends on is called a *collaborator*—our code collaborates with it to get its work done. The collaborator can be a component, an object, a layer, or a subsystem. It can be local, it can be kept internal to our object, it can be passed in as a parameter, or it can even be remote. Our object can't function without the collaborator. However, we need to replace it for the sake of testing.

A mock stands in for the collaborator (see *Stubs vs. Mocks*, on page 278). It does not do any real work. It simply gives expected responses to calls from our code in order to get the test working.

When running our application, we want our code to depend on the real object it needs (the collaborator). This is also the case when integration-testing our application. However, when unit-testing, we want our code to instead depend on the mock. So, we need to find a way to switch our code's dependency between a mock and a real object.

In a statically typed language like Java, we can achieve this by using an interface, as shown in the following figure. Frameworks in Java—such as EasyMock, JMock, Mockito, and so on—make mocking easier. Some of these even let us mock a class without having to create an interface. Using a proxy-based mechanism, they intercept our call and route our request to the mock instead of the real dependent object.

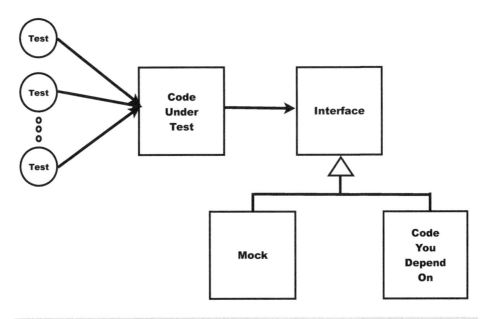

Figure 17—Mocking during unit testing

Groovy's dynamic nature and metaprogramming capabilities provide a great advantage in this area. There are a few ways to create mocks in Groovy. We can use the following:

- Method overriding
- Categories
- ExpandoMetaClass
- Expando
- Map
- Groovy's mock library

In the rest of this chapter we'll discuss techniques to create and use mocks in Groovy.

18.5 Mocking by Overriding

Suppose we have a class that depends on a method that does some significant work and takes substantial time and resources, such as the following myMethod():

UnitTestingWithGroovy/com/agiledeveloper/CodeWithHeavierDependencies.groovy

```
package com.agiledeveloper

public class CodeWithHeavierDependencies
{
  public void myMethod()
  {
    def value = someAction() + 10

    println(value)
  }

  int someAction()
  {
    Thread.sleep(5000) // simulates time consuming action

    return Math.random() * 100 // Simulated result of some action
  }
}
```

We're interested in testing myMethod() (which belongs to CodeWith-HeavierDependencies). However, the method depends on someAction(), which simulates a time- and resource-consuming operation.

If we simply write a unit test for myMethod(), it will be slow. There is yet another problem—we can't assert any result from a call to myMethod(), because it doesn't return anything. Instead, it prints a value to standard output. We need to figure out a way to capture what it prints and assert that. So, we have a method that is hard to test; it's slow and complicated.

To address these concerns, let's override the offending methods:

```groovy
import com.agiledeveloper.CodeWithHeavierDependencies

class TestCodeWithHeavierDependenciesUsingOverriding extends GroovyTestCase {
  void testMyMethod() {
    def testObj = new CodeWithHeavierDependenciesExt()

    testObj.myMethod()

    assertEquals 35, testObj.result
  }
}

class CodeWithHeavierDependenciesExt extends CodeWithHeavierDependencies {
  def result

  int someAction() { 25 }

  def println(text) { result = text }
}
```

Let's run the code and ensure the test passes fairly quickly:

```
.
Time: 0.015

OK (1 test)
```

In this code, we created a new class called CodeWithHeavierDependenciesExt—a mock—that extends class CodeWithHeavierDependencies. In this class, we mocked the methods someAction and println(). (We took advantage of the Groovy convention to call System.out.println() simply as println() and provided a local implementation of println()—savvy?) Run this test code and see how it succeeds. There's no delay in running the test and no messing with standard output.

We are still testing behavior, but by making the non-deterministic behavior deterministic, we're able to write an assertion against it. We must find a clever way to mock out dependencies so we can focus on unit-testing the behavior of our code.

In the previous example, we tested a method in a Groovy class. We can use this approach for testing Java classes, as well.

Mocking by overriding our own Java methods, such as someAction(), is not a problem. However, unlike the Groovy code that called println(), the Java code would be calling System.out.println(). So, creating a println() in our derived class, which is the mock, will not help. However, we can extend PrintStream and replace

System.out. Let's look at a Java class that is equivalent to the previous Groovy code we tested:

UnitTestingWithGroovy/com/agiledeveloper/JavaCodeWithHeavierDependencies.java
```java
package com.agiledeveloper;

public class JavaCodeWithHeavierDependencies
{
  public int someAction()
  {
    try
    {
      Thread.sleep(5000); // simulates time consuming action
    }
    catch(InterruptedException ex) {}

    return (int) (Math.random() * 100); // Simulated result of some action
  }

  public void myMethod()
  {
    int value = someAction() + 10;

    System.out.println(value);
  }
}
```

The Groovy code to test the preceding Java code is as follows:

UnitTestingWithGroovy/TestJavaByOverride.groovy
```groovy
import com.agiledeveloper.JavaCodeWithHeavierDependencies

class TestCodeWithHeavierDependenciesUsingOverriding extends GroovyTestCase {
  void testMyMethod() {
    def testObj = new ExtendedJavaCode()

    def originalPrintStream = System.out
    def printMock = new PrintMock()
    System.out = printMock

    try {
      testObj.myMethod()
    } finally { System.out = originalPrintStream }

    assertEquals 35, printMock.result
  }
}

class ExtendedJavaCode extends JavaCodeWithHeavierDependencies {
  int someAction() { 25 }
}
```

```groovy
class PrintMock extends PrintStream {
  PrintMock() { super(System.out) }

  def result

  void println(int text) { result = text }
}
```

The output from the preceding code is the expected result of the test passing:

```
.
Time: 0.026

OK (1 test)
```

myMethod(), the method being tested, is part of the JavaCodeWithHeavierDependencies class. We created ExtendedJavaCode to extend that class and overrode the some-Action() method. We also created a class PrintMock that extends PrintStream, and assigned an instance of that to System.out. This helps intercept the call to System.out.println() and directs it to our mock implementation.

18.6 Mocking Using Categories

In Section 13.1, *Injecting Methods Using Categories*, on page 193, we discussed how categories provide controlled aspect-oriented programming (AOP) in Groovy. In this section we'll see how we can use it to create mocks.

UnitTestingWithGroovy/TestUsingCategories.groovy
```groovy
import com.agiledeveloper.CodeWithHeavierDependencies

class TestUsingCategories extends GroovyTestCase {
  void testMyMethod() {
    def testObj = new CodeWithHeavierDependencies()

    use(MockHelper) {
      testObj.myMethod()

      assertEquals 35, MockHelper.result
    }
  }
}

class MockHelper {
  def static result

  def static println(self, text) { result = text }

  def static someAction(CodeWithHeavierDependencies self) { 25 }
}
```

MockHelper has two static methods, one for each method we want to mock—someAction() and println(). Within the test, we ask the category to intercept calls to methods and substitute these two methods where appropriate by using use(MockHelper). This is much like the advice used in AOP.

The output from the previous bit of code is a reassuring pass of the test, as shown here:

```
.
Time: 0.027

OK (1 test)
```

Categories are useful only with Groovy code. They does not help to mock methods called from within compiled Java code.

The override approach we saw in Section 18.5, *Mocking by Overriding*, on page 280, is useful for both Java and Groovy code. However, we can't use that approach if the class being tested is final. The categories approach shines in that case.

18.7 Mocking Using ExpandoMetaClass

We can intercept method calls in Groovy in another way, using the ExpandoMetaClass (see Section 13.2, *Injecting Methods Using ExpandoMetaClass*, on page 198, and Section 13.3, *Injecting Methods into Specific Instances*, on page 203). We don't have to create a separate class as in the two approaches we've seen so far. Instead, we can create a closure for each method we want to mock, and set that into MetaClass for the instance being tested. Let's look at an example.

Create a separate instance of ExpandoMetaClass for the instance being tested. This MetaClass will carry the mock implementation of collaborator methods.

In this example, shown in the following code, we create a closure for mocking println() and set that into an instance of ExpandoMetaClass for ClassWithHeavierDependencies in line number 7. Similarly, we create a closure for mocking someAction() in line number 8. The advantage of creating an instance of ExpandoMetaClass specifically for the instance under test is that we don't globally affect the metaclass for CodeWithHeavierDependencies. That means if we have other tests, the method we mock does not affect them (remember to keep the tests isolated from each other).

UnitTestingWithGroovy/TestUsingExpandoMetaClass.groovy

```
Line 1  import com.agiledeveloper.CodeWithHeavierDependencies

    -   class TestUsingExpandoMetaClass extends GroovyTestCase {
```

```
     void testMyMethod() {
 5     def result
       def emc = new ExpandoMetaClass(CodeWithHeavierDependencies, true)
       emc.println = { text -> result = text }
       emc.someAction = { -> 25 }
       emc.initialize()
10
       def testObj = new CodeWithHeavierDependencies()
       testObj.metaClass = emc

       testObj.myMethod()
15
       assertEquals 35, result
     }
   }
```

The output from the previous code confirms that the test passes:

```
.
Time: 0.031

OK (1 test)
```

In this example, when myMethod() calls the two methods println() and someAction(),
the ExpandoMetaClass intercepts those calls and routes them to our mock
implementation. Again, this is similar to the advice in AOP.

Creating the mock, setting up its expectations, and using it in the test are
nicely contained within the test method in this case. There are no additional
classes to create. If we have other tests, we can create in a concise way the
mocks necessary to satisfy those tests.

This approach of using ExpandoMetaClass for mocking is useful only with Groovy
code. It does not help to mock methods called from within precompiled Java
code.

18.8 Mocking Using Expando

So far in this chapter we've looked at ways to mock instance methods called
from within another instance method. In the rest of this chapter, we'll look
at ways to mock other objects on which our code depends.

Let's take a look at an example. Suppose the methods of a class we're interested in testing depend on a File. That'll make it hard to write a unit test. We
need to find ways to mock this object so our unit tests on our class can be
quick and automated:

```groovy
package com.agiledeveloper

public class ClassWithDependency
{
  def methodA(val, file)
  {
    file.write "The value is ${val}."
  }
  def methodB(val)
  {
    def file = new java.io.FileWriter("output.txt")
    file.write "The value is ${val}."
  }
  def methodC(val)
  {
    def file = new java.io.FileWriter("output.txt")
    file.write "The value is ${val}."
    file.close()
  }
}
```

In this code, we have three methods with different flavors of dependency. methodA() receives an instance of what appears to be a File. The other two methods, methodB() and methodC(), instantiate an instance of FileWriter internally. The Expando class will help us with the first method only. Given that, we'll consider only methodA() in this section. We'll see how to test the other two methods in Section 18.10, *Mocking Using the Groovy Mock Library*, on page 289.

methodA() writes a message to the given File object using its write() method. We want to test methodA(), but without actually having to write to a physical file and then read its contents back to assert.

We can take advantage of Groovy's dynamic typing here because methodA() does not specify the type of its parameter. So, we can send any object that can fulfill the intended parameter's capability, such as having the write() method (see Section 3.4, *Design by Capability*, on page 56). Let's do that now. We'll create a class HandTossedFileMock with the write() method. We don't have to worry about all the properties and methods that the real File class has. All we care about is what the method being tested really calls. The code is as follows:

```groovy
import com.agiledeveloper.ClassWithDependency
class TestWithExpando extends GroovyTestCase {
  void testMethodA() {
    def testObj = new ClassWithDependency()
```

```
    def fileMock = new HandTossedFileMock()
    testObj.methodA(1, fileMock)

    assertEquals "The value is 1.", fileMock.result
  }
}

class HandTossedFileMock {
  def result
  def write(value) { result = value }
}
```

The output from the previous code confirms a passing test:

```
.
Time: 0.015

OK (1 test)
```

In this code, the mock implementation of write() that we created within Hand-TossedFileMock simply saves the parameter it receives into a result property. We're sending an instance of this mock class to methodA() instead of the real File. methodA() is quite happy to use the mock, thanks to dynamic typing.

That was not too bad; however, it would be great if we did not have to hand-toss that separate class. This is where Expando comes in (see Section 15.1, *Creating Dynamic Classes with Expando*, on page 225).

Simply tell an instance of Expando to hold a property called text and a mock implementation of the write() method. Then pass this instance to methodA(). Let's look at the code:

UnitTestingWithGroovy/TestUsingExpando.groovy
```
import com.agiledeveloper.ClassWithDependency

class TestUsingExpando extends GroovyTestCase {
  void testMethodA() {
    def fileMock = new Expando(text: '', write: { text = it })

    def testObj = new ClassWithDependency()
    testObj.methodA(1, fileMock)
    assertEquals "The value is 1.", fileMock.text
  }
}
```

The output is as follows:

```
.
Time: 0.022

OK (1 test)
```

In both of the previous examples, no real physical file was created when we called methodA(). The unit test runs quickly, and we don't have any files to read or clean up after the test.

Expando is useful when we pass the dependent object to the method being tested. If, on the other hand, the method is creating the dependent object internally (such as the methods methodB() and methodC()), it is of no help. We'll address this in Section 18.10, *Mocking Using the Groovy Mock Library*, on page 289.

18.9 Mocking Using Map

We saw an example of using Expando as a mock object. We can also use a Map. A map, as we know, has keys and associated values. The values can be objects or even closures. We can take advantage of this to use a Map in place of a collaborator.

Here's a rewrite of the example using Expando from Section 18.8, *Mocking Using Expando*, on page 285, this time using a Map:

UnitTestingWithGroovy/TestUsingMap.groovy
```
import com.agiledeveloper.ClassWithDependency

class TestUsingMap extends GroovyTestCase {
  void testMethodA() {
    def text = ''
    def fileMock = [write : { text = it }]

    def testObj = new ClassWithDependency()
    testObj.methodA(1, fileMock)

    assertEquals "The value is 1.", text
  }
}
```

The output is as follows:

```
.
Time: 0.029

OK (1 test)
```

Just like Expando, Map is useful when we pass the dependent object to the method being tested. It does not help if the collaborator is created internally in the method being tested. We'll address this case next.

18.10 Mocking Using the Groovy Mock Library

Groovy's mock library implemented in the groovy.mock.interceptor package is useful for mocking deeper dependencies—that is, instances of collaborators/dependent objects created within the methods we're testing. StubFor and MockFor are the two classes that take care of this. Let's look at them one at a time.

StubFor and MockFor are intended to intercept calls to methods like categories do (see Section 18.6, *Mocking Using Categories*, on page 283). However, unlike with categories, we don't have to create separate classes for mocking. We introduce the mock methods on instances of StubFor or MockFor, and these classes take care of replacing the MetaClass for the object we're mocking.

In *Stubs vs. Mocks*, on page 278, we discussed the difference between stubs and mocks. Let's start with an example using StubFor to understand the strengths and weaknesses of stubs. Then we'll use MockFor to look at the advantage mocks offer.

Using StubFor

Let's use Groovy's StubFor to create stubs for the File class:

```
UnitTestingWithGroovy/TestUsingStubFor.groovy
Line 1  import com.agiledeveloper.ClassWithDependency

   -    class TestUsingStubFor extends GroovyTestCase {
   -      void testMethodB() {
   5        def testObj = new ClassWithDependency()

   -        def fileMock = new groovy.mock.interceptor.StubFor(java.io.FileWriter)
   -        def text
   -        fileMock.demand.write { text = it.toString() }
  10        fileMock.demand.close {}

   -        fileMock.use {
   -          testObj.methodB(1)
   -        }
  15
   -        assertEquals "The value is 1.", text
   -      }
   -    }
```

When creating an instance of StubFor, we provided the class we're interested in stubbing—in this case, the java.io.FileWriter. We then created a closure for the write() method's stub implementation. On line number 12, we called the use() method on the stub. At this time, it replaces the MetaClass of FileWriter with a ProxyMetaClass. Any call to an instance of FileWriter from within the attached closure will be routed to the stub.

Stubs and mocks, however, do not help intercept calls to constructors. In the previous example, FileWriter's constructor is called, and it ends up creating a file named output.txt on the disk.

StubFor helped us test whether our method, methodB(), is creating a proper instance of FileWriter and writing the expected content to this instance. However, it has one limitation. It failed to test whether the method was well-behaved by closing the file. Even though we demanded the close() method on the stub, it ignored checking whether close() was actually called. The stub simply stands in for the collaborator and verifies the state. To verify behavior, we have to use a mock (see *Stubs vs. Mocks*, on page 278)—specifically, the MockFor class.

Using MockFor

Let's make one change to the previous test code:

UnitTestingWithGroovy/TestUsingMockFor.groovy
```
//def fileMock = new groovy.mock.interceptor.StubFor(java.io.FileWriter)
def fileMock = new groovy.mock.interceptor.MockFor(java.io.FileWriter)
```

We replaced StubFor with MockFor—that's the only change. When we run the test now, it fails, as shown here:

```
.F
Time: 0.093
There was 1 failure:
1) testMethod1(TestUsingStubFor)junit.framework.AssertionFailedError:
verify[1]: expected 1..1 call(s) to 'close' but was never called.
```

Unlike the stub, the mock tells us that even though our code produced the desired result, it did not behave as expected. That is, it did not call the close() method that was set up in the expectation using demand.

methodC() does the same thing as methodB(), but it calls close(). Let's test that method using MockFor:

UnitTestingWithGroovy/TestMethodCUsingMock.groovy
```
import com.agiledeveloper.ClassWithDependency

class TestMethodCUsingMock extends GroovyTestCase {
  void testMethodC() {
    def testObj = new ClassWithDependency()

    def fileMock = new groovy.mock.interceptor.MockFor(java.io.FileWriter)
    def text
    fileMock.demand.write { text = it.toString() }
```

```
    fileMock.demand.close {}
    fileMock.use {
      testObj.methodC(1)
    }
    assertEquals "The value is 1.", text
  }
}
```

In this case, the mock tells us that it is quite happy with the collaboration. The test passes, as shown here:

```
.
Time: 0.088

OK (1 test)
```

In the previous examples, the method under test created only one instance of the object being mocked—FileWriter. What if the method creates more than one of these objects? The mock represents all of them, and we have to create the demands for each one. Let's look at an example of using two instances of FileWriter. The useFiles() method in the following code copies the given parameter to the first file and writes the parameter's size to the second:

```
class TwoFileUser {
  def useFiles(str) {
    def file1 = new java.io.FileWriter("output1.txt")
    def file2 = new java.io.FileWriter("output2.txt")
    file1.write str
    file2.write str.size()
    file1.close()
    file2.close()
  }
}
```

Here's the test for that code:

UnitTestingWithGroovy/TwoFileUserTest.groovy
```
class TwoFileUserTest extends GroovyTestCase {
  void testUseFiles() {
    def testObj = new TwoFileUser()
    def testData = 'Multi Files'
    def fileMock = new groovy.mock.interceptor.MockFor(java.io.FileWriter)
    fileMock.demand.write() { assertEquals testData, it }
    fileMock.demand.write() { assertEquals testData.size(), it }
    fileMock.demand.close(2..2) {}
    fileMock.use {
      testObj.useFiles(testData)
    }
  }
```

```
void tearDown() {
    new File('output1.txt').delete()
    new File('output2.txt').delete()
  }
}
```

The output from running the previous test is as follows:

```
.
Time: 0.091

OK (1 test)
```

The demands we created are to be satisfied collectively by both of the objects created in the method being tested. The mock is flexible to support more than one object. Of course, if we have a lots of objects being created, the mock can get hard to implement. The ability to specify multiplicity of calls, discussed next, may help.

The MockFor was quite capable of mocking the FileWriter class's methods, but it did not prevent the actual constructor from running, so unfortunately, empty files named output1.txt and output2.txt will be created when the tests run. We clean it up in the tearDown() method.

The mock keeps track of the sequence and number of calls to a method, and if the code being tested does not exactly meet the expectation we have demanded, the mock raises an exception, failing the test.

We can easily set up expectations for multiple calls to the same method. Here is an example:

```
def someWriter() {
  def file = new FileWriter('output.txt')
  file.write("one")
  file.write("two")
  file.write(3)
  file.flush()
  file.write(file.getEncoding())
  file.close()
}
```

Suppose we care only to test the interaction between our code and the collaborator. We need to set up an expectation for three calls to write(), followed by a call to flush(), a call to getEncoding(), a call to write(), and, finally, a call to close().

We can specify the cardinality or multiplicity of a call using a range with the demand. For example, mock.demand.write(2..4) {...} says that we expect the method write() to be called at least two times, but no more than four times. Let's write a test for the previous method to see the ease with which we can express the expectations for multiple calls and the return values, and also assert that the parameter values received are as expected.

```
void testSomeWriter() {
  def fileMock = new groovy.mock.interceptor.MockFor(java.io.FileWriter)
  fileMock.demand.write(3..3) {} // If you want to say upto 3 times, use 0..3
  fileMock.demand.flush {}
  fileMock.demand.getEncoding { return "whatever" } // return is optional
  fileMock.demand.write { assertEquals 'whatever', it.toString() }
  fileMock.demand.close {}

  fileMock.use {
    testObj.someWriter()
  }
}
```

In this example, the mock asserts that write() was called three times; however, it failed to assert the parameters passed in. We can modify the code to assert for parameters, as shown here:

```
def params = ['one', 'two', 3]
def index = 0
fileMock.demand.write(3..3) { assert it == params[index++] }
  // If you want to say upto 3 times, use 0..3
```

In this chapter we saw the unit-testing and mocking facilities that are baked into the Groovy library. Some powerful and fluent third-party libraries make unit testing easier and more fun. For mocking, check out gmock.[1] The testing tool Spock provides greater fluency and ease for writing and expressing unit tests.[2] In Spock, we can write assertions using simple expect: expected == expression, provide a table of data values of input and expectations, and easily create mocks.

Unit testing takes quite a bit of discipline. However, the benefits outweigh the cost. Unit testing is critical in dynamic languages that offer greater flexibility than statically typed languages.

We've explored techniques for managing dependencies via stubs and mocks. We can use Groovy to unit-test our Java code. We can use our existing unit-testing and mock frameworks, and override methods to mock our Groovy and Java code. To unit-test our Groovy code, we can use categories and ExpandoMetaClass. Both let us mock by intercepting method calls. ExpandoMetaClass makes it so we don't have to create extra classes and our tests are concise.

---

1. http://code.google.com/p/gmock/
2. http://code.google.com/p/spock

For simple mocking of parameter objects, we use Maps or Expando. If we want to set up expectations for multiple methods and mock dependencies that are internal to methods being tested, we use StubFor. To test the state as well as the behavior, we use MockFor.

We saw how Groovy's dynamic nature along with its metaprogramming capability makes unit testing a breeze. As we evolve our code, refactor it, and get a better understanding of our application requirements, unit testing with Groovy can help maintain our velocity of development. It'll give us confidence that our application is continuing to meet our expectations—we can use it as a carabiner as we ascend through the application-development complexities.

CHAPTER 19

Creating DSLs in Groovy

Domain-specific languages (DSLs) are "targeted at a particular type of problem."—see the reference to Martin Fowler's discussions on DSLs in Appendix 1, *Web Resources*, on page 309. Their syntax is focused on the intended domain or problem. We don't use them for general-purpose programming like we use Java, Groovy, or C++, because DSLs have a very limited scope and capability.

A DSL is small, simple (it may not be simple to design, though), expressive, and focused on a problem area or domain. DSLs have two characteristics: they're context-driven and fluent.

DSLs have been around for a long time. Chances are we've worked with them in applications with special keyword input files used to communicate with external applications. Ant and Gant (see Appendix 1, *Web Resources*, on page 309, for the latter) are examples of DSLs. Specifically, Gant is a wrapper around Ant that uses Groovy instead of XML to specify build tasks.

Groovy's dynamic nature and its metaprogramming capabilities makes it attractive for building DSLs. In this chapter, we'll talk about DSLs and how to use Groovy to build them.

19.1 Context

Context is one of the characteristics of a DSL. As humans, we rely heavily on context when we communicate. We're efficient, and context provides for continuity in our conversations. The other day I heard my friend Neal holler, "Venti latte with two extra shots!" He was using the Starbucks DSL. Nowhere did he mention the word "coffee," but he sure got one, at a high price. That's context-driven.

Let's look at Java code to order pizza. This code lacks context. The reference joesPizza is used repeatedly:

CreatingDSLs/OrderPizza.java
```java
//Java code
package com.agiledeveloper;

public class OrderPizza {
  public static void main(String[] args) {
    PizzaShop joesPizza = new PizzaShop();
    joesPizza.setSize(Size.LARGE);
    joesPizza.setCrust(Crust.THIN);
    joesPizza.setTopping("Olives", "Onions", "Bell Pepper");
    joesPizza.setAddress("101 Main St., ...");
    int time = joesPizza.setCard(CardType.VISA, "1234-1234-1234-1234");
    System.out.printf("Pizza will arrive in %d minutes\n", time);
  }
}
```

The same code written in Groovy is less cluttered, thanks to the with() method (see Section 7.1, *Using Object Extensions*, on page 128):

CreatingDSLs/OrderPizza.groovy
```groovy
import com.agiledeveloper.*

PizzaShop joesPizza = new PizzaShop()
joesPizza.with {
    setSize(Size.LARGE)
    setCrust(Crust.THIN)
    setTopping("Olives", "Onions", "Bell Pepper")
    setAddress("101 Main St., ...")
    int time = setCard(CardType.VISA, "1234-1234-1234-1234")
    printf("Pizza will arrive in %d minutes\n", time)
}
```

Since typing is optional and parentheses are almost always optional in Groovy (see Section 19.9, *The Parentheses Limitation and a Workaround*, on page 303), we can make the previous code a tad lighter:

CreatingDSLs/OrderPizza2.groovy
```groovy
import com.agiledeveloper.*

PizzaShop joesPizza = new PizzaShop()
joesPizza.with {
    setSize Size.LARGE
    setCrust Crust.THIN
    setTopping "Olives", "Onions", "Bell Pepper"
    setAddress "101 Main St., ..."
    time = setCard(CardType.VISA, "1234-1234-1234-1234")
    printf "Pizza will arrive in %d minutes\n", time
}
```

Context makes things terse (in a good way), less cluttered, and more effective.

19.2 Fluency

Fluency is another characteristic of a DSL. It helps make code readable and naturally flowing. It's not easy to design for fluency, but we should do it for our users. We'll now discuss some examples of fluency and explore a few ways to write loops in Groovy:

```groovy
CreatingDSLs/FluentLoops.groovy
// Traditional Looping
for(int i = 0; i < 10; i++) {
  println(i);
}
// Groovy ways
for(i in 0..9) { println i }

0.upto(9) { println it }

10.times { println it }
```

All the previous loops produce the same result. Groovy provides fluency for looping, among other things. Fluency is not restricted to Groovy, though. EasyMock (which inspired the Groovy mock library) exhibits fluency in setting up the mock expectations in Java:

```
//Java code
    expect(alarm.raise()).andReturn(true);
    expect(alarm.raise()).andThrow(new InvalidStateException());
```

The previous code indicates that the alarm mock should return true on the first call and throw an exception on the second.

We can find another good example of a DSL in Grails/GORM. For example, we can specify data constraints on an object's properties using the following Groovy syntax:

```
class State
{
    String twoLetterCode
    static constraints = {
        twoLetterCode unique: true, blank: false, size: 2..2
    }
}
```

Grails smartly recognizes this fluent and expressive syntax for expressing the constraints and generates the validation logic for both the front end and the back end.

Groovy builders (see Chapter 17, *Groovy Builders*, on page 253) are good examples of DSLs. They're fluent and built on context.

19.3 Types of DSLs

When designing a DSL, we have to decide between two types—external and internal.

An external DSL defines a new language. We have the flexibility to choose the syntax. We then parse the commands in our new language to take actions. When I started my first job, the company asked me to maintain a DSL that needed extensive use of lex and yacc. (I first thought they asked me to do it because I was good. I later understood they don't ask new employees to do stuff because they're good, but rather because no one else wants to do it!) The parsing was a lot of "fun." We can use languages such as C++ and Java, and the support of extensive parsing capabilities and libraries, to do the heavy lifting for us. For example, we can use ANTLR to build DSLs (see Terence Parr's *The Definitive ANTLR Reference: Building Domain-Specific Languages* [Par07]).

An internal DSL, also called an *embedded DSL*, defines a new language, but within the syntactical confines of an existing language. We don't use any parsers, but we have to construe the syntax by tactfully mapping to constructs such as methods and properties in the underlying language. Our internal DSL's users might not realize they're using syntax of a broader language. However, creating the internal DSL takes significant design effort and clever tricks to make the underlying language work for us.

I mentioned Ant and Gant earlier. Ant, which uses XML, is an example of an external DSL. Gant, on the other hand, uses Groovy to solve the same problem and is an example of an internal DSL.

19.4 Designing Internal DSLs

Dynamic languages are well suited to designing and implementing internal DSLs. They have good metaprogramming capabilities and flexible syntax, and we can easily load and execute code fragments.

Not all dynamic languages are created equal, however.

I find it very easy to create DSLs in Ruby, for example. It is dynamically typed, parentheses are optional, the colon symbol (:) can be used instead of double quoting strings, and so on. Ruby's elegance heavily favors creating internal DSLs.

Creating internal DSLs in Python can be a bit of a challenge. The significant whitespace can be a hindrance.

Groovy's dynamic typing and metaprogramming capabilities help a great deal in creating internal DSLs. However, it's picky about parentheses and does not have the elegant colon symbol that Ruby does. We will have to work around some of these restrictions, as we'll see later.

It takes significant time, patience, and effort to design an internal DSL. We must be creative, work around issues tactfully, and be willing to compromise to succeed in our design efforts.

19.5 Groovy and DSLs

Groovy has a number of key capabilities to help create internal DSLs, including the following:

- Dynamic and optional typing (Section 3.5, *Optional Typing*, on page 61)

- The flexibility to load scripts dynamically, plus manipulate and execute them (Section 10.8, *Using Groovy Scripts from Groovy*, on page 167)

- Open classes, thanks to categories and ExpandoMetaClass (see Chapter 13, *MOP Method Injection*, on page 193)

- Closures that provide a nice context for execution (Chapter 4, *Using Closures*, on page 71)

- Operator overloading helps freely define operators (Section 2.8, *Operator Overloading*, on page 31).

- Builder support (Chapter 17, *Groovy Builders*, on page 253)

- Flexible parentheses

Groovy's handling of flexible parentheses is useful and annoying at the same time. Groovy requires no parentheses for calling methods that take parameters, but insists on having them for methods with no parameters. See Section 19.9, *The Parentheses Limitation and a Workaround*, on page 303, for a simple trick to work around this annoyance.

In the rest of this chapter, we'll look at examples of creating DSLs in Groovy using these capabilities.

19.6 Using Command-Chain Fluency

We can achieve some level of fluency simply using a Groovy feature that allows commands, or method calls, to be chained. Groovy does not require parentheses when methods take arguments. Also, if a method returns a result, we can make subsequent calls on that instance without using a dot (.). Using simple plain-vanilla Groovy code, with no metaprogramming magic, we can execute fluent code like the following:

CreatingDSLs/CommandChain.groovy
```
move forward and then turn left
jump fast, forward and then turn right
```

That looks like a data file, but it's 100 percent executable Groovy code. Let's analyze it and figure out the Groovy code needed to execute it.

In the first line, we don't have any commas. Groovy will read the words move and forward and assume we're calling a move() method with forward as an argument. We define a move() method and also a variable named forward with a desired value like "forward." Once Groovy reduces the first two words, it expects to have an object on which to call the and() method. To facilitate this, from the move() method we return an instance that will support this method. Since a comma is used on the second line, the jump() method will take two parameters. We can continue to analyze along these lines to figure out what methods, variables, and parameters we'd need. To process the previous fluent datalike code, we need to create a bunch of variables and methods like the following:

CreatingDSLs/CommandChain.groovy
```
def (forward, left, then, fast, right) =
  ['forward', 'left', '', 'fast', 'right']

def move(dir) {
  println "moving $dir"
  this
}

def and(then) { this }

def turn(dir) {
  println "turning $dir"
  this
}

def jump(speed, dir) {
  println "jumping $speed and $dir"
  this
}
```

We used multiple assignments to define the needed variables. The methods move(), and(), turn(), and jump() each return this, the object on which they're invoked. This allows the methods to be nicely chained in those two lines.

Place the previous code and the fluent two lines in the same file and execute it using the groovy command to produce the output:

```
moving forward
turning left
jumping fast and forward
turning right
```

The command-chaining feature in Groovy makes it quite easy to create simple DSLs with fairly good fluency. To create more-complex DSLs and to execute them within a context, we'll have to go beyond this capability, which we'll do next.

19.7 Closures and DSLs

The with() method helps delegate calls within a closure, giving us an execution context. We can take advantage of this approach to create our own methods with context and fluency.

Let's revisit the pizza-ordering example. Say we want to create a syntax that flows naturally. We don't want to create an instance of PizzaShop because that is more of an implementation detail. We want the context to be implicit. Let's look at the following code (in the next section we'll see how to make this more fluent and context-driven):

CreatingDSLs/ClosureHelp.groovy
```
time = getPizza {
  setSize Size.LARGE
  setCrust Crust.THIN
  setTopping "Olives", "Onions", "Bell Pepper"
  setAddress "101 Main St., ..."
  setCard(CardType.VISA, "1234-1234-1234-1234")
}

printf "Pizza will arrive in %d minutes\n", time
```

The getPizza() method accepts a closure within which we call methods to order pizza using the instance methods of a PizzaShop class. However, the instance of that class is implicit. The delegate (see Section 4.9, *Closure Delegation*, on page 86) takes care of routing the methods to the implicit instance, as we can see in the implementation of the following getPizza() method:

CreatingDSLs/ClosureHelp.groovy
```
def getPizza(closure) {
  PizzaShop pizzaShop = new PizzaShop()
  closure.delegate = pizzaShop
  closure()
}
```

The output from executing the call to the getPizza() code is as follows:

```
Pizza will arrive in 25 minutes
```

Wait a second; how did we get the time value printed in the output? Because the last statement in getPizza() was a call to the closure, whatever it returned, getPizza() returned. The last statement within the closure is setCard(), so its result was returned to the caller. This DSL imposes ordering: the setCard() must be the last method called to order pizza. We can work on improving the interface so the ordering is more obvious. Also, we can replace calls to set methods like setSize Size.LARGE with assignment statements such as size = Size.LARGE.

19.8 Method Interception and DSLs

We can implement the DSL for ordering pizza without really using a PizzaShop class. We can do that by purely intercepting method calls. Let's start with the code to order pizza (stored in a file named orderPizza.dsl):

CreatingDSLs/orderPizza.dsl
```
size large
crust thin
topping Olives, Onions, Bell_Pepper
address "101 Main St., ..."
card visa, '1234-1234-1234-1234'
```

It hardly looks like code. It looks more like a data file. However, that's pure Groovy code, and we're going to execute it (everything we see in that file, except the strings in double quotes, is either method names or variable names). But before that, we have to perform a few tricks...er, I mean design our DSL.

Let's create a file named GroovyPizzaDSL.groovy, and in it define the variables large, thin, and visa (we can define other variables, such as small, thick, and masterCard, at will). Now define a method acceptOrder() to call into a closure that will eventually execute our DSL. Also implement the methodMissing() method that will be called for any method that does not exist (pretty much all methods called in our DSL file orderPizza.dsl).

CreatingDSLs/GroovyPizzaDSL.groovy
```
def large = 'large'
def thin = 'thin'
def visa = 'Visa'
def Olives = 'Olives'
def Onions = 'Onions'
def Bell_Pepper = 'Bell Pepper'

orderInfo = [:]
```

```groovy
def methodMissing(String name, args) {
  orderInfo[name] = args
}

def acceptOrder(closure) {
  closure.delegate = this
  closure()
  println "Validation and processing performed here for order received:"
  orderInfo.each { key, value ->
    println "${key} -> ${value.join(', ')}"
  }
}
```

We have to figure out a way to put these two files together and execute. We can do that quite easily (see Section 10.8, *Using Groovy Scripts from Groovy*, on page 167), as shown next. Invoke GroovyShell, load the previous two scripts, form them into a cohesive script, and evaluate it.

CreatingDSLs/GroovyPizzaOrderProcess.groovy
```groovy
def dslDef = new File('GroovyPizzaDSL.groovy').text
def dsl = new File('orderPizza.dsl').text

def script = """
${dslDef}
acceptOrder {
  ${dsl}
}
"""

new GroovyShell().evaluate(script)
```

Here is the output from the previous code:

```
Validation and processing performed here for order received:
size -> large
crust -> thin
topping -> Olives, Onions, Bell Pepper
address -> 101 Main St., ...
card -> Visa, 1234-1234-1234-1234
```

As we can see, designing and executing a DSL in Groovy (as we did in orderpizza.dsl) is pretty easy if we know how to exploit Groovy's metaobject protocol capabilities.

19.9 The Parentheses Limitation and a Workaround

Let's leave the pizza example behind and look at a simple register. This section will show how to create a DSL for a simple register, the device that lets us total amounts. Here is the first attempt to create that:

CreatingDSLs/Total.groovy
```groovy
value = 0
def clear() { value = 0 }
def add(number) { value += number }
def total() { println "Total is $value" }

clear()
add 2
add 5
add 7
total()
```

The output from the previous code is as follows:

```
Total is 14
```

In this code, we wrote total() and clear() instead of total and clear, respectively. Let's drop the parentheses and try to call total:

CreatingDSLs/Total.groovy
```groovy
try {
  total
} catch(Exception ex) {
  println ex
}
```

Executing the previous code gives the following result:

```
groovy.lang.MissingPropertyException:
  No such property: total for class: Total
```

Groovy thinks that the call to total refers to a (nonexistent) property. Working with a language to design a DSL is like playing with a two-year-old—we don't fight with the kid when he gets cranky; we go along a little bit. So, in this case, tell Groovy that it's OK and work with it. Simply create the properties it wants:

```groovy
value = 0
def getClear() { value = 0 }
def add(number) { value += number }
def getTotal() { println "Total is $value" }
```

We wrote properties with the names total and clear by writing the methods getTotal() and getClear(). Now Groovy is quite happy (like the kid) to play with us, and we can call these properties without parentheses:

```groovy
clear
add 2
add 5
add 7
total
clear
total
```

The output from the previous code is as follows:

```
Total is 14
Total is 0
```

We've seen ways to create fluent syntax. Next we'll discuss how to intercept and synthesize method calls in a DSL.

19.10 Categories and DSLs

Using categories, we can intercept method calls in a controlled fashion (see Section 13.1, *Injecting Methods Using Categories*, on page 193). We can put that to use in creating a DSL. Let's figure out ways to implement the following fluent call: 2.days.ago.at(4.30).

2 is an instance of Integer, and we know that days is not a property on it. We'll inject that, using categories, as a property (the getDays() method). The days is just noise here, but in another context it may be useful to differentiate between five days ago and five minutes ago. It provides connectivity in the sentence "two days ago at 4.30." We can implement the method getDays() that accepts Integer and returns the received instance. In the getAgo() method (for the ago property), we accept an instance of Integer and return so many days before the current date using the operations on the Calendar class. Finally, in the at() method, we set the time on that date to the time given as the parameter (4.30), and return an instance of Date. We can perform all this within the use() block, as shown in the following code. (We're not performing error checking on the time we provide, so we can send 4.70 if we'd like instead of 5:10; it's an undocumented feature. Also, we may want to clone the instance of Calendar on which the at() method is called and modify the clone to avoid any side effects.)

CreatingDSLs/DSLUsingCategory.groovy
```groovy
class DateUtil {
  static int getDays(Integer self) { self }

  static Calendar getAgo(Integer self) {
    def date = Calendar.instance
    date.add(Calendar.DAY_OF_MONTH, -self)
    date
  }

  static Date at(Calendar self, Double time) {
    def hour = (int)(time.doubleValue())
    def minute = (int)(Math.round((time.doubleValue() - hour) * 100))
    self.set(Calendar.HOUR_OF_DAY, hour)
    self.set(Calendar.MINUTE, minute)
    self.set(Calendar.SECOND, 0)
```

```
      self.time
    }
  }
}

use(DateUtil) {
  println 2.days.ago.at(4.30)
}
```

The output from the previous code is as follows:

```
Thu Jan 31 04:30:00 MST 2008
```

A final concern with the DSL syntax created here is that we used
2.days.ago.at(4.30). It's more natural to use 4:30 instead of 4.30, so it would be
nice to instead use 2.days.ago.at(4:30). Groovy can accept a Map as a parameter
to methods.

By defining the at() method's parameter as Map instead of Double, we can achieve
that:

CreatingDSLs/DSLUsingCategory2.groovy
```
class DateUtil {
  static int getDays(Integer self) { self }

  static Calendar getAgo(Integer self) {
    def date = Calendar.instance
    date.add(Calendar.DAY_OF_MONTH, -self)
    date
  }

  static Date at(Calendar self, Map time) {
    def hour = 0
    def minute = 0
    time.each {key, value -> hour = key.toInteger()
      minute = value.toInteger()
    }
    self.set(Calendar.HOUR_OF_DAY, hour)
    self.set(Calendar.MINUTE, minute)
    self.set(Calendar.SECOND, 0)
    self.time
  }
}

use(DateUtil) {
  println 2.days.ago.at(4:30)
}
```

The output from the previous code is as follows:

```
Thu Jan 31 04:30:00 MST 2008
```

The only restriction in this categories approach is that we can employ the DSL only within the use() blocks. This restriction might actually be beneficial, because the method injection is controlled. Once we leave the block of code, the methods injected are forgotten from the context and are no longer available, which might be desirable. In Section 19.11, *ExpandoMetaClass and DSLs*, on page 307, we will see how to implement the same syntax using ExpandoMetaClass.

19.11 ExpandoMetaClass and DSLs

Categories apply only within the use blocks, and their effect is fairly limited in scope. If we want the method injection to be effective throughout our application, we can use the ExpandoMetaClass instead of categories. Let's use the ExpandoMetaClass to implement the DSL syntax we saw in the previous section:

```
CreatingDSLs/DSLUsingExpandoMetaClass.groovy
Integer.metaClass{
  getDays = { ->
    delegate
  }

  getAgo = { ->
      def date = Calendar.instance
      date.add(Calendar.DAY_OF_MONTH, -delegate)
      date
    }
}

Calendar.metaClass.at = { Map time ->
    def hour = 0
    def minute = 0
    time.each {key, value ->
      hour = key.toInteger()
      minute = value.toInteger()
    }

    delegate.set(Calendar.HOUR_OF_DAY, hour)
    delegate.set(Calendar.MINUTE, minute)
    delegate.set(Calendar.SECOND, 0)
    delegate.time
}

println 2.days.ago.at(4:30)
```

We added the desired methods to the ExpandoMetaClasses of the Integer class and the Calendar class. The calls to these fluent methods get routed to the methods we added, as we can see here:

```
Fri Feb 03 04:30:00 MST 2012
```

The solution to add methods using the ExpandoMetaClass is a lot cleaner than writing static methods with categories.

We now know that creating an internal DSL in Groovy is fairly easy. The dynamic nature and optional typing helps us create a fluent interface. Closures help us create context. Groovy's categories and ExpandoMetaClass are helpful to inject, intercept, and synthesize method calls and properties. Finally, Groovy's ability to load and execute arbitrary scripts comes in handy for executing the DSLs.

I hope you enjoyed your journey through the capabilities of this powerful and dynamic language. I've used Groovy in everything from small scripts in performing automated routine tasks on my systems to scripts that run enterprise applications. Groovy's conciseness and ease of integration with Java drew me in. The productivity gain I realized kept me there. I sincerely hope the concepts in this book will help you program responsibly and reap the dynamic productivity of this incredibly powerful language on the Java Virtual Machine. I wish you all the best!

Web Resources

A Bit of Groovy History . . . . http://glaforge.free.fr/weblog/index.php?itemid=99
A blog by Guillaume Laforge on Groovy history.

API for FactoryBuilderSupport . . . .
. . . . http://groovy.codehaus.org/api/groovy/util/FactoryBuilderSupport.html
API for the FactoryBuilderSupport class, which is the new base class for SwingBuilder.

ASTTest Annotation . . http://groovy.codehaus.org/gapi/groovy/transform/ASTTest.html
Groovy annotation for testing and debugging AST transformations.

Clip from *Raiders of the Lost Ark* . . http://www.youtube.com/watch?v=Epw-LSC3L2U
Swordfight scene from the movie *Raiders of the Lost Ark*.

CodeNarc . . . . http://codenarc.sourceforge.net
CodeNarc is a Groovy-based static code-analysis tool.

Crash of the Mars Orbiter . . http://www.cnn.com/TECH/space/9909/30/mars.metric.02
CNN coverage of the crash of the Mars Orbiter.

Duck Typing . . . . http://c2.com/cgi/wiki?DuckTyping
What's duck typing?

E Text Editor . . . . http://www.e-texteditor.com
TextMate-like editor for Windows.

easyb . . . . http://www.easyb.org
easyb is a automated testing tool with nice fluency for functional and integration testing.

Eclipse Plug-in for Groovy . . . . http://groovy.codehaus.org/Eclipse+Plugin
Plug-in for Groovy development on the Eclipse IDE.

FactoryBuilderSupport . . . . http://groovy.codehaus.org/FactoryBuilderSupport
Groovy's FactoryBuilderSupport class, which is the new base class for SwingBuilder.

Gant Home . . . . http://gant.codehaus.org
A site for Gant, which is like Ant but uses Groovy instead of XML.

The GDK . . . . http://groovy.codehaus.org/groovy-jdk
List of the methods that are part of the Groovy JDK—Groovy extensions to
the JDK.

Getting Started with Grails . . . . http://www.infoq.com/minibooks/grails
Jason Rudolph's book on working with Grails.

Good, Bad, and Ugly of Java Generics . . . .
. . . . http://www.agiledeveloper.com/articles/GenericsInJavaPartI.pdf
An article discussing the good, the bad, and the ugly of Java Generics.

GPars . . . . http://gpars.codehaus.org
GPars is a library that provides a variety of concurrent programming options
a great deal of Groovy fluency.

Gradle . . . . http://gradle.org
Gradle is a lightweight build-management tool to help programmers easily
configure builds with little configuration and no XML.

Grails Home . . . . http://grails.org/
Home of the Grails project for documentation and downloads.

Griffon Project . . . . http://griffon.codehaus.org
Groovy-based framework to build desktop applications.

Groovy API Javadoc . . . . http://groovy.codehaus.org/api
Javadoc for the Groovy API.

Groovy Closures Definition . . http://groovy.codehaus.org/Closures+-+Formal+Definition
Discussions and definition of Groovy closures.

Groovy Collections Support . . http://groovy.codehaus.org/groovy-jdk/java/util/Collection.html
Extensions and features Groovy has added to collections.

Groovy Daily Build . . . . .http://build.canoo.com/groovy
Place to download current builds of the Groovy project (for those who like to
stay on the bleeding edge).

Groovy Download Page . . . . .http://groovy.codehaus.org/Download
Direct link to the Groovy download page for latest released version and previous versions.

Groovy Home .http://groovy.codehaus.org
Home of the Groovy project for documentation and downloads.

Groovy Looping . . . . .http://groovy.codehaus.org/Looping
Shows different ways to loop in Groovy.

Groovy Mailing Lists . . . . .http://groovy.codehaus.org/Mailing+Lists
List and details of Groovy mailing lists.

Groovy Operator Overloading . . .http://groovy.codehaus.org/Operator+Overloading
Groovy operator overloads and their method mapping.

Groovy Scriptom API . . . . .http://groovy.codehaus.org/COM+Scripting
Groovy API that allows you to interact with Windows ActiveX and COM.

Groovy String Support . .http://groovy.codehaus.org/groovy-jdk/java/lang/String.html
Extensions and support for Strings in Groovy.

Groovy's Support for java.math Classes . .http://groovy.codehaus.org/Groovy+Math
Groovy support of java.math classes to provide better accuracy.

Groovy's Support for Map . . . .
. . . . .http://groovy.codehaus.org/groovy-jdk/java/util/Map.html
Extensions and features Groovy has added to Java's Map.

GVM . . . . .http://gvmtool.net
The Groovy Environment Manager, a tool to manage multiple versions of
Groovy and related tools.

Higher-Order Function . . . . http://c2.com/cgi/wiki?HigherOrderFunction
Discussions on higher-order functions.

IntelliJ IDEA . . . . http://www.jetbrains.com/idea
Popular Java IDE with exceptional Groovy support.

Java Download . . http://www.oracle.com/technetwork/java/javase/downloads/index.html
Download page for Java and JDK.

JRuby Home . . . . http://jruby.codehaus.org
Home of the JRuby project for documentation and downloads.

Languages and Idioms . . . .
. . http://blog.agiledeveloper.com/2007/05/its-not-languages-but-their-idioms-that.html
A blog entry discussing languages and idioms.

Markmail for Groovy Mailing List . . . . http://groovy.markmail.org
Convenient place to search for any topics discussed in the Groovy users
mailing list.

MetaClass and Method Interception . . . .
. . http://graemerocher.blogspot.com/2007/06/dynamic-groovy-groovys-equivalent-to.html
A blog by Graeme Rocher on Groovy's metaprogramming capabilities and
open classes.

Mocks Aren't Stubs . . . . . . http://martinfowler.com/articles/mocksArentStubs.html
Martin Fowler discussing the similarities and differences between mocks and
stubs.

No Fluff Just Stuff . . . . http://www.nofluffjuststuff.com
A popular traveling Java conference.

The Official Website for the Book http://pragprog.com/titles/vslg2
Official website for this book, with links to download all the example source
code from this book, file errata, and provide feedback.

The Pragmatic Programmers . . . . http://pragprog.com
Website of the publisher of this book.

Runtime vs. Compile Time/Static vs. Dynamic . . . .
. . . . . . http://groovy.codehaus.org/Runtime+vs+Compile+time,+Static+vs+Dynamic
Discussions and rationale for Groovy's support of dynamic typing.

Selenium . . . . http://seleniumhq.org/download
Automation tool that facilitates testing web applications.

Some Differences Between Java and Groovy . . . .
. . . . http://groovy.codehaus.org/Differences+from+Java
List and details of some differences between Java and Groovy.

Spock Library . . . . http://spockframework.org
Home of the Spock testing library.

State of IDE Support for Groovy . . . . . . http://groovy.codehaus.org/IDE+Support
Different IDEs that support Groovy development and their current state.

Sun/Java Scripting Project Home . . . . https://scripting.dev.java.net
Details about scripting languages and JSR 223: Scripting for the Java Platform.

Technical Debt . . . . http://martinfowler.com/bliki/TechnicalDebt.html
Martin Fowler discussing the term *technical debt*.

TextMate . . . . http://macromates.com
TextMate, a popular editor on the Mac.

TextMate Groovy Bundle . . . . . http://docs.codehaus.org/display/GROOVY/TextMate
Groovy bundle for TextMate, a popular editor on the Mac.

Treating a Java Method as a Closure . . . .
. . . . http://www.jroller.com/melix/entry/coding_a_groovy_closure_in
Cédric Champeau shows how to treat a Java method as a closure on the Groovy side.

Tweaking the Groovy Bundle for TextMate Editor . . . http://tinyurl.com/ywotsj
Venkat's blog on a tweak to the Groovy bundle for easy/quick display of output.

Unit tests that illustrate the build from Spec DSL . . . .
. . http://svn.codehaus.org/groovy/trunk/groovy/groovy-core/src/test/org/code-
haus/groovy/ast/builder/AstBuilderFromSpecificationTest.groovy
A series of test cases that illustrate the use of the build from specification DSL.

Using JUnit 4 with Groovy . . http://groovy.codehaus.org/Using+JUnit+4+with+Groovy
Steps to use JUnit 4.0 with Groovy.

Using Notepad2 . . . . http://tinyurl.com/yqfucf
A blog entry showing how to use Notepad2 to edit and run Groovy on Windows.

Why Copying an Object Is a Terrible Thing to Do . . . .
. . . . http://www.agiledeveloper.com/articles/cloning072002.htm
An article that addresses issues with object-copying in Java.

Why Getter and Setter Methods Are Evil . . . .
. . . . http://www.javaworld.com/javaworld/jw-09-2003/jw-0905-toolbox.html
An article by Allen Holub.

Why Scripting Languages Matter http://www.oreillynet.com/pub/wlg/3190
Tim O'Reilly discussing the nature of applications and the role played by scripting languages.

Xerces XML Parser . . . . http://xerces.apache.org/xerces-j
Popular Java-based XML parser.

Bibliography

[AS96]   Harold Abelson and Gerald Jay Sussman. *Structure and Interpretation of Computer Programs*. MIT Press, Cambridge, MA, 2nd, 1996.

[Bec02]   Kent Beck. *Test Driven Development: By Example*. Addison-Wesley, Reading, MA, 2002.

[Bec96]   Kent Beck. *Smalltalk Best Practice Patterns*. Prentice Hall, Englewood Cliffs, NJ, 1996.

[Blo08]   Joshua Bloch. *Effective Java*. Addison-Wesley, Reading, MA, 2008.

[ES90]   Margaret A. Ellis and Bjarne Stroustrup. *The Annotated C++ Reference Manual*. Addison-Wesley Longman, Reading, MA, 1990.

[Eck06]   Bruce Eckel. *Thinking in Java*. Prentice Hall, Englewood Cliffs, NJ, Fourth, 2006.

[Fri97]   Jeffrey E. F. Friedl. *Mastering Regular Expressions*. O'Reilly & Associates, Inc., Sebastopol, CA, 1997.

[GHJV95]   Erich Gamma, Richard Helm, Ralph Johnson, and John Vlissides. *Design Patterns: Elements of Reusable Object-Oriented Software*. Addison-Wesley, Reading, MA, 1995.

[Gra07]   James Edward Gray II. *TextMate: Power Editing for the Mac*. The Pragmatic Bookshelf, Raleigh, NC and Dallas, TX, 2007.

[Knu97]   Donald Ervin Knuth. *The Art of Computer Programming: Fundamental Algorithms*. Addison-Wesley Longman, Reading, MA, Third, 1997.

[Lad03]   Ramnivas Laddad. *AspectJ in Action: Practical Aspect-Oriented Programming*. Manning Publications Co., Greenwich, CT, 2003.

[Mey97]   Bertrand Meyer. *Object-Oriented Software Construction*. Prentice Hall, Englewood Cliffs, NJ, Second, 1997.

[Par07]   Terence Parr. *The Definitive ANTLR Reference: Building Domain-Specific Languages*. The Pragmatic Bookshelf, Raleigh, NC and Dallas, TX, 2007.

[Rai04]   J. B. Rainsberger. *JUnit Recipes: Practical Methods for Programmer Testing*. Manning Publications Co., Greenwich, CT, 2004.

[Seb04]   Robert W. Sebesta. *Concepts of Programming Languages*. Addison-Wesley, Reading, MA, 2004.

[TH03]   David Thomas and Andrew Hunt. *Pragmatic Unit Testing In Java with JUnit*. The Pragmatic Bookshelf, Raleigh, NC and Dallas, TX, 2003.

Index

Long Live the Command Line!

Use tmux and vim for incredible mouse-free productivity.

Your mouse is slowing you down. The time you spend context switching between your editor and your consoles eats away at your productivity. Take control of your environment with tmux, a terminal multiplexer that you can tailor to your workflow. Learn how to customize, script, and leverage tmux's unique abilities and keep your fingers on your keyboard's home row.

Brian P. Hogan
(88 pages) ISBN: 9781934356968. $16.25
http://pragprog.com/book/bhtmux

Vim is a fast and efficient text editor that will make you a faster and more efficient developer. It's available on almost every OS—if you master the techniques in this book, you'll never need another text editor. In more than 100 Vim tips, you'll quickly learn the editor's core functionality and tackle your trickiest editing and writing tasks.

Drew Neil
(346 pages) ISBN: 9781934356982. $29
http://pragprog.com/book/dnvim

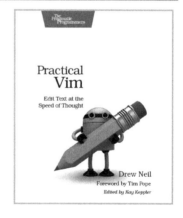

Seven Databases, Seven Languages

There's so much new to learn with the latest crop of NoSQL databases. And instead of learning a language a year, how about seven?

Data is getting bigger and more complex by the day, and so are your choices in handling it. From traditional RDBMS to newer NoSQL approaches, *Seven Databases in Seven Weeks* takes you on a tour of some of the hottest open source databases today. In the tradition of Bruce A. Tate's *Seven Languages in Seven Weeks*, this book goes beyond your basic tutorial to explore the essential concepts at the core of each technology.

Eric Redmond and Jim R. Wilson
(354 pages) ISBN: 9781934356920. $35
http://pragprog.com/book/rwdata

You should learn a programming language every year, as recommended by *The Pragmatic Programmer*. But if one per year is good, how about *Seven Languages in Seven Weeks*? In this book you'll get a hands-on tour of Clojure, Haskell, Io, Prolog, Scala, Erlang, and Ruby. Whether or not your favorite language is on that list, you'll broaden your perspective of programming by examining these languages side-by-side. You'll learn something new from each, and best of all, you'll learn how to learn a language quickly.

Bruce A. Tate
(330 pages) ISBN: 9781934356593. $34.95
http://pragprog.com/book/btlang

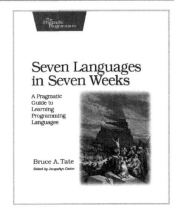

The Joy of Math and Programming

Rediscover the joy and fascinating weirdness of pure mathematics, or get your kids started programming in JavaScript.

Mathematics is beautiful—and it can be fun and exciting as well as practical. *Good Math* is your guide to some of the most intriguing topics from two thousand years of mathematics: from Egyptian fractions to Turing machines; from the real meaning of numbers to proof trees, group symmetry, and mechanical computation. If you've ever wondered what lay beyond the proofs you struggled to complete in high school geometry, or what limits the capabilities of the computer on your desk, this is the book for you.

Mark C. Chu-Carroll
(250 pages) ISBN: 9781937785338. $34
http://pragprog.com/book/mcmath

You know what's even better than playing games? Creating your own. Even if you're an absolute beginner, this book will teach you how to make your own online games with interactive examples. You'll learn programming using nothing more than a browser, and see cool, 3D results as you type. You'll learn real-world programming skills in a real programming language: JavaScript, the language of the web. You'll be amazed at what you can do as you build interactive worlds and fun games.

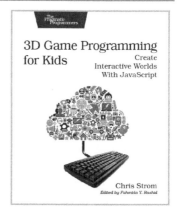

Chris Strom
(250 pages) ISBN: 9781937785444. $36
http://pragprog.com/book/csjava

Tinker, Tailor, Solder, and DIY!

Get into the DIY spirit with Raspberry Pi or Arduino. Who knows what you'll build next...

The Raspberry Pi is a $35, full-blown micro computer that runs Linux. Use its video, audio, network, and digital I/O to create media centers, web servers, interfaces to external hardware—you name it. And this book gives you everything you need to get started.

New Updates

The Raspberry Pi's greatest feature is its creative and amazingly productive community, which releases updates and new products on a daily basis. It's hard to keep up with the pace, but thanks to our Pragmatic eXpress series you'll always get the latest and most accurate information about your favorite mini computer. This book now contains an all-new chapter about sensors. It explains how to use digital and analog sensors with the Pi—even though the Pi doesn't have analog input ports! We've added a small section about the new PiStore and we've updated the GPIO chapter to cover the differences between the different revisions of the Pi boards. And, even more updates are coming soon for this book!

Maik Schmidt
(149 pages) ISBN: 9781937785048. $17
http://pragprog.com/book/msraspi

Arduino is an open-source platform that makes DIY electronics projects easier than ever. Even if you have no electronics experience, you'll be creating your first gadgets within a few minutes. Step-by-step instructions show you how to build a universal remote, a motion-sensing game controller, and many other fun, useful projects. This book has now been updated for Arduino 1.0, with revised code, examples, and screenshots throughout. We've changed all the book's examples and added new examples showing how to use the Arduino IDE's new features.

Maik Schmidt
(272 pages) ISBN: 9781934356661. $35
http://pragprog.com/book/msard

Kick Your Career Up a Notch

Ready to blog or promote yourself for real? Time to refocus your personal priorities? We've got you covered.

Technical Blogging is the first book to specifically teach programmers, technical people, and technically-oriented entrepreneurs how to become successful bloggers. There is no magic to successful blogging; with this book you'll learn the techniques to attract and keep a large audience of loyal, regular readers and leverage this popularity to achieve your goals.

Antonio Cangiano
(288 pages) ISBN: 9781934356883. $33
http://pragprog.com/book/actb

You're already a great coder, but awesome coding chops aren't always enough to get you through your toughest projects. You need these 50+ nuggets of wisdom. Veteran programmers: reinvigorate your passion for developing web applications. New programmers: here's the guidance you need to get started. With this book, you'll think about your job in new and enlightened ways.

Ka Wai Cheung
(160 pages) ISBN: 9781934356791. $29
http://pragprog.com/book/kcdc

Put the "Fun" in Functional

Elixir puts the "fun" back into functional programming, on top of the robust, battle-tested, industrial-strength environment of Erlang.

You want to explore functional programming, but are put off by the academic feel (tell me about monads just one more time). You know you need concurrent applications, but also know these are almost impossible to get right. Meet Elixir, a functional, concurrent language built on the rock-solid Erlang VM. Elixir's pragmatic syntax and built-in support for metaprogramming will make you productive and keep you interested for the long haul. This book is *the* introduction to Elixir for experienced programmers.

Dave Thomas
(240 pages) ISBN: 9781937785581. $36
http://pragprog.com/book/elixir

A multi-user game, web site, cloud application, or networked database can have thousands of users all interacting at the same time. You need a powerful, industrial-strength tool to handle the really hard problems inherent in parallel, concurrent environments. You need Erlang. In this second edition of the best-selling *Programming Erlang*, you'll learn how to write parallel programs that scale effortlessly on multicore systems.

"A gem; a sensible, practical introduction to functional programming."

—*Gilad Bracha* – Co-author of the Java language and Java Virtual Machine specifications, creator of the Newspeak language, member of the Dart language team

Joe Armstrong
(510 pages) ISBN: 9781937785536. $42
http://pragprog.com/book/jaerlang2

The Pragmatic Bookshelf

The Pragmatic Bookshelf features books written by developers for developers. The titles continue the well-known Pragmatic Programmer style and continue to garner awards and rave reviews. As development gets more and more difficult, the Pragmatic Programmers will be there with more titles and products to help you stay on top of your game.

Visit Us Online

This Book's Home Page
http://pragprog.com/book/vslg2
Source code from this book, errata, and other resources. Come give us feedback, too!

Register for Updates
http://pragprog.com/updates
Be notified when updates and new books become available.

Join the Community
http://pragprog.com/community
Read our weblogs, join our online discussions, participate in our mailing list, interact with our wiki, and benefit from the experience of other Pragmatic Programmers.

New and Noteworthy
http://pragprog.com/news
Check out the latest pragmatic developments, new titles and other offerings.

Save on the eBook

Save on the eBook versions of this title. Owning the paper version of this book entitles you to purchase the electronic versions at a terrific discount.

PDFs are great for carrying around on your laptop—they are hyperlinked, have color, and are fully searchable. Most titles are also available for the iPhone and iPod touch, Amazon Kindle, and other popular e-book readers.

Buy now at *http://pragprog.com/coupon*

Contact Us

Online Orders:	*http://pragprog.com/catalog*
Customer Service:	*support@pragprog.com*
International Rights:	*translations@pragprog.com*
Academic Use:	*academic@pragprog.com*
Write for Us:	*http://pragprog.com/write-for-us*
Or Call:	+1 800-699-7764

CPSIA information can be obtained at www.ICGtesting.com
Printed in the USA
LVOW01s0318141113

361173LV00022B/86/P

9 781937 785307